CRATER

 Wilderness Press

1986 Supplement to

CRATER LAKE NATIONAL PARK AND VICINITY

p. vi: Acknowledgments. "John Gemerys" should be "John Zcemerys."

p. 2: Diamond Lake Recreation Area—Mt. Thielsen. This prominent peak is the focal point of the new Mt. Thielsen Wilderness, created in 1984. No wilderness permit is required.

p. 2: Sky Lakes proposed wilderness. "I find it quite disconcerting that southern Oregon's most popular mountain trails have not been incorporated into an official wilderness." Well, it became an official wilderness in 1984. No wilderness permit is required.

p. 3: Mountain Lakes Wilderness. Wilderness permits are no longer required.

p. 9: Wilderness permits. Only Crater Lake National Park still requires these. If you write the park for a permit, please include this in their address: P.O. Box 7.

pp. 30, 31: Baby elephant heads. The specific scientific name for this plant is *attollens*, not *attolens*.

p. 45: Parasitic cinder cones. It was once thought that these cinder cones fed off the large magma chamber that fueled Mt. Mazama. However, the newer interpretation is that these cinder cones were not parasitic, but rather had their own sources of magma.

p. 45: Forgotten Crater. Now it is officially Williams Crater, after Prof. Howel Williams (p. 41) of University of California, Berkeley's Geology Department.

p. 48, Map 8, and index: Williams Cone. This tentative name has been changed to Williams Crater.

p. 79: Mt. Thielsen area. In 1984 this area officially became the Mt. Thielsen Wilderness. No wilderness permit is required.

p. 83: Route 6. Now there is a shorter way from Diamond Lake Corrals to the slopes of Mt. Thielsen. About 1.0 mile up Howlock Mountain Trail 1448 you meet the new Spruce Ridge Trail 1458. This waterless, spruce-free, generally viewless route makes a usually gentle, 2.6-mile climb to the new Mt. Thielsen Trail 1456. See next entry for that trail.

pp. 83–84: Route 7. Climbing east to the Pacific Crest Trail, old Mt. Thielsen Trail 1456 averaged a 13% gradient. This may have been a bit steep for some people, but certainly was not out of line for anyone climbing Mt. Thielsen. Above the PCT, the gradient averages about 22%. Anyway, the old trail has been abandoned and a longer one built. The trouble is, it no longer starts from Diamond Lake. Instead, it starts from Highway 138 about ½ mile north of where the old route crossed the highway. No longer can you start a hike from your campsite unless you're good at cross-country orienteering. (See this supplement's map for the location of the area's old and new trails.) The new Mt. Thielsen Trail averages a comfortable 9¼% gradient, and from Highway 138 it climbs 1.7 miles up

to a junction with Spruce Ridge Trail 1458 (see previous entry). Ahead, it climbs 2.3 miles to the Pacific Crest Trail, meeting it on Mt. Thielsen's west ridge. To find the old Mt. Thielsen Trail, which climbs to the summit, walk ⅓ mile south on the PCT.

p. 86, col. 2: Natural Bridge Geologic Site. The Forest Service strongly discourages swimming anywhere in this area. There is now a bridge spanning the small gorge just downstream from the lava tube, so you can get good views from both sides of the Rogue River.

pp. 87–112: Sky Lakes proposed wilderness. Sky Lakes became an official wilderness in 1984. No wilderness permit is required.

p. 97: Route 14. Above Hemlock Lake the trail is officially abandoned.

p. 97–98: Route 16. Beyond the Wickiup campsites the trail is officially abandoned.

p. 98: Route 17. The Red Lake Trail is officially abandoned all the way up to the No Name Trail.

p. 107, col. 2, line 22: "South Rock Trail" should be "South Rock Creek Trail."

pp. 115–120: Mountain Lakes Wilderness. Wilderness permits are no longer required.

p. 121–122: Distances, Snow Lakes Trail onward. These should read: 23.5 miles to Snow Lakes Trail, 25.9 miles to Devils Peak/Lee Peak saddle, 29.0 miles to Seven Lakes Trail, 31.6 miles to Sevenmile Trail, 33.4 miles to Sevenmile Marsh Campground.

p. 127: Smith. This entry has been updated: Smith, James G. 1983. *Geologic Map of the Sky Lakes Roadless Area and Mountain Lakes Wilderness, Jackson and Klamath Counties. Oregon.* Washington, D.C.: U.S. Geological Survey, Map MF-1507A. Also: Smith, James G., and John R. Benham, Fredrick L. Johnson. 1983. *Mineral Resource Potential Map of the Sky Lakes Roadless Area and Mountain Lakes Wilderness, Jackson and Klamath Counties, Oregon.* Washington, D.C.: U.S. Geological Survey, Map MF-1507B. Also useful: Luedke, Robert G., and Robert L. Smith. 1982. *Map Showing Distribution, Composition and Age of Late Cenozoic Volcanic Centers in Oregon and Washington.* Washington, D.C.: U.S. Geological Survey, Map I-1091-D.

p. 128: Whitney. At the last minute his book got increased to 288 pages. Interestingly enough, the identical book is published in Canada by Douglas & McIntyre, Ltd. under an entirely different title: *A Field Guide to the West Coast Mountains.*

p. 131: Legend. This should include a declination, which averages about 18°E.

Map 1, east of 138, and Map 2: Trail changes. A new Mt. Thielsen Trail 1456 has been constructed, and part way up it, the new Spruce Ridge Trail 1458 leaves it for a northward descent to Howlock Mountain Trail 1448. All these trails are shown on the accompanying supplementary map, which is drawn at the same scale as are Maps 1 and 2, 1:62,500.

Maps 11–22: Sky Lakes proposed wilderness. The wilderness became official in 1984, and its boundaries are similar to those shown on these maps.

Map 16: Alta Lake. This lake should have been labeled on the map. The lake is the long, narrow lake immediately west of Violet Hill, both features being in the southern part of the map.

Map 19: South Fork Rock Creek Trail. It is signed South Rock Creek Trail.

Maps 21, 22 and 24: Cascade Canal. Since this canal is seasonal, it should have been drawn as such.

Map 24: Fish Lake Resort, Pacific Crest Trail. Fish Lake Trail 1014, which is 1.7 miles long, connects these two features. This new lateral trail leaves the Pacific Crest Trail about ¼ mile southeast of its Highway 140 crossing and ends at the southern part of the resort's campground.

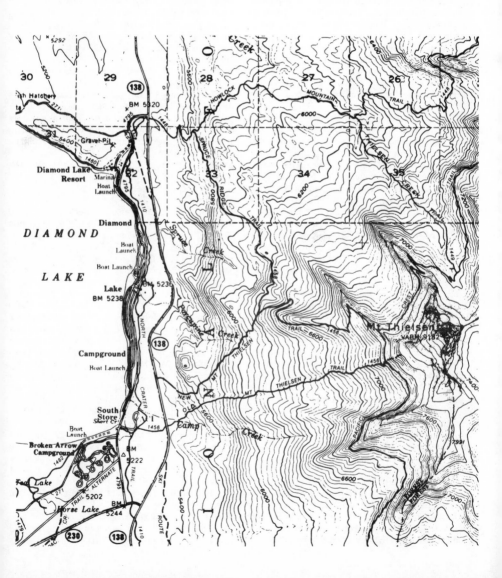

LAKE

National Park and Vicinity

Jeffrey P. Schaffer

FIRST EDITION August 1983
Second printing August 1992

Copyright © 1983 by Jeffrey P. Schaffer

Design by the author
Photographs, maps and illustrations by the author, except as noted
Topographic maps revised and updated by author, based on U.S. Geological Survey maps
Cover design by Larry Van Dyke and Noëlle Imperatore

Library of Congress Card Catalog Number 82-62810
International Standard Book Number 0-89997-020-6

Manufactured in the United States of America
Published by Wilderness Press
        2440 Bancroft Way
        Berkeley, CA 94704
        (510) 843-8080

Write for free catalog

Front cover: **Crater Lake and the Phantom Ship, viewed from the crater's rim**
Title page: **Crater Lake and Wizard Island, viewed from Sinnott Memorial**

For Ken Ng

Acknowledgments

With time for only two months of field work, I tried to map all of the area's maintained trails and most of the roads to the trailheads. While doing this, I also tried to identify as many plants as possible and tried to gain a fairly comprehensive understanding of the area's geology. Add to these objectives all the other kinds of information needed to produce a comprehensive guidebook, and I was pushed to the limit. To create a complete and (I hope) accurate guidebook, I relied on help and criticism from others.

I am particularly indebted to Ron Warfield and Charlie Bacon. Ron Warfield, the chief naturalist at Crater Lake National Park, reviewed all portions of the manuscript that dealt with the park. Dr. Bacon, a U.S. Geological Survey geologist and *the* geological expert on Crater Lake National Park, reviewed most of my sections on geology, Chapter 8 in particular. Without his dozens of critical comments, that chapter would have been woefully dated and inaccurate.

I also want to acknowledge Hank Tansky, the park's assistant naturalist, who reviewed a short section of the manuscript. Furthermore, I had fruitful conversations with Dr. Jim Smith (U.S. Geological Survey) on the area's overall geology, and with David Sherrod (a graduate student at U.C. Santa Barbara) on the geology of the area north of Crater Lake. Not being a fisherman, I relied heavily on trout information supplied by John Toman and Mick Jennings (both of the Oregon Department of Fish & Wildlife). While claiming to be more of a botanist than a fisherman, I was shown by Joan Fosback, an expert local botanist, that I still have ample room for improvement. I've incorporated most of her comments into the botany chapter, though I have chosen to disagree with her on the taxonomy of several species, preferring to side with the taxonomical biases of my former mentor, Dr. Ted Niehaus. From John Gemerys (Rogue River National Forest) and William Deese (Winema National Forest) I received maps showing the potential boundary of the proposed Sky Lakes Wilderness. Finally, Ken Ng accompanied me for part of the field work, giving me encouragement to continue my 12-hour workdays.

Tom Winnett, editor and publisher of Wilderness Press, also provided encouragement during extremely stressful times, while Noëlle Liebrenz, the company's manager, was always cheerful and a delight to do business with.

Drafting the book's 26 topographic maps proved to be a gargantuan task, one which took several hundred hours. Without the help of two people, the map work would have taken considerably longer, and the book might have been published in 1984 instead of '83. My wife, Bonnie Myhre, spent many monotonous hours painting some map overlays *gratis* (a fate of authors' wives), while Jim Thompson, a drafting student at our local Sonoma Valley High School, worked on more technical, though still tedious, aspects of map production.

In creating the final product, I've tried to be as accurate as possible. However, writing a perfect book seems to be an elusive goal, and I take responsibility for whatever errors and/or misrepresentations may occur.

—Jeffrey P. Schaffer
Boyes Hot Springs, CA
May 16, 1983

Contents

1　The Crater Lake Area

The Park and Related Lands

Introduction　Southern Oregon's High Cascades are a glacier-sculpted, volcanic wonderland with a repertory of recreational opportunities that is bound to please almost every outdoor enthusiast. Sightseeing, day hiking, backpacking, horseback riding, nature study, exploring, photography, camping, hunting, fishing, swimming, sunbathing, boating, sailing, water skiing, ski touring, snowmobiling and just plain relaxing—they're all here. For 99% of Oregon's residents, this area is less than a tankful of gas away. The same is true for California residents living in Redding, Chico, Oroville, Red Bluff and other northern communities.

Crater Lake, "the Gem of the Cascades," is the foremost attraction for out-of-state visitors, and as such it serves as the focus for southern Oregon's High Cascades, a region that the author calls "Crater Lake National Park & Vicinity" (see area map, pages 129-130). This Crater Lake area, as used in this book, extends from Lake of the Woods north to Diamond Lake. This area is composed of the following geographic units: foremost, Crater Lake National Park, then Diamond Lake Recreation Area, Sky Lakes proposed wilderness, Lake of the Woods Recreation Area and Mountain Lakes Wilderness.

Crater Lake National Park. (Chapters 8-10) This national park typically receives about half a million visitors each year, almost one half of them from California, and only one fourth of them from Oregon. About three fourths of the visitors come during summer, and the average visitor stays but a few hours before driving on to the next destination on his itinerary. Thus, visitation is brief, as at the Grand Canyon, though the Crater Lake tourist usually visits between 10 a.m. and 3 p.m., while the Grand Canyon tourist tries to take in a sunset and/or sunrise.

The park can be divided into two areas of use: 1) Crater Lake, its Rim Drive and associated north- and south-access roads, and 2) park's backcountry. The first, about 1/5 of the park's area, receives about 99¾% of the summer visitors, while the second, about 4/5 of the area, receives the remaining ¼%.

The typical summer tourist visits Rim Village, which on an average summer day is jammed with hundreds of other camera-toting tourists. Most tourists also drive along the lake's two-way west-rim road, stopping at several prominent turnouts for more snapshots. Less than half drive completely around the lake, and only about a tenth descend the Cleetwood Cove Trail and take the boat tour around the lake. Those who do, about 500 per day, make that overly steep, fairly viewless utility trail the most popular trail in the park. However, its popularity is rivaled by the park's most scenic trail (at least in the author's opinion)—the Garfield Peak Trail, which conveniently starts from Rim Village. Only about one fourth of the sightseers camp overnight in the park.

The other type of park visitor, the wilderness enthusiast, has most of the park to himself. On a typical summer night, there are only about a dozen hikers camped in the park's backcountry. And most of them are camped along the Pacific Crest, the Lightning Springs or the Dutton Creek Trail. What this means is that roughly three fourths of the park is rarely, if ever, visited. There is an explanation for this dearth of humanity—most of this area is waterless, viewless and, in most people's minds, monotonous.

1

Unless you're thoroughly steeped in natural history, you won't appreciate it. Like backpacking, both fishing and swimming are both best pursued outside the park, both particularly at Diamond Lake—see Chapter 4.

Diamond Lake Recreation Area (Chapter 11) If this book's title had been based on an area's popularity, then I would have had to call it "Diamond Lake & Vicinity," for this area receives about one million visitors annually, roughly twice the number at Crater Lake. Unlike that lake, Diamond Lake is very popular among Oregonians. It more or less sits at the hub of a ring of southern and central Oregon cities: Klamath Falls, Ashland, Medford, Grants Pass, Roseburg, Eugene-Springfield and Bend. From any of these, you can tow your boat to the lake and back on less than a tank of gas, making the lake a highly desirable weekend outing destination.

And water sports are what Diamond Lake is all about, with fishing as the paramount activity. Indeed, of the approximately five dozen trout-stocked lakes mentioned in Chapter 4, Diamond Lake by itself receives over half of each year's planted trout. If you don't own a boat, you can rent or charter one at the lake's capacious Diamond Lake Resort. Because this 3015-acre lake has an average depth of only about 20 feet, it tends to be quite warm. During the height of the visitor season, from Fourth of July through Labor Day, the water temperature stays at the respectable mid- to upper-60s, occasionally topping the 70° mark. Because boats are limited to 10 mph, speed boats and water skiers are absent, which is a blessing to fishermen, sailors and swimmers.

Since the water sports are obvious, this guidebook emphasizes the nonobvious—the trails in and around the recreation area. Between your water sports you can get in some fine hiking or horseback riding, horses being rented from the resort's stables. And for the expert mountain climber, this area contains one of Oregon's most serious challenges, the north face of Mt. Thielsen.

If you drive up to Diamond Lake via Highway 62, you'll discover that the highway-side Rogue River offers plenty of recreation potential. It is, in fact, a recreation area unto itself. Rafting may be the most exciting attraction, though fishing, swimming and sunbathing sure have their adherents. This stretch of river is well supplied with logistical necessities such as campgrounds, R.V. parks, resorts, motels, restaurants, gas stations, stores and other services.

Sky Lakes proposed wilderness (Chapters 12 and 13) As a naturalist who has mapped and described more miles of mountain trails than anyone else in the United States, I find it quite disconcerting that southern Oregon's most popular mountain trails have not been incorporated into an official wilderness. I've seen lots of inferior mountain scenery that has such protection, and if any area in Oregon deserves such protection, it is the Sky Lakes. Indeed, the Forest Service treats it as an official wilderness, asking that you fill out wilderness permits and obey all wilderness rules and practices. Although this proposed wilderness is several times larger than nearby Mountain Lakes Wilderness, its lakes are nevertheless more accessible. The author found he could backpack to any of the Sky Lakes' several dozen lakes in 2 hours or less. The Mountain Lakes Wilderness, with longer, steeper trails to its lakes, makes you work harder.

Being southern Oregon's most lake-blessed area, Sky Lakes also must be one of its most mosquito-cursed. Before August, a tent is essentially a necessity just to give you temporary asylum from these bloodthirsty beasties. By August, their numbers have declined sufficiently that they can be kept at bay with just insect repellent.

The Sky Lakes proposed wilderness is overwhelmingly a landscape of virgin forest punctuated with clusters of shimmering lakes and lakelets. But there is one notably different feature, Mt. McLoughlin, which rises as the highest peak in the southern half of Oregon. As such, it is the wilderness' most popular destination, having, on clear days, a steady stream of pilgrims inching their way up its very steep trail.

Lake of the Woods Recreation Area (Chapter 14) Like Diamond Lake, Lake of the Woods is a boater's paradise, though on a smaller scale. However, the emphasis is different, for there is no speed limit. Consequently speed boats and ski boats ply the lake, and some of their unmuffled engines send reverberations across the lake basin. The noise, however, is usually lost in the din of everyday activities and only becomes really apparent after dusk, when occasional boats race around the lake. Fishermen make do by rising early, hauling in their morning catch, then retreating about midmorning. The lake has four public picnic areas, each with an adjacent roped-in, safe swimming area. Water temperatures are comparable to those at Diamond Lake, conducive to swimming and sunbathing. Unlike the Diamond Lake environs, this area lacks a good network of hiking and riding trails, though of course the Sky Lakes and Mountain Lakes wildernesses are just minutes away.

Three other large lakes are peripheral to this book's area. These are Fish Lake, which is a few miles west of Lake of the Woods via Highway 140, and Howard Prairie and Hyatt lakes, which are both to the southwest via Dead Indian Road. Fish Lake, a natural lake that has been dammed to increase its volume, is an excellent fishermen's lake and a favorite among many southern Oregonians. Howard Prairie and Hyatt lakes, both shallow, manmade lakes, are appealing through midsummer, but by late summer they've lost most of their volume, and much of their bottom has become either grassy meadow or mud flat. Fish Lake also drops significantly, leaving a late-season bathtub ring. Lake of the Woods can also drop several feet, causing its marshy north end to dry up, but otherwise not significantly affecting the rest of the lake.

Mountain Lakes Wilderness (Chapter 15) This compact, pint-sized wilderness, only one township large, has all the features found in many larger wildernesses. Basically, it is the glacier-gouged remains of several overlapping, fault-torn volcanoes. When the glaciers retreated, they left about a half dozen respectable lakes and dozens of mosquito ponds. Fortunately, most of the ponds are away from the popular lakes, so the mosquito problem, while bad before August, is not desperate, as it it in the Sky Lakes wilderness. Surrounded by ridges and peaks, the Mountain Lakes have finer backdrops than do the Sky Lakes. And while the Mountain Lakes' Aspen Butte can't furnish the far-ranging views of Sky Lakes' Mt. McLoughlin, it nevertheless tenders very respectable views for considerably less effort. About 10 other, lower summits, each with revealing views, are attained by safe, relatively easy cross-country jaunts.

Seasons and Seasonal Sports

Climate The climate of the Crater Lake area can be divided into two major seasons. The primary one is the summer season, which is in full swing from about the Fourth of July through the Labor Day weekend. The second one is the winter season, from about Thanksgiving through April. Crater Lake, which attracts more than its share of snow, has a ski-touring season that can last from late October through mid-July. The following table presents a few basic statistics of the climate at Crater Lake National Park Headquarters, and we can generalize from them.

Crater Lake National Park Headquarters, at 6480 feet elevation

	Jan.	Feb.	Mar.	Apr.	May	Jun.	Jul.	Aug.	Sep.	Oct.	Nov.	Dec.
Extreme max. temp.	58	66	67	70	80	83	90	89	86	76	75	62
Av. max. temp.	33	35	37	43	51	58	70	69	63	52	41	34
Av. min. temp.	17	18	19	23	28	34	42	41	37	31	25	20
Extreme min. temp.	−21	−18	− 7	0	5	11	18	21	18	10	− 7	−9
Av. rainfall (in.)	11½	8	8	4½	3	2½	¾	1	2	5¾	9	11¾
Av. snowfall (in.)	121	91	94	45	23	5	3½	2¾	6	27	59	101

Yearly precipitation, 69 inches; yearly snowfall, 50 feet

At 6480 feet elevation, the Park Headquarters is roughly at the same elevation as the lakes of the Sky Lakes and Mountain Lakes wildernesses, so in them you can expect similar temperatures, though less snowfall. Note that in the table, the temperature extremes can be well above or below the monthly averages.

In general the summer season is quite pleasant, neither too hot nor too cold, and precipitation is relatively uncommon. As a rule, the lower a spot is, the warmer it is. Hence at Diamond Lake and Lake of the Woods, the summer days typically warm to about 80°F or so, not 70°F, which is common in the park and the wilderness areas. Surprisingly, the minimum temperatures are about the same, averaging about 40°F at the break of dawn. This is because as the air cools, it contracts, becomes denser, and therefore sinks to lower elevations. Diamond Lake and Lake of the Woods, lying in basins, collect this cold air. (Fort Klamath, lying near the base of the park, experiences the same chilling effect.) During my stay at various campgrounds, I recorded minimum summer temperatures from about the low 30s to the mid-50s. The lowest temperatures were after starry, low-humidity nights, during which lots of heat radiated out to space. The warmest temperatures were after cloudy, muggy nights.

Just after the Labor Day weekend, temperatures usually drop markedly. Autumn is in the air and fall colors—mostly from huckle-berries—begin to appear. Days typically climb into the 60s or high 50s. Lakes, which got into the mid-to-upper 60s a few weeks earlier, are now in the low 60s, which is too cool for most swimmers. Although the area's higher peaks—those above 8000 feet—can get dusted with snow *anytime* during the summer, the first major snow storm doesn't usually appear until late September, when it gives the park and the wilderness areas a momentary ermine coat. Fall can be a pleasant time in the mountains, for most of the people are gone, yet the days are usually mild enough for one to enjoy the quiet solitude.

By mid-October, Crater Lake's Rim Drive is usually buried under snow, and the road stays closed until June or July of the following year. Also about this time, the Forest Service roads leading up to wilderness trailheads are closed.

Winter usually arrives in the Crater Lake area by Thanksgiving, sooner at the higher elevations. At 5000 feet the snowpack usually lasts through April, and during winter months you'll find brave souls fishing on the icy surfaces of Fish Lake and Lake of the Woods. At 6000 feet the snowpack usually lasts through May, and at 7000 feet, through June. Snow patches can persist weeks after the first bit of ground is exposed. Some snow patches last well into August, particularly along Crater Lake's east rim, which causes that rim's one-way road to open later than the two-way west-rim road (about mid-July and late June, respectively).

Hiking season Most of the trails are liberated from their icy captors by mid-June, though some remain shackled till mid-July. Where such snow problems exist, they are mentioned in the appropriate trail description.

As the snow melts, mosquito populations swell to intolerable numbers, particularly in the Sky Lakes basin. From late May through late July, you should carry a tent if you plan to backpack into the wilderness; otherwise you'll have

no recourse from their incessant attacks. Long-sleeved shirts can be a necessity, even though the weather can turn hot and muggy. Unfortunately for you, the hiker, wildflowers are showiest at the peak of the mosquito season, which means you'll have to endure their needling attacks if you're a flower fancier. Since mosquitoes are major pollinators, it is important that they are present when the flowers are blooming.

August is about the only tent-free month for backpackers, for by September storms can sweep through every few days. Still, September hiking is usually quite safe, though by early October you should certainly check the weather report before you head into the mountains. A major snowstorm could give you some very serious problems.

Winter sports season Since the area is usually covered with snow from late November through April or May, winter recreationists have about six months to enjoy their sports. Both Diamond Lake and Lake of the Woods have major staging areas for snowmobilers, and at mid-elevations on both sides of the Cascades there are dozens of snowbound roads for snowmobilers to enjoy. They are even permitted up Crater Lake's north-rim access road for winter-wonderland views of the lake.

Ski tourers can take the same routes, but they generally look for quieter places. They can find such solitude among the northern and southern flatter parts of Crater Lake National Park. Because ski tourers are allowed to go into high-elevation areas closed to snowmobilers, their season is longer. In and around the Sky Lakes wilderness, they can make forays as late as May.

Ice fishing on some of the area's larger lakes tends to be a truly winter sport—January through March. After that, the ice may get dangerously thin.

One winter sport is conspicuously absent—downhill skiing. Certainly the topography is available for many fine runs, but no ski resort has been built. To skiers, this is a major disappointment; to most environmentalists, a cause for elation. For downhill skiing, you'll have to visit Bend's Mt. Bachelor or Ashland's Mt. Ashland, both outside this book's area.

2 Towns, Resorts, Lodges and Campgrounds

Introduction Of the sights found in southern Oregon's High Cascades, Crater Lake is foremost, and it attracts a lion's share of the tourists. During the summer the typical Crater Lake tourist visits the lake's environs for only a few hours before driving on. In one respect this short stay is fortunate, since Crater Lake National Park's lodge, cabins and campgrounds can accommodate only about one-fourth of the daily 4000 or so summer tourists. Folks who want to reside a few days in the southern Cascades usually camp or lodge outside the park, and they drive up with most of their gear. Again, this is fortunate, since major supplies are lacking; not a single respectable-sized town lies in the area. Should you need a doctor or an auto mechanic, you'll probably have to go all the way to Medford or Klamath Falls. Alas, the area's four towns are not particularly tourist oriented.

Towns

Butte Falls, with a few hundred people, is the area's largest town. Actually, this logger-oriented town lies just west of our area, and only a very few of this book's users will even pass through it. You can buy gas, food and some supplies and sometimes get a meal. No lodging or camping.

Fort Klamath, located on eastside Highway 62 betwixt Crater Lake and Highway 97, is very short on residents, but nevertheless offers gas, food, supplies, meals, lodging and camping.

Prospect, located just off westside Highway 62 below the Highway 230 junction, doesn't get the share of tourists it once had when the old highway went through the town. Today it offers gas, food, supplies and a *choice* of eating establishments, but no lodging or camping.

Rocky Point is a "town" only in the eyes of some of its few inhabitants. The town basically consists of a small general store, a gas station and the Harriman Springs Resort. The Rocky Point Resort lies about a mile north of "town." The town caters to Klamath Falls' fishermen.

Resorts and Lodges

It's best to make reservations in advance, since the following resorts and lodges may be full.

Some are open seasonally, and their schedules vary from year to year. Others attempt to stay open all year, but only the large Diamond Lake Resort has a successful all-year activity schedule.

Crater Lake Lodge On the southwest rim of Crater Lake, it approaches Mt. Hood's Timberline Lodge, Yosemite's Ahwahnee Hotel and Grand Canyon's El Tovar Hotel in setting and appointments. You need not be a guest to use the lodge's dining room, bar, lobby or lounge. The concessioner also operates 20 nearby cabins, plus adjacent store and cafeteria, and offers bus and boat tours. Mid-June through mid-September. Phone: 594-2511. **Map 9.**

Crater Lake R.V. Park It also has several cabins, a small store, a trout pond and an excellent swimming hole with treetop high-diving. Along Highway 62, 4⅔ miles northwest of Fort Klamath and 1⅔ miles southeast of Crater Lake National Park's south boundary. Mid-May through mid-October. Phone: 381-2275. **Area map,** p. 130, at upper-right corner.

Diamond Lake Resort This large resort is more self-sufficient than many small towns—meals, lodging, gas, supplies, boat charters and rentals. It sponsors events that attract hundreds of visitors, but in general caters to the lake's large summertime fishermen population. Open all year. Phone: 793-3333. Along northeast shore of Diamond Lake. **Map 1.**

Fish Lake Resort A small resort with store, cafe, gas, boat rentals, cabins and trailer park. Friendly, unhurried atmosphere. May be open all year. Phone: Operator, Fish Lake Toll Station #1. At Fish Lake. **Map 24.**

Fort Klamath Lodge and R.V. Park Very economical accommodations—motel, youth hostel, cabins. Phone: 381-2234. Adjacent to the popular Cattle Crossing Cafe. In Fort Klamath. **Area map,** p. 130, near upper-right corner.

Harriman Springs Resort Similar to Rocky Point Resort, below. Phone: 356-2323. Along Rocky Point Road. **Map 23.**

Lake of the Woods Resort A small-scale Diamond Lake Resort with similar, though scaled-down facilities. May be open all year. Phone: Operator, Lake of the Woods Toll Station #1. Along northeast shore of Lake of the Woods. **Map 25.**

Rocky Point Resort Cabins, restaurant, bar, marina. Mid-April through October. Phone: 356-2287. Near north end of Rocky Point Road. **Map 23.**

Union Creek Resort A small resort with lodge, cabins, cafe, store and gas. Open all year. Phone: 560-3565. Along Highway 62, 1¼ miles southwest of the Highway 230 junction. **Area map,** p. 129, near left edge.

Campgrounds

The great majority of multiday visitors stay in the area's campgrounds. In the following list, these are designated by size: small, about 2 to 15 sites; medium, about 20 to 50 sites; large, about 60 to 100 sites; and very large, well over 100 sites. The small campgrounds usually have minimal outhouses and no tap water. The large and very large campgrounds have electrified bathrooms. The medium campgrounds are in between. Private campgrounds typically have hot water, showers and laundry. Primitive campgrounds tend to be free; the other public campgrounds generally cost a few dollars per day. Private campgrounds can cost substantially more, particularly if you are driving or pulling a big rig. Public campgrounds are open typically June through September, though the lower ones are open longer. Private campgrounds are usually open longer.

Crater Lake National Park

Lost Creek Campground (5980') Small. Along the Pinnacles road, 3.1 miles south of Rim Drive. **Map 10.**

Mazama Campground (6000') Very large. Along south-rim road, 0.3 mile north of Highway 62. **Map. 12.**

Rogue River National Forest

Beaver Dam Campground (4530') Small. Along Road 3706, 1.5 miles north of Dead Indian Road. **Area map,** p. 130, near lower-left corner.

Big Bend Campground (4072') Small. Along Road 37, 0.9 mile south of Road 34. **Map 18.**

Daley Creek Campground (4500') Small. Along Road 3706, 1.7 miles north of Dead Indian Road. **Area map,** p. 130, near lower left corner.

Doe Point Campground (4650') Medium. Near Highway 140 at Fish Lake. **Map 24.**

Farewell Bend Campground (3420') Large. Along Highway 62, ⅓ mile southwest of the Highway 230 junction. **Area map,** p. 129, near middle of left edge.

Fish Lake Campground (4650') Medium. Near Highway 140 at Fish Lake. **Map 24.**

Fourbit Ford Campground (3200') Small. Near junction of Forest Routes 30 and 37. **Area map,** p. 130, near middle of left edge.

Hamaker Campground (3980') Small. From Highway 230 midway between Highways 62 and 138, start southeast on Road 6530. **Map 3.**

Huckleberry Mountain Campground (5400') Small. Isolated. Best reached from north end of Forest Route 60. **Map 11.**

Imnaha Campground (3780') Small. Just east of Forest Route 37 and opposite Imnaha Guard Station. **Map 15.**

Mill Creek Campground (2780') Small. One mile northeast on Road 030. Leave Highway 62 just 1.8 miles north of Prospect Ranger Station. **Area map,** p. 129, near lower left corner.

Natural Bridge Campground (3210') Medium. Just west of Highway 62, about 1 mile south of Union Creek settlement. **Area map,** p. 129, near lower-left edge.

North Fork Campground (4580') Small. West of Fish Lake and just off Road 3706, about 1 mile southwest of that road's junction with Highway 140. **Map 24** (left edge).

Parker Meadows Campground (4980') Small. Campground's road is about ½ mile north of the Forest Route 37/Road 3770 junction. **Map 18.**

River Bridge Campground (2820') Small. At Rogue River along Kiter Creek Road, which leaves Highway 62 3.8 miles north of Prospect Ranger Station. **Area map,** page 129, lower left edge.

Snowshoe Campground (4020') Small. Along Road 3065, just west of Forest Route 37. **Map 18.**

South Fork Campground (3980') Small. Just above both Rogue River and Forest Route 34. **Map 15.**

Sumpter Creek Campground (3900') Small. About ⅓ mile west of Forest Route 37 and 1½ miles south of Imnaha Campground. **Map 15.**

Union Creek Campground (3300') Large. Just west of Highway 62's Union Creek settlement. **Area map,** page 129, near left edge.

Upper South Fork Campground (4350') Small. Along the Rogue River about ¾ mile north of Forest Route 37's river bridge. **Map 18.**

Whiskey Spring Campground (3510') Medium. Near junction of Forest Routes 30 and 37. **Area map,** p. 130, near middle of left edge.

Willow Prairie Campground (4400') About 1¼ miles west on Road 3634, which leaves Forest Route 37 about 1½ miles northwest of Highway 140. **Area map,** p. 130, near lower left edge.

Umpqua National Forest

Broken Arrow Campground (5200') Very large. Near southeast shore of Diamond Lake. **Map 1.**

Diamond Lake Campground (5200') Very large. By east shore of Diamond Lake. **Map 1.**

Thielsen View Campground (5190') Large. Along west shore of Diamond Lake. **Map 1.**

Winema National Forest

Aspen Point Campground (4970') Large. Along northeast shore of Lake of the Woods. **Map 25.**

Cold Springs Campground (5850') Small. At end of Road 3651. **Map 19.**

Fourmile Lake Campground (5750') Medium. At end of Road 3661. **Map 22.**

Odessa Campground (4150') Small. Near west shore of Upper Klamath Lake. **Map 23.**

Sevenmile Marsh Campground (5480') Small. At end of Road 3334. **Map 17.**

Sunset Campground (4970') Large. Along east shore of Lake of the Woods. **Map 25.**

Kimball State Park

Kimball Campground (4200') Small. Along Route 232, about 2.9 miles north of its junction with Highway 62, and immediately north of its junction with the east end of Dixon Road. **Area map,** p. 130, at upper right corner.

Private

Crater Lake R.V. Park (4290') Medium. Along Highway 62, 4⅔ miles northwest of Fort Klamath and 1⅔ miles southeast of Crater Lake National Park's south boundary. **Area map,** p. 130, near upper-right corner. Also see entry under "Resorts and Lodges."

Diamond Lake Park, ACI (5240') Medium. Above southeast corner of Diamond Lake. **Map 1.**

Fort Klamath Lodge and R.V. Park (4180') Medium. In Fort Klamath. **Area map,** p. 130, near upper-right corner.

Harriman Springs Resort (4150') Medium. Along Rocky Point Road. **Map 23.**

Lake of the Woods Resort (4980') Medium. Along northeast shore of Lake of the Woods. **Map 25.**

Rocky Point Resort (4160') Medium. Near north end of Rocky Point Road. **Map 23.**

Ken Ng, on the Union Peak summit (page 78), identifies landmarks with the aid of topographic maps. Mt. McLoughlin, in the background, lies 27 miles to the south.

3 Exploring the Crater Lake Area on Foot, Horseback or Skis

Introduction Over half of this book is devoted to trails—where they go, what they are like, what lakes, peaks or views you'll see, and what significant plants, animals or geologic formations you're likely to encounter along the trails. This book is aimed mainly at hikers, not at equestrians or skiers, though they will find some merit in the text and in the 26 topographic maps. The rules that apply to hikers also apply to equestrians and skiers, though they have a few more points to consider, points which are mentioned at the end of this chapter. To camp overnight in some areas, all will need wilderness permits.

Wilderness Permits

To camp in the Crater Lake National Park back-country or in any part of the Mountain Lakes Wilderness, you'll need a wilderness permit. It doesn't matter whether you are on foot, horse-back or skis, or whether you are entering on a popular summer weekend or in the dead of winter—they are still required. In Crater Lake National Park, you can get a permit either at the Park Headquarters or at the Rim Village Visitor Center. For Mountain Lakes Wilderness, you can get a permit at any of the wilderness' three trailheads.

Since the Sky Lakes "wilderness" is merely proposed and therefore not official, wilderness permits are not required. Nevertheless, you'll find them at all the official trailheads. By completing them, you'll provide the Forest Service with visitor-use information, which will allow planners to optimize their management of the area. In the National Forest lands north of Crater Lake National Park, no wilderness permits are required.

Though you don't have to write a govern-mental agency for wilderness permits, you may want to contact one for other information. Their addresses and phone numbers are:

Superintendent
Crater Lake National Park
Crater Lake, OR 97604
(503) 594-2211

Forest Supervisor
Rogue River National Forest
P.O. Box 520
Medford, OR 97501
(503) 776-3600

Forest Supervisor
Umpqua National Forest
P.O. Box 1008
Roseburg, OR 97470
(503) 672-6601

Forest Supervisor
Winema National Forest
P.O. Box 1390
Klamath Falls, OR 97601
(503) 882-7761

These agencies limit the size of each back-country party: 12 persons and 8 stock in Crater Lake National Park; a combination of persons and stock, 20 maximum, in Sky Lakes proposed wilderness; and a combination of persons and stock, 10 maximum, in Mountain Lakes Wilderness.

Day Hiking and Backpacking

General Most, if not all, of the routes in this book can be done as day hikes rather than as overnight hikes—although you may want to take more than one day to do many of them. Generally, however, many are suitable day hikes and you can do them with very little planning or preparation. Novices to hiking and backpacking can learn the art by reading Thomas Winnett's *Backpacking Basics*— aimed directly at them.

Because accurate, up-to-date maps are included in this guide, mileage figures within the text are kept to a minimum. The one or more figures at the beginning of each route are mostly the author's, based on his field mapping and measurements. For Crater Lake National Park, the official park figures were generally used, since most of the Government's topographic base map was too inaccurate for the author to determine accurate distances.

If you're hiking in spring or fall, you can often follow a trail even when parts of it are snowbound. Along a few trails there are trees bearing metal markers. Along most others, there are blazes. A *blaze* is a spot on a tree's trunk where a patch or two of bark has been removed to leave a conspicuous, manmade scar.

Minimum-impact hiking If thousands of hikers walk through a mountain landscape, with its fragile soils, they are almost bound to degrade it. The following suggestions are offered in the hope they will reduce the human imprint on the landscape, thus keeping it attractive for those who might follow.

First, if you're healthy enough to make an outdoor trip into a wilderness area, you're in good enough condition to do so on foot. If possible, leave horses behind. (However, some hunters who enter mountain areas in autumn may certainly not want to carry a deer out on their shoulders.) One horse can do more damage than a dozen backpackers. It will contribute at least as much excrement as all of them, but moreover, it will do so indiscriminately, sometimes in creeks or on lakeshores. Another problem with horses is that they can trample meadow trails into a string of muddy ruts, particularly in early season. And they selectively graze the meadows, causing a change in the native flora.

On foot, if at all possible, day-hike rather than overnight-hike. In one day's time you can reach *any* destination mentioned in this book and return to your trailhead. Most lakes are a moderate hike, round trip. No lake in this entire area is more than 6 miles from the nearest trailhead. Fishermen may object to day hiking, since the best times for fishing are early morning and evening. And who wants to get up at four in the morning to fish a lake at dawn? For them, backpacking is a must.

Why do day hikers have less impact on the environment? For one thing, they usually use toilets at campgrounds or near trailheads rather than soil near lakes. A month's worth of backpackers in the Sky Lakes wilderness could contribute about a ton of human waste to the area, and the bulk of this is within 100 yards of some lake, stream or trail. Around a popular lake, excrement can lead to deterioration of its water quality. Always defecate *at least 50 yards* away from any lake or stream and bury feces 6 to 8 inches deep. In part because of this human-waste problem, Park and Forest Service officials recommend you boil or otherwise treat the water you drink. Three to five minutes is sufficient time to kill a microscopic organism, *Giardia lamblia,* which is a common cause of backpacker diarrhea. If you do get sick after you've been in the mountains, then suspect this organism. To minimize your chances of getting sick, drink from springs or creeks rather than lakes or ponds. Day hikers have an advantage over backpackers in that they can carry in their own supply of fresh water.

If, in order to have a satisfactory wilderness experience, you decide to backpack, then you should consider the following advice.

1. Pack out toilet paper. Popular lakes can receive hundreds of visitors during summer, and there's a limit to how much paper can be buried.

2. Don't build a campfire unless you absolutely have to, as in an emergency. They aren't prohibited, but downed wood is already too scarce at popular sites, and cutting or defacing standing vegetation, whether living or dead, is strictly prohibited. Use a stove instead. Stoves cook meals faster, leave pots and pans cleaner, and save downed wood for the soil's organisms, which are, in turn, food for larger animals. Campfires can leave an unsightly mess and, as a winter's snowpack melts, campfire ashes can be carried into lakes, reducing the water quality.

3. Don't pollute lakes and streams by washing clothes or dishes in them or throwing fish guts into them. And don't lather up in them, even with biodegradable soap. *All* soaps pollute. Do your washing and pot scrubbing well away from streams and lakes, and bury fish entrails ashore rather than throwing them back into the water.

4. Set up camp at least 100 feet away from streams, trails and lakeshores. Always camp on mineral soil (or perhaps even on bedrock, if you've brought sufficient padding), but never in meadows or other soft, vegetated areas. It's best

to use a site already in existence rather than to brush out a new campsite. That would result in one more human mark upon the landscape.

5. Leave your campsite clean. Don't leave scraps of food behind, for this only attracts mice, bears and other camp marauders. If you can carry it in, you can carry it out. After all, your pack is lighter on the way out.

6. Don't build structures. Rock walls, large fireplaces and bough beds were fine in the last century, but not today. There are just too many humans on this planet, and one goes up into the wilderness for a bit of solitude. The hiker shouldn't have to be confronted with continual reminders of man's presence. Leave the wilderness at least as pure as you found it.

7. Noise and loud conversations, like motor vehicles, are inappropriate. Have some consideration for other campers in the vicinity. Also, camp far enough from others to assure privacy to both them and you.

Regardless of whether you are day hiking or backpacking, you should observe the following advice.

1. If you are 14 or older, you will need a valid Oregon fishing license if you plan to fish—see the next chapter.

2. Destruction, injury, defacement or disturbance in any manner of any natural feature or public property is prohibited. This includes molesting any animal; picking flowers or other plants; cutting, blazing, marking, driving nails into or otherwise damaging growing trees or standing snags; writing, carving or painting names or other inscriptions anywhere; destroying, defacing or moving signs; collecting rocks or minerals.

3. Smoking is not allowed while traveling through vegetated areas. You may stop and smoke in a safe place.

4. Although you are unlikely to meet any pack or saddle animals on a trail, be aware that they have the right of way. Hikers should get completely off the trail, on the downhill side if possible, and remain quiet until the stock has passed.

5. When traveling on a trail, stay on the trail. Don't cut switchbacks, since this destroys trails. When going cross country, don't mark your route in any way. Let the next person find his way as you did. Use a compass and map.

6. Be prepared for sudden adverse weather. It's good to carry a poncho even on a sunny day hike; it can also double as a ground cloth or an emergency tent. A space blanket (2 oz. light) is also useful. Some day hikes accidentally turn into overnight trips, due to injury, getting lost or bad weather. Early-season and late-season

Two very bad camping practices: hikers bivouacking at the shore of Alta Lake (across the trail at that!); stock tied only a few yards away from Eb Lake.

hikers may encounter snow flurries and, rarely, full-fledged storms; and if they plan to camp out overnight, they should have a tent or at least a tube tent. Before you drive off to your trailhead, find out what the weather is supposed to be like, but be prepared for the worst. Never climb to a mountaintop if clouds are building above it, particularly if you hear thunder in the cloudy distance. And if you see lightning, turn back.

7. The farther you are from your trailhead, the greater is the problem if you are injured. You shouldn't hike alone, since you might have no one but yourself to rescue you in an emergency. However, many trails covered in this book are popular enough that you are likely to meet other hikers, should you need help. Vehicles, including bicycles and motorcycles, are forbidden on almost every trail mentioned in this book.

The following regulations apply to Crater Lake National Park *only*.

1. Dogs, cats and other pets are not permitted in the backcountry or on any trail. Elsewhere in the park, they must be on leash.

2. Firearms and other hunting devices are prohibited.

Equestrians

In the 1950s and 60s, with an increase in mountain roads and the development of reliable lightweight backpacking equipment, every mountain destination became attainable on foot. Horses were no longer needed. Some people still prefer to pack in with horses, and they can do so, particularly in Mountain Lakes Wilderness and Sky Lakes proposed wilderness. The northwest quadrant of the proposed wilderness is admirably suited for horses, since backpackers tend to shun this area. Both McKie Camp and Solace Cow Camp have adequate grazing areas.

If you are bringing stock into the mountains, you should heed the following Forest Service advice. Pasture or tether stock outside the camp areas and at least 200 feet from lakeshores, creeks or springs. Use hobbles, hitchlines, natural barriers and stock-handling facilities where provided. Stock should not be picketed or tied to trees overnight, since this leads to stomp holes dug by their shifting hoofs. Graze pack and saddle animals wisely and avoid overuse of meadows. Since forage is inadequate at most campsites, plan to bring in supplemental grain or pelletized feed. Grazing is discouraged in Crater Lake National Park.

Cross Country Skiers

From mid-October through early June, Crater Lake National Park, Mountain Lakes Wilderness and Sky Lakes proposed wilderness are largely mantled with snow. For some folks, this is the best time to experience wilderness, for solitude abounds and the marks of man are largely buried beneath the snow. The same rules that apply to hikers apply to ski tourers.

Certainly the most scenic ski touring is along the rim of Crater Lake. You can start from Rim Village, since the road up to it is kept open year 'round. When skiing along the rim, watch for icy spots, snow cornices and avalanche areas. From Highway 138, you can also ski up the north-rim access road to the Crater Lake rim, but this is certainly the long way in, and is a route used by snowmobilers. Because the park's north lands are flat, they lend themselves to winter camping. Should you camp, be sure you have your wilderness permit.

Due to the rather rugged topography, most of this book's area is not suitable for ski touring. Where the terrain is relatively flat, as around Diamond Lake and Lake of the Woods, snowmobilers prevail, and their noise and speed are annoying to most ski tourers.

Some snow-mantled landscapes can pose orientation problems. If you are not expert with map and compass, you could easily get lost. In a blinding snowstorm, you could get lost no matter how expert you are. Never travel alone. If you are unfamiliar with the area or with mountain navigation and winter survival, restrict your activities to the shorter, more popular routes, and do so after March, when there's less chance of storms and of severely cold weather. Isolated winter camping can be either rewarding or deadly.

4 Lakes and Fish of Southern Oregon's High Cascades

Introduction The lakes—not the mountains or the forests—are the magnets that attract most of us to the High Cascades of southern Oregon. Indeed, the area's prime attraction is a giant lake, not the ruins of Mt. Mazama, which hold this lake. Geologists, I'm sure, would rather have no lake at all, for then they could examine the floor of Crater Lake and resolve some intriguing geological questions. Some botanists, too, may be indifferent toward the lake, for they'd rather study every plant community there, for each is very youthful—only a few thousand years old. Scientists aside, the rest of us come to the lakes to boat, swim, fish or camp, to enjoy their beauty, or simply to take a break from life's hectic pace.

Boating Most of the boating lakes lie outside the area covered by this book. In fact, there are only four lakes—all relatively large—onto which you can launch boats. Southernmost is Lake of the Woods, which sports a plethora of watercraft. This is the only lake open to speed boats and ski boats. Diamond Lake, the northernmost, is three times the size of Lake of the Woods, but is nevertheless restricted to slow boats. It is unquestionably the finest lake for sailboats and probably the best one for fishing boats. Some diehard fishermen, however, prefer aptly named Fish Lake, along Highway 140. Finally, Fourmile Lake rewards fishermen willing to drive a few miles out of the way. The lake lacks a boat-launch ramp, so this limits the size of watercraft to whatever you can carry.

Of course you can pack in a nonmotorized raft or foldboat to many of the mountain lakes, if you're willing to make the effort. One exception is Crater Lake, which has its own fleet of boats for tourist rides only.

Swimming Considerably fewer people go to lakes to swim, the author being one of them. Like hiking, jogging and bicycling, swimming is an excellent form of aerobic exercise, and swimming in a nonchlorinated, nonrestricted body of water can be a pure joy. In the area there are two kinds of swimming lakes: the large, lower-elevation lakes and the small, higher-elevation lakes.

The first category includes Diamond Lake, Lake of the Woods and Fish Lake. At each you'll find a resort, campgrounds, picnic areas and summer homes. When you swim or play in the water, you usually have company. The typical bathers are children, who splash around while their parents suntan nearby. Being large, these lakes tend to be windy, particularly in late afternoon, when waves slap upon the windward shore. While this is an inconvenience to swimmers emerging from water, it does clear the air of mosquitoes—a definite blessing. These lakes typically warm up to the mid-60s (acceptable swimming temperatures) by late June, peak around 70°F by late July, then steadily slide to below the mid-60s around mid-September. The lakes are so massive that summer storms do little to lower their temperatures.

That is not true for the higher, "wilderness" lakes. Lakes in this category can drop several degrees when a one-day storm passes by, particularly if they are shallow or only a few acres in size. On the other hand, such lakes can warm to the high 60s only a few days after the last remaining snowpatches begin to wane. When this happens is extremely variable: a few in mid-June, larger, deeper ones by mid-July. From late July through mid-August are idyllic days for the wilderness swimmer: lake temperatures are generally in the high 60s, and most mosquitoes are gone. By the Labor Day weekend, however, the smaller, shallower lakes have cooled noticeably, though the larger ones have dropped by only a degree or two.

Fishing Diamond Lake, with about 400,000 fingerling trout planted in it each year, is a fishermen's mecca. In all likelihood, more fish are pulled from this lake than the combined total at Lake of the Woods, Fish Lake, Fourmile Lake and Crater Lake. Crater Lake, the area's largest, deepest lake, presents a problem for fishermen, since there are only two locations from where they can fish. Both require you to walk down the fairly steep Cleetwood Cove Trail. You can fish at trail's end beyond the boat dock, or you can take a boat ride to Wizard Island, fish there, and take a later boat ride back to the dock. Most Crater Lake fishermen come back empty-handed. If you catch one, odds are that it will be a rainbow trout or a kokanee salmon, though in 1981 a small population of brown trout—thought to have died out—was rediscovered. This trout, *Salmo trutta,* is brown to olive-brown on the back, brown on the sides, and white or yellow on the belly. It has large black spots and sometimes red spots, both often surrounded by a lighter halo.

The chart on the previous page lists the fish you can expect to catch in the area. The fish data are based solely on Fish and Wildlife information, and are subject to change. Lake size and elevation are largely from the author's data, and lake depth is a combination of the author's and Fish and Wildlife's data. Generally, the wilderness lakes are stocked with brook trout, while the larger, lower lakes are stocked with rainbow trout. In this guidebook, "rough fish" and juveniles are not described.

Eastern brook trout, *Salvelinus fontinalis.* Back is olive green, with distinct wavy lines. Sides also olive green, but with reddish spots, some having bluish halos; no black spots. Leading edges of fins are whitish.

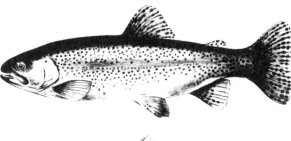

Rainbow trout, *Salmo Gairdnerii.* Many small, dark spots, especially on back; none with halos. Conspicuous reddish lateral band along length of some fish.

Kokanee salmon, *Oncorhynchus nerka.* Dark blue back and silvery sides. Fish turn deep red in spawning season. Anal fin usually has 13-17 rays, as opposed to trout's usual 9–12 rays.

Brown bullhead, *Ictalurus nebulosus.* A catfish with typical whiskers. This species has a squarish tail. Found at Lake of the Woods.

Calif. Dept. of Fish and Game

Lakes and Fish of Southern Oregon's High Cascades

Lake's name	Map	Chapter	Elevation (feet)	Size (acres)	Depth (feet)	Fish
Alta Lake	16	12	6805	16	13	E
Avalanche Lake	25,26	15	6795	2	5	—
Badger Lake	22	13	5910	12	11	E
Beal Lake	18	12	5550	4	9	E
Bert Lake	22	13	5950	2	10	E
Blue Canyon Lake	21	12	6155	2	18	E
Blue Lake	21	12	5635	9	33	E
Boulder Pond	16	12	6640	½	3	—
Carey Lake	21	12	6030	6	31	E
Center Lake	22	13	5950	4	2	—
Cliff Lake	16	12,13	6270	8	30	E
Clover Lake	26	15	6700	2	8	E
Como, Lake	26	15	6540	6	32	E,R
Crater Lake	8,9,10	8,9	6176	13,100	1932	R,K,B
Dee Lake	19,22	13	5910	16	13	E
Deep Lake (by Donna Lake)	19	13	5950	4	17	E
Deep Lake (by Heav. Twin Lks.)	19	13	5975	1	5	—
Deer Lake	19	13	6070	4	15	E
Diamond Lake	1	11	5183	3,015	52	R
Donna Lake	19	13	5940	2	9	E
Eb Lake	26	15	6770	2	8	—
Echo Lake	26	15	6670	4	16	E
Elizabeth, Lake	19	13	6020	4	8	E
Finch Lake	19	12	6590	1	12	E
Fish Lake	24	2	4642	450	45	R,E
Fourmile Lake	21,22	13	5744	677	170	E,K,R
Francis, Lake	20	13	6510	4	12	E
Freye Lake	21	12	6230	4	3	—
Frog Lake	16	12	6310	2	5	—
Gladys, Lake	20	13	6670	3	5	—
Grass Lake	16	12,13	6030	25	8	E
Harriette, Lake	26	15	6735	35	63	E,R
Heavenly Twin Lake, north	19	13	5975	25	13	E,R
Heavenly Twin Lake, south	19	13	5978	6	17	E
Hemlock Lake	19	12	6105	6	20	E
Hemlock Lake	26	15	6390	4	3	—
Holst Lake	19	12	6110	4	12	E
Horse Lake	1	11	5198	6	8	R
Horseshoe Lake	21	12	5718	25	12	R,E
Isherwood Lake	19	13	5980	18	17	E
Island Lake	19,22	13	5906	40	17	E
Ivern, Lake	16	12	5690	3	10	E
Lake of the Woods	25	14	4949	1,113	52	E,R,K,BB
Land, Lake	19	13	5970	3	8	—
Lilly Pond	22	13	5910	1	2	—
Liza, Lake	19	13	6020	2	5	—
Long Lake	22	13	6050	37	9	E
Margurette Lake	19	13	6010	15	29	E,R
Martin Lake	19	13	6030	1	3	—
McKee Lake	18	12	5790	4	10	E
Meadow Lake	21	12	5625	1	3	E,R
Middle Lake	16	12,13	6100	26	20	E
Mud Lake	18,19,21	12	5630	4	3	R,E
Mystic Lake	26	15	7270	2	14	E
Norris Pond	21	13	5750	2	3	—
North Lake	16	12	6045	6	5	—
Notasha, Lake	19	13	6030	5	27	E,R
Orris Pond	21	13	5758	1	4	—
Paragon Lake	26	15	6980	3	8	E
Pear Lake	21	12	5755	20	33	R,E
Puck Lake, north	19,20	13	6470	7	18	E
Puck Lake, south	19,20	13	6475	24	10	E
Red Lake	19	13	5830	29	6	E
Round Lake	18	12	5860	3	12	E
Snow Lakes (by Pacific Cr. Tr.)	19	13	6640	½	6	—
Snow Lakes (near Wind Lake)	19	13	6070	3	8	E
Sonya, Lake	19	13	5860	8	38	E,R
South Lake	16	12	6380	8	10	—
South Pass Lake	26	15	6510	9	15	E,R
Squaw Lake	21	13	5750	30	11	E
Storm Lake	26	15	6510	½	4	—
Summit Lake	21	13	5740	2	3	—
Teal Lake	1	11	5197	1½	5	—
Trapper Lake	19	13	5938	17	11	E
Waban, Lake	25	15	6330	4	3	—
West, Lake	4	10	5110	5	6	—
Weston Lake	25	15	6420	1½	16	E
Wind Lake	19	13	6035	2	8	E
Wizzard Lake	19	13	5910	5	17	E
Woodpecker Lake	22	13	5910	3	11	E
Woods, Lake of the	25	14	4949	1,113	52	E,R,K,BB
Zeb Lake	26	15	6770	2½	10	E
Zepher Lake	26	15	6630	5	5	—

Fish   B: brown trout   BB: brown bullhead   E: "eastern" brook trout   K: kokanee salmon   R: rainbow trout

Author diving into Cliff Lake   *Ken Ng*

Now that you've been introduced to the game fish, you have to know the rules. If you are 14 years or older, you'll need a valid Oregon state angling license (except at Crater Lake National Park, where none is required, though special regulations apply). You can pick one up at most sporting goods stores or at the Diamond Lake, Fish Lake and Lake of the Woods resorts. The fishing season at Diamond Lake runs from the last Saturday in April to the last day in October. At all the other lakes in the area, the season is year-round. Of course, the wilderness lakes are completely snowed in for about half the year. Winter fishermen can ice-fish at Lake of the Woods or Fish Lake. The trout limit for all fishermen is ten fish per day, 6 inch minimum length; no more than five may be over 12 inches, and of these no more than two may be over 20 inches. For further information, contact the Oregon Department of Fish and Wildlife, P.O. Box 3503 (506 SW Mill Street),

Portland, OR 97208; tel. (503) 229-5403. The regional office for the southern Cascades lands west of the crest is at 3140 NE Stephens, Roseburg, OR 97470; tel (503) 440-3353. The regional office for lands east of the crest is 61374 Parrell Road, Bend, OR 97701; phone is (503) 388-6363.

Camping Diamond Lake, Lake of the Woods, Fish Lake and Fourmile Lake all have lake-shore campgrounds, and these are listed in Chapter 2. Camping anywhere else by these lakes is expressly prohibited. At the lakes of the Sky Lakes "wilderness" and the Mountain Lakes Wilderness, you should camp at least 100 feet away from the lakeshore. Often, the local topography makes this impossible, since the only level ground around some lakes is just a few yards away from the shore. If you must camp close to the lake, be sure to follow mininum-impact backcountry practices, which are described in the previous chapter.

5 Geology

Introduction Mountains. We take them for granted. But why should we have mountains in the first place—and, since the earth has been around for a long, long time, why haven't the mountains eroded away to the sea? The answer to both questions lies with plate tectonics—the ceaseless movements of the earth's crust and its associated upper mantle. This composite outer layer is made up of a few giant plates plus more abundant smaller ones, all interacting with one another. Some movements lead to the formation of mountain ranges, others to ocean basins. This plate tectonics has been occurring perhaps since our planet's infancy, when its crust solidified about 4½ billion years ago. And the process should continue until the sun, running out of hydrogen, expands to become a red giant, vaporizing planet Earth in the process.

Western North America, about 15 million years ago (left) and today (right). The Juan de Fuca plate (gray) is producing new oceanic crust along its western edge, causing sea-floor spreading (large, dark arrows). This plate is bordered by the Pacific plate on its west and south edges, and by the North American plate on its east edge. Note that in the 15-million-year time lapse, the Juan de Fuca plate has changed its orientation with respect to North America, and that it has migrated considerably eastward and northward while diving under the continent (open arrows). Note that the directions of sea-floor spreading and plate diving are very different. In another 15 million years, the Juan de Fuca plate will all but disappear beneath the North American plate. In the map on the right the stars are major Cascade Range volcanoes and the small rectangle is this chapter's geologic map.

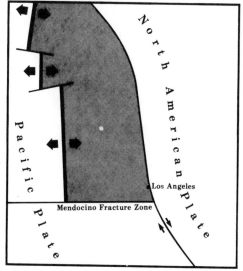
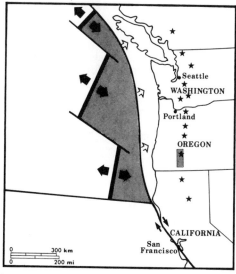

17

The tectonic setting Fortunately, we need not look billions of years back in time to unravel the story of the Cascade Range. A few tens of millions of years are sufficient and, for the Crater Lake area, the time span is considerably less.

We can begin our brief story about 50 million years ago. Back then, oceanic plates were diving under continental plates, much as they do today, along their interfacing edges. One oceanic plate, the Farallon plate, was diving east under the continental North American plate, being consumed in the process. This plate had a narrow middle section, which was totally consumed by about 30 million years ago, leaving a southern part and a northern part. That northern part is called the Juan de Fuca plate. Like the larger Farallon plate, the Juan de Fuca plate continued diving under the North American plate.

There is a definite relationship between a diving plate and a volcanic range. Geologists once thought that as a plate dived and encountered increasing temperatures and pressures, it began to melt, and the melted material rose as magma ("subsurface lava"), which in turn could build up volcanoes. Today, however, there is no general consensus on magma generation; the subterranean picture is more complex than we once thought. Nevertheless, it's fairly safe to say that if the Juan de Fuca plate weren't diving beneath western North America, we wouldn't have today's Cascade Range. Around the world you see volcanic ranges associated with diving plates. And this is why we will never run out of mountains. Plates continually move—though sometimes in pulses—and the movements lead to the generation of new magma. This magma can solidify beneath the earth's crust and later give rise to a granitic Sierra Nevada or North Cascades, or it can erupt to form an Oregon Cascades. Plate movement can also create or destroy ocean basins. For example, magma is rising along the west edge of the Juan de Fuca plate, where two plates are spreading apart, to fill the gap with new sea floor, which enlarges the ocean basin. (Near Asia the sea floor is diving under a continental plate at a *faster* rate, so overall the Pacific Ocean basin is actually shrinking.)

The Oregon Cascades The oldest rocks of the Cascades, about 45 million years old, may have been the result of early movement of the ancestral Farallon plate. Since those early times, episodes of volcanism have produced volcanoes, lava flows and ash deposits, building up the range layer by layer. Apparently, in southern Oregon uplift has played only a minor role, although it played a major role in the Sierra Nevada. In the Crater Lake area, shown on the accompanying geologic map, only the more recet layers are exposed, the oldest of these being in canyon bottoms, such as in the Red Blanket and Middle Fork Rogue River canyons, and they also make up much of the Mountain Lakes Wilderness. Elsewhere in our area, most of the rocks are less than five million years old and the main peaks are less than one million years old.

These younger rocks, with their high peaks, fresh flows and glaciated canyons, are known, appropriately, as the High Cascades. This range is constructed upon the eastern third of the older, more eroded, essentially unglaciated Western Cascades. Basically, our book is about the southern one-fourth of the High Cascades, from Mts. Bailey and Thielsen south to the Mountain Lakes Wilderness.

High Cascades volcanoes the geologic map shows our area's main volcanoes, the dominant one being former Mt. Mazama. In its prime, it stood 11,000-12,000 feet above sea level, dominating the landscape much as Mts. Hood and Shasta dominate their landscapes today. But the mountain "made the mistake" of becoming too silicic (silicon-rich) and consequently paid the price—self destruction—about 6900 years ago. This event led to the formation of Crater Lake within the mountain's ruins. Chapter 8, the Crater Lake Rim Drive, documents this mountain's rise and fall.

Just why a volcano looks the way it does depends, essentially, on two major variables: what kind of magma is present and how much of it is erupted. The particular combination of kind and amount gives rise to one of four types of volcanoes—though, as is so true in nature, each type can grade into another type. These four are shield volcanoes, cinder cones, stratovolcanoes and domes.

Shield volcanoes are composed mostly of basalt, a rock that is rich in iron and magnesium and relatively poor in silica (silicon dioxide). Generally, the less silica that is present in a lava flow, the less viscous it is. Hence, basalt flows tend to be "runny," and they'll stream for miles away from the summit area. Consequently, shield volcanoes, which are composed of dozens of layers of basalt flows, tend to be low and spreading, roughly several miles across. In our area Union Peak is an excellent example.

However, the best examples are the Hawaiian Islands. The island of Hawaii and its underwater base are an amalgamation of five overlapping shield volcanoes, a complex that is tens of miles across and is composed of hundreds of layers of basalt flows.

Cinder cones are the most common volcanoes in our area. They can form independently or on top of another volcano, such as atop the Union Peak and Timber Crater shield volcanoes. Basically, a cinder cone is a ring of loose rocks, violently ejected in solid or semisolid form from a central vent. Being composed largely of unconsolidated rock, a cinder cone is subject to relatively rapid erosion, particularly by an ensuing lava flow from the volcano's vent. These cones are formed by relatively mild, short-lived eruptions, so they are small, usually less than 1000 feet high and less than a mile wide. In composition they tend to be like shield-volcano lava flows—basaltic—though they can be andesitic. Red Cone, Rodley Butte, Crater Peak and the Goose Nest are but a few of our area's several dozen cones.

Stratovolcanoes, also known as composite cones or stratocones, are, like shield volcanoes, the products of many eruptive episodes. They are composed of a more silicic lava, usually andesite, which typically produces shorter, thicker, *slower* lava flows. Because the lava doesn't flow away as readily, the volcano can build up to great heights (after all, andesite is named for the pervasive rock found in the Andes). Because andesite is pastier than basalt, it can hold more gas, and this leads to more violent eruptions. These don't form a ring around the vent, but rather shower the mountain with assorted debris. At Crater Lake you can see alternating layers of lava flows and pyroclastic rocks. Mt. Mazama was the prime example of a stratovolcano, but today the only standing, clear-cut example is Mt. McLoughlin. Mt. Bailey, Pelican Butte and others are intermediate between shield volcanoes and stratovolcanoes.

Domes form when the lava is so pasty that it essentially wells up in place, barely flowing at all. Such lava is usually dacite, rhyodacite or rhyolite, and each of these can get extremely charged with gas, leading to catastrophic eruptions. Later in its life, Mt. Mazama tended toward these more silicic lavas, which ultimately led to a series of devastating eruptions. Don't expect to see Shasta-sized domes, for domes are blown apart before they can reach

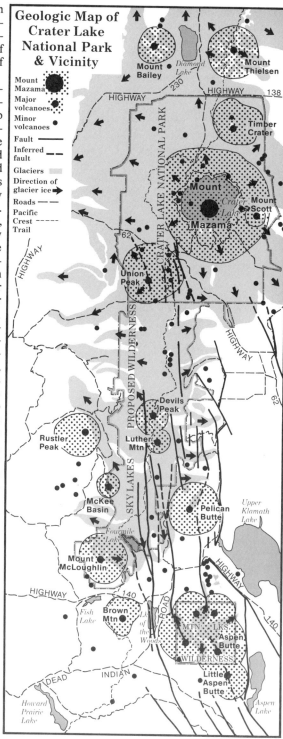

such proportions. Typically, domes are about the size of cinder cones or a bit larger. In our area Llao Rock is to some extent an example of a lava dome, though it is more of a stubby flow than a dome. Excellent examples of domes rise in northern California: Lassen Peak and the Chaos Crags.

Geologically speaking, all volcanoes are short-lived. Mt. Mazama, the area's largest, had a life span of roughly ½ million years. Most of our area's other volcanoes had considerably shorter lives. Since the High Cascades are several million years old, they contain relicts of ancient volcanoes in all stages of erosion. Youthful Mt. McLoughlin, Pelican Butte and Brown Mountain are unmistakable volcanoes, but you have to look more closely to see that there was once a volcano over Devils Peak. Immediately south of the peak, you have to use quite a bit of imagination or insight to recognize that there was also a volcano over Luther Mountain. And all but the more experienced volcano hunters will fail to note the ancient (relatively speaking) volcano above Bessie Rock. Thanks to plate tectonics, we can expect to see new volcanoes replacing the old ones. Perhaps in the distant future our area will be blessed with another Mt. Mazama to glorify the southern Oregon landscape.

Faults Glancing at the geologic map, you can't help but notice the area's faults. Faulting and volcanism seem to go hand in hand. Magma, pushing its way to the earth's surface, fractures the crust. Conversely, rifting of the earth's crust provides magma with an escape route. Faulting has probably been around as long as volcanism, and it is still going on today. Basically, faulting in our area is restricted to the east side of the Cascade divide, where the range is slumping down to the Klamath Lake basin. During the Ice Age, roughly the last 1-2 million years, east-side glaciers carried prodigious amounts of materials into this basin, though today the basin shows no

such accumulations. The reason for this is two-fold. First, late in the Ice Age, Upper Klamath Lake's water level was a bit higher, and it lapped against the base of the mountains. Second, the basin's west side is sinking along a fault zone, taking the glacial sediments down with it.

Glaciers Were it not for glaciers, many of us probably wouldn't visit southern Oregon's High Cascades, for they would be nearly lakeless. The overwhelming majority of the area's lakes owe their origin to glaciers, which excavated the bedrock basins that now hold them. Only the area's larger lakes—Crater Lake, Diamond Lake, Lake of the Woods and Fish Lake—are nonglacial in origin. Crater Lake partly fills a collapsed magma chamber, while the other three lakes are dammed by lava flows.

The geologic map shows the approximate extent of the area's glaciers and the directions they flowed, though it doesn't show their intensity. Where there has been relatively little volcanic activity to alter the landscape, as in the Sky Lakes Area, glaciers have operated for a long time, perhaps over a million years, gouging deep, flat-floored canyons that have lake-studded basins at their heads. Where there are youthful volcanoes, glaciers have had less time to operate. On this book's topographic maps, compare youthful Mt. McLoughlin's mildly glaciated slopes (Map 24) with those of considerably older, severely glaciated Mt. Thielsen (Map 2). But we must be cautious with such comparisons, for a volcano can produce flank eruptions, instantly excavating a bowl that looks very much like a cirque (a glacial bowl). Mts. Mazama, Thielsen, Bailey and McLoughlin probably had such eruptions, which provided favorable sites for the germination of glaciers.

Throughout much of their history, the High Cascades have experienced the interplay of generally constructional volcanic processes and of generally erosional glacial processes. Together they have largely created the terrain we see today, a landscape of "fire and ice."

6 Botany

Introduction In May 1980 southern Washington's Mt. St. Helens produced a large eruption. In a matter of minutes, the mountain violently ejected about ¾ cubic mile of matter, which destroyed about 230 square miles of adjacent forest lands. This eruption was directed northward, so most of the devastation lay in an arc from northwest to northeast. Comparatively little damage was done to the forest lands south of the volcano.

About 4900 B.C. southern Oregon's Mt. Mazama produced a series of tremendously large eruptions, which lasted perhaps a matter of days, according to a Klamath Indian legend. In that time the mountain violently ejected about 12-14 cubic miles of matter, far more than was erupted at Mt. St. Helens. Furthermore, the final eruptions were in all directions. The legend tells how "burning ashes" fell like rain and how some people sought refuge in the waters of distant Klamath Lake. After the last volcanic ash settled, a vast, previously forested landscape lay in utter desolation, looking as lifeless as a moonscape. Today, about 600 species of plants thrive in this once lifeless area, which is a testimony to nature's resiliency. Viewing this largely forested landscape today, you'd hardly guess that it had been denuded in the geologically recent past.

Plant dispersion Mazama's death throes occurred at a time when the climate was a bit warmer than it is today. Truly alpine species may have existed back then only above 9000 feet, and if so they disappeared with the mountaintop. At that time, borderline alpine species existed on or near the summits of Union Peak, Mt. Bailey and Mt. Thielsen. Though Mazama's eruptions may have destroyed every plant on these summits, some seeds and rootstocks undoubtedly survived. Within as little as perhaps a few years, these survivors significantly re-established their local populations, and in time their seeds were dispersed, largely indirectly through birds, to the slopes of Mazama (Crater Lake's outer slopes). In all likelihood, plants of lower elevations reseeded Mazama's ravaged slopes considerably faster than did subalpine plants, for the source areas of such plants were far more extensive.

But a few alpine plants never re-established themselves. We can only speculate what they were. Three likely candidates, all in the mustard family, are short-fruited smelowskia, golden draba and alpine bittercress. All are fairly common in many of Washington's alpine environments, but their distributions become increasingly sporadic southward to Lassen Peak. In fact, there is a large gap for the smelowskia, which is sporadic through Oregon south to the Three Sisters, then reappears once more at Lassen Peak, 250 miles south of them. (Logic tells us it should be seen on Mt. Shasta, but that volcano's recurrent eruptions have decimated much of its alpine and subalpine flora.)

How could smelowskia end up 250 miles south of its last stand? Perhaps its seeds were carried south in the gut of some migrating bird. But this hypothesis is a shot in the dark, even though such processes are very important for plant dispersion. The solution to the question more likely lies in realizing that over roughly the last two million years, while giant Cascade volcanoes have come and gone, Oregon's climate has been generally cooler. We are, in fact, in a temporary interglacial period. The *typical* Cascade environment is one with many glaciers (note their distribution on the geology chapter's map).

During these typical, glacial times, alpine plants could easily compete with lower plants

21

down to about 6000 feet elevation. In other words, as recently as about 15,000 years ago, when glacier ice still gripped much of the High Cascades, there existed an almost continuous crestline alpine zone south through Oregon to Mt. McLoughlin. The subalpine zone extended farther south, past Lassen Peak to the Sierra Nevada, reaching these destinations by a loop through the Klamath Mountains, which today contain abundant species from both the Cascades and the Sierra Nevada. As the glaciers' stranglehold was broken by a warming Oregon climate, lower plants expanded into higher territories, and the increased competition forced the alpine and subalpine plants into the harsh, restricted areas we see them in today.

Plant distribution   Today Oregon's southern High Cascades host about 600 species of vascular plants—ferns, herbs, shrubs and trees. Every plant growing here has certain water, temperature, mineral and biological requirements, and these limit its distribution. Some plants, such as sticky cinquefoil and woolly sunflower, have wide tolerances and consequently enjoy greater-than-average distributions. In contrast, some plants, such as Crater Lake currant and Mazama collomia, have very limited distributions.

Because plants are more or less limited by the environment and by interacting plants and animals, we can look for each of them in rather specific places. We wouldn't expect to find plants of shady forest floors growing on sunny, gravelly slopes. This is convenient for plant identification, for often two otherwise similar plants can be identified by their habitat—their biological neighborhood. For example, the sticky currant does well in forests while the very similar squaw currant does well in dry, rocky places. Of course, a forest can grade into a rocky area, and in such a zone of gradation you'd be likely to see both species.

Identifying herbs   With the preceding limitation in mind, the author nevertheless arranged the seven following plates of wildflowers (really, herbs) on the basis of habitat, since this is the easiest method for plant identification for the neobotanist. First determine, from the following list of plates, the proper plate, then on it look for the proper candidate. Since many plants grow in more than one habitat, you may have to check several plates. Also be aware that since only about half of the area's "wildflowers" are described, you may not find the proper candidate (however, virtually every showy-flowered,

common herb is described). Some plants are borderline between herb and shrub, so, if in doubt, also check the shrubs plate, Plate 8.

Once you find a suitable candidate on a plate, note its family and its scientific name. Both are listed alphabetically in the list of herbs below, which includes a common name, a few key plant characteristics and an elevation range. (If two or more plants in the same genus are listed, the genus name for all but the first is represented by its initial, such as "*P.*"

Experienced botanists, recognizing the family that a particular candidate belongs to, may find it easier to turn directly to that family, read the plant descriptions, and then turn to the proper plate for visual confirmation.

Plate 1. Shady forests   If you're hiking between 3000 and 5000 feet—our area's lowest zone—you're likely to see the herbs on this plate. This is the only plate that shows the area's *non*green, usually parasitic, herbs, which are typically white-to-red. Type localities: Red-blanket Canyon, Middle Fork Canyon, forested parts of Crater Lake rim.

Plate 2. Open forests; flowers whitish, pale violet or bluish white.   These forests may be interspersed with small meadows, pumice slopes or rocky areas. Sunlight is fairly abundant. Type localities: much of Lake of the Woods area and the lower Mountain Lakes Wilderness: much of the west slopes of Crater Lake National Park.

Plate 3. Open forests; flowers creamy yellow, yellow, orange, scarlet, red, pink or purple. Same habitats as for Plate 2.

Plate 4. Wet areas; flowers white, greenish white, yellow or partly yellow.   Wet areas include springs, creeks, bogs, wet meadows, lakes and snowmelt puddles. Type localities: Castle Crest Wildflower Garden, Boundary Springs, Sky Lakes basin.

Plate 5. Wet areas; flowers pink, red, violet, blue or brown. Same habitats as for Plate 4.

Plate 6. Dry, sunny areas; sunflowers, buckwheats and pussy paws.   Dry areas, mostly in the area's *higher* elevations, composed of gravel, pumice or rock. Sunflowers are quite easy to recognize. Buckwheats and pussy paws have clusters of tiny flowers, usually white, yellow or pink. Type localities: Mts. Bailey, Thielsen, Scott and McLoughlin and most of the Crater Lake rim.

Plate 7. Dry, sunny areas; all other kinds of flowers. Same habitats as for Plate 6.

Plate 1. Shady forests.

1 *Asarum caudatum* (Aristolochiaceae family), **2** *Achlys triphylla* (Berberidaceae), **3** *Vancouveria hexandra* (Berberidaceae), **4** *Cornus canadensis* (Cornaceae), **5** *Clintonia uniflora* (Liliaceae), **6** *Trillium ovatum* (Liliaceae), **7** *Corallorhiza Mertensiana* (Orchidaceae), **8** *Eburophyton Austinae* (Orchidaceae), **9** *Trientalis latifolia* (Primulaceae), **10** *Allotropa virgata* (Pyrolaceae), **11** *Chimaphila umbellata* (Pyrolaceae), **12** *Hypopithys monotropa* (Pyrolaceae), **13** *Pterospora andromedea* (Pyrolaceae), **14** *Pyrola picta* (Pyrolaceae), **15** *Pyrola secunda* (Pyrolaceae), **16** *Anenome deltoidea* (Ranunculaceae)

Herbs

Apocynaceae (Dogbane Family)

Apocynum androsaemifolium, **spreading dogbane.** Flowers small, usually absent, pink-to-white and urn-shaped. Leaves opposite, turning bright yellow in fall. Plant low, spreading. Common on dry forest floors, up to 7000'. **Plate 3:1.**

Aristolochiaceae (Birthwort Family)

Asarum caudatum, **wild ginger.** Flowers, usually absent, are brownish, 3-petaled, and below plant's round leaves. Ginger odor. Plant up to 6" tall. On damp floors of shady forests, up to 5000'. **Plate 1:1.**

Berberidaceae (Barberry Family)

Achlys triphylla, **vanilla leaf.** Flowers tiny, whitish, clustered on stem above 3 large leaflets, each with wavy margins. Plant ½-1½' tall. On damp floors of shady forests, up to 5500'. **Plate 1:2.**

Berberis nervosa, **Oregon grape.** Flowers small, cream-to-yellow, usually absent, yielding to bluish gray berries. Leaves shiny, hollylike. Stems reddish. Plant spreading, about 1' tall. On shady forest floors, up to 6000'. **Plate 3:2.**

Vancouveria hexandra, **northern inside-out flower.** Flowers small, drooping, with reflexed white petals. Note distinctive, broad leaflets, usually in clusters of 3. Plant ½-1½' tall. On shady forest floors, up to 6000'. **Plate 1:3.**

Boraginaceae (Borage Family)

Hackelia micrantha, **Jessica's stickseed.** Pinwheel flowers, blue with white centers, yielding to barbed seed pods. Plant 1-2' tall. In moist-to-wet places, 4500-7500'. **Plate 2:1.** *H. californica,* **California stickseed,** is similar, but flowers are entirely white. Plant 1½-2½' tall. In open forests, up to 6500'.

Mertensiana paniculata, **tall lungwort.** Flowers blue, bell-shaped, hanging. Leaves fleshy, lancelike. Plant 1-5' tall. In moist-to-wet places, up to 6500'. **Plate 2:2.**

Caprifoliaceae (Honeysuckle Family)

Linnaea borealis, **twinflower.** Pink, drooping flowers, when present, in pairs. Leaves oval, shiny, ½" long, sometimes forming mats. Plant 1-6" tall. On forest floors, up to 5500'. **Plate 3:3.**

Caryophyllaceae (Pink Family)

Arenaria pumicola, **pumice sandwort.** Flowers small, with 5 white, notched petals. Stem leaves few, paired, linear and ascending. Stems spreading, from 2-8" long. On dry, open, gravelly soils, 6000-8000'. **Plate 7:1.**

Compositae (Sunflower Family)

Note: These flowers are usually "daisy-like." Each "sunflower" is usually composed of several to many *ray* flowers, the "petals," and several to many central *disk* flowers. In some species the ray flowers may be lacking; in others, the disk flowers may be lacking.

Achillea lanulosa, **yarrow.** Flowers small, whitish, in dense, umbrellalike clusters. Leaves lacy, highly divided. Plant 2-24" tall. In moist, open places, up to 6500'. **Plate 2:3.**

Adenocaulon bicolor, **trail plant.** Flowers few, small, whitish, tubular, on delicate stem. Leaves triangular, mostly basal. Plant 1-2' tall. On shady forest floors. **Plate 2:4.**

Agoseris aurantiaca, **orange agoseris.** Disk flowers only. Inch-wide sunflowers dandelion-like, but orange. Grasslike leaves, many with paired spurs. Plants ½-1½' tall. Usually on dry, grassy slopes, up to 6500'. **Plate 3:4.**

Anaphalis margaritacea, **pearly everlasting.** Disk flowers only, small and yellow, surrounded by white, paperlike bracts. Leaves dull-green. Plant 1-3' tall. In several habitats, up to 7500'. **Plate 2:5.**

Antennaria alpina var. *media,* **alpine everlasting.** Disk flowers only, white-to-pink. Leaves silvery green, mostly basal, about ½" long. Plant 2-4" tall. In rocky or gravelly places, 6000-8000'. **Plate 2:6.** *A. Geyeri,* **pinewoods everlasting,** and *A. rosea,* **rosy everlasting,** are similar. The first has leaves up to 1¼" long, is 2-6" tall, and usually grows in open pine forests, up to 7000'. The second has dull-green leaves, about ½" long, is 6-10" tall, and grows in many habitats, up to 7000'.

Arnica cordifolia, **heart-leaved arnica.** Sunflower large, yellow, usually solitary. Leaves gray-green, broad, in 2 to 4 pairs, the lower ones heart-shaped. Plant ½-1' tall. On open slopes, 4500-9000'. **Plate 6:1.**

A. mollis, **soft arnica.** Sunflowers yellow, usually 1 *or* 3. leaves green, in 2 to 4 pairs, the basal leaves 6-10" long, the top leaves about 2" long. Plant 1-2' tall. In wet places, up to 7500'. **Plate 4:1.** *A. longifolia,* **seep-spring arnica,** is similar, but its sticky, strong-smelling leaves are narrower, about 3-6 times longer than wide, and usually in 5 or more pairs. Plant ½-1½' tall, in both wet and rocky places, up to 8000'.

A. viscosa, **gummy arnica.** Sunflowers many, each of yellowish disk flowers. Leaves paired, hairy, sticky, aromatic, and up to 1½" long. Plant bushy, 1-2' tall. Uncommon on talus slopes, 6000-8000'. **Plate 6:2.**

Erigeron compositus, **cut-leaved daisy.** Sunflowers about ½" across. Disk flowers yellow; ray flowers, when present, white or violet. Leaves dull-green, forked, short-haired, in dense mat. Plant 1-3" tall. In gravelly places, 6500-9000'. **Plate 6:3.**

E. peregrinus, **wandering daisy.** Inch-wide sunflowers few to many. Disk flowers yellow, ray flowers violet. Stems few to many. Plant ½-2' tall. Common in wet places, 5000-7000'. **Plate 4:2.**

Eriophyllum lanatum, **woolly sunflower.** Flowers yellow, numerous, each on a tall stem. Leaves mainly at base and, like stems, hairy. Plant ½-2' tall. In dry, open places, up to 7000'. **Plate 6:4.**

E. lanatum var. *integrifolium,* **dwarf woolly sunflower.** Flowers yellow. Leaves whitish, woolly, about ¼" long. Plant 1-3" tall. In gravelly or rocky places, 6500-9000'. **Plate 6:5.**

Hieracium albiflorum, **white hawkweed.** Ray flowers only, small and white. Leaves mostly basal, somewhat hairy. Plant 1-2½' tall. In dry, open woods, up to 7000'. **Plate 2:7.**

H. horridum, **shaggy hawkweed.** Ray flowers only, small and yellow. Leaves very hairy. Plant 3-12" tall. In dry places, 6500-9000'. **Plate 6:6.**

Hulsea nana, **dwarf hulsea.** Both disk and ray flowers of the inch-wide sunflower are yellow. Leaves dull-green, hairy, with wavy margins. Plants 1-6" tall. In gravelly or rocky places, 6500-9000'. **Plate 6:7.**

Microseris alpestris, **alpine microseris.** Ray flowers only, yellow, dandelion-like. Leaves basal, grasslike, often with several spurs. Plant ½-1' tall. Common in dry, open places, 5500-8000'. **Plate 6:8.** *M. nutans,* **nodding microsersis,** is very similar, but some leaves are usually present on flowering stems as well as at base. Common in moist woods and grassy meadows, up to 7000'. *Agoseris glauca,* **pale agoseris,** is also similar, but leaves are gray-green and usually spurless. Plant 2-8" tall, in open areas, up to 8500'.

Raillardella argentea, **silky raillardella.** Disk flowers only, few in number, composing solitary sunflower. Leaves basal, hairy, gray-green. Plant ½-4" tall. In rocky, usually subalpine places, 6500-9000'. **Plate 6:9.**

Rudbeckia californica, **California cone flower.** Disk flowers brown, many, forming a cone. Ray flowers, when present, pointed, yellow. Plant 2-5' tall. In wet places, usually meadows, 4500-6500'. **Plate 4:3.** *Helenium Bigelovii,* **Bigelow's sneezeweed,** is similar, but its disk flowers form a

Plate 2. Open forests; flowers whitish, pale violet or bluish white.

1 *Hackelia micrantha* (Boraginaceae), **2** *Mertensia paniculata* (Boraginaceae), **3** *Achillea lanulosa* (Compositae), **4** *Adenocaulon bicolor* (Compositae), **5** *Anaphalis margaritacea* (Compositae), **6** *Antennaria alpina* (Compositae), **7** *Hieracium albiflorum* (Compositae), **8** *Phacelia heterophylla* (Hydrophyllaceae), **9** *Monardella odoratissima* (Labiatae), **10** *Lupinus lepidus* (Leguminosae), **11** *Smilacina stellata* (Liliaceae), **12** *Fragaria virginiana* (Rosaceae), **13** *Horkelia fusca* (Rosaceae), **14** *Mitella trifida* (Saxifragaceae), **15** *Chamaesaracha nana* (Solanaceae), **16** *Valeriana sitchensis* (Valerianaceae).

sphere and its ray flowers are 3-lobed. In wet places, up to 6000'.

Senecio canus, **woolly butterweed.** Flowers yellow, many, ¾" across. Leaves light gray-green and densely hairy, mostly spatulate and basal. Plant ½-1½' tall. In gravelly or rocky places, up to 9000'. **Plate 6:10.**

S. integerrimus, **single-stemmed butterweed.** Flowers like those of woolly butterweed. Leaves green, large at base but reducing upward. Plant 1-3' tall. In dry, open forests, up to 7000'. **Plate 3:6.**

S. triangularis, **arrowhead butterweed.** Flowers like those of woolly butterweed. Leaves bright green, arrowhead-shaped, strongly toothed. Usually along streams, 4000-7000'. **Plate 4:4.**

Taraxacum officinale, **common dandelion.** Ray flowers only, yellow. Leaves basal, long and notched. Plant 2-8" tall. Common in moist places, up to 6500'. **Plate 3:7.**

Cornaceae (Dogwood Family)

Cornus canadensis, **bunchberry.** Flowers tiny, surrounded by 4 large, white, petallike leaves. Berries red. Whorl of leaves, usually 6. Plant 2-6" tall. On shady forest floors, up to 5000'. **Plate 1:4.**

Crassulaceae (Stonecrop Family)

Sedum oregonense, **creamy stonecrop.** Flowers whitish green with 5-pointed, rusty center. Leaves succulent, dull gray-green, turning rusty. Plant 4-10" tall. On rocky outcrops, 5000-8000'. **Plate 7:2.**

Cruciferae (Mustard Family)

Arabis platysperma, **pioneer rock cress.** Flowers 4-petaled, lavender-to-white. Seed pods flat, ⅛-¼" wide, erect. Basal leaves 1-1½" long. Plant 2-16" tall. In gravelly or rocky places, 6000-8500'. **Plate 7:3.** *A. suffrutescens,* **woody rock cress,** is similar, but the flat seed pods are horizontal or hanging, and plant base is usually woody. Habitat similar.

A. Lemmonii, **Lemon's rock cress,** differs from both in having narrow (1/16"), round, horizontal seed pods and ½" long basal leaves. Habitat similar,

Fumariaceae (Bleeding Heart Family)

Dicentra formosa, **bleeding heart.** Flowers violet, heart-shaped. Leaves fernlike. Plants ½-1½' tall. In wet, often shady, places, up to 7700'. **Plate 5:1.**

Hydrophyllaceae (Waterleaf Family)

Phacelia hastata var. *compacta,* **dwarf silver-leaved phacelia.** Flowers creamy, on a coiled stem. Leaves hairy, dull-green. Plant 1-4" tall. In gravelly or rocky places, 5500-9000'. **Plate 7:4.** Regular, lower-elevation variety is similar, but 1-2' tall.

P. heterophylla, **vari-leaf phacelia.** Flowers creamy, on a coiled stem. Leaves hairy, dull-green, the upper ones entire, but the lower ones composed of 3 or 5 leaflets. Plant 1-2' tall. In open areas, up to 8000'. **Plate 2:8.**

Hypericaceae (St. John's Wort Family)

Hypericum perforatum, **Klamath weed.** Petals 5, yellow, with black dots along margin. Leaves opposite, growing on secondary stalks as well as main stalk. Plant 1-3' tall. In dry, open places, up to 5000'. **Plate 3:8.**

Labiatae (Mint Family)

Monardella odoratissima, **coyote mint.** Flowers white-to-violet. Leaves opposite, aromatic. Stems squarish. Plant ½-2' tall. Common on open slopes, up to 7500'. **Plate 2:9.**

Leguminosae (Pea Family)

Lupinus latifolius, **broad-leaved lupine.** Pea flowers blue-violet and white, in whorls on stalks. Leaves composed of 7-9 radiating leaflets. Plant 1½-4' tall. In wet places, 4000-7000'.

Plate 5:2. *L. polyphyllus,* **blue-pod lupine,** is similar, but larger, with hollow lower stems. Leaflets 9-15. In wet places, up to 5000'.

L. lepidus, **elegant lupine.** Flowers and leaves similar to preceding, but plant is much smaller, about 2-8" tall. Common in dry, gravelly places, up to 9000'. **Plate 2:10.** *L. albicaulis,* **pine lupine,** is similar, but has drab, whitish flowers. Plant 1-2' tall. Very common in open forests, up to 8200'.

Vicia americana, **American vetch.** Pea flowers rose-purple, ½" long. Leaves composed of 4 or 5 pairs of leaflets, ending in tendrils (grasping threads). Plant ½-1½' tall. In open places, up to 5500'. **Plate 3:9.**

Liliaceae (Lily Family)

Clintonia uniflora, **queen's cup.** Flowers white, usually 1 or 2. Leaves basal, usually 2 or 3. Plant 1-6" tall. In shady forests, up to 6200'. **Plate 1:5.**

Fritillaria atropurpurea, **spotted mountain bells.** Inch-wide flowers, with 6 brownish purple petals. Stem and linear leaves pale-green. Plant ½-2' tall. Usually in sunny, moist-to-wet places, up to 6500'. **Plate 5:3.**

Lilium pardalinum, **leopard lily.** Flowers showy, yellow-orange to scarlet, with purple spots. Lower leaves usually in whorls of 7 or more leaves. Plant 3-8' tall. In wet places, up to 5500'. **Plate 5:4.**

Smilacina stellata, **star Solomon's seal.** Flowers white, about ½ dozen, at end of crooked, somewhat ascending stem. Berries red-to-black. Stem 1-2' long. Usually in forests, up to 7700'. **Plate 2:11.** *S. racemosa,* **branched Solomon's seal,** is somewhat similar, but usually has several dozen smaller flowers (or berries), and has broader leaves. Usually in forests, up to 6500'.

Trillium ovatum, **western trillium.** Solitary flower with 3 white-to-pink petals, on stalk above 3 broad leaves. Plant ½-1½' tall. In shady forests, up to 6000'. **Plate 1:6.**

Veratrum viride, **green corn lily** (green false hellebore). Flowers many, green to yellow-green. Leaves cornlike. Plant 2-6' tall. In wet places, up to 8000'. **Plate 4:5.** *V. californicum,* **California corn lily,** is similar, but has white flowers and grows up to 6000'.

Malvaceae (Mallow Family)

Sidalcea oregana, **Oregon checker.** Flowers pink, to 1" wide, in terminal cluster that flowers from the bottom up. Note tube in center of each flower. Leaves roundish, deeply cleft. Plant highly variable, ½-3' tall. In wet places, up to 5500'. **Plate 5:5.**

Nymphaceae (Water Lily Family)

Nuphar polysepalum, **yellow pond lily.** Flowers large, yellow. Leaves large, floating. In ponds and lakes, up to 6500'. **Plate 4:6.**

Onagraceae (Evening Primrose Family)

Epilobium angustifolium, **red fireweed.** Inch-wide flowers with 4 rose-to-magenta petals. Upper stem is same color. Plant 2-6' tall. In open, moist areas, up to 7000'. **Plate 3:10.**

Gayophytum diffusum, **spreading gayophytum.** Flowers whitish, tiny, 4-petaled. Leaves linear. Plant delicate, ½-1' tall. In dry, open places, up to 8000'. **Plate 7.4**

Orchidaceae (Orchid Family)

Corallorhiza Mertensiana, **Mertens' coralroot.** Lower petal striped red. Entire plant orange-to-red, ½-2' tall. In shady forests, up to 7500'. **Plate 1:7.** *C. maculata,* **spotted coralroot,** is similar, but lower petal has red spots and plant grows only up to 6000'.

Eburophyton Austinae, **phantom orchid.** Flowers white-to-pinkish white. Stem pale-white to dull-yellow, no green. In shady forests, up to 6000'. **Plate 1:8.**

Plate 3. Open forests; flowers creamy yellow, yellow, orange, scarlet, red, pink or purple.

1 *Apocynum androsaemifolium* (Apocynaceae), **2** *Berberis nervosa* (Berberidaceae), **3** *Linnaea borealis* (Caprifoliaceae), **4** *Agoseris aurantiaca* (Compositae), **5** *Verbascum Thapsus* (Scrophulariaceae), **6** *Senecio integerrimus* (Compositae), **7** *Taraxacum officinale* (Compositae), **8** *Hypericum perforatum* (Hypericaceae), **9** *Vicia americana* (Leguminosae), **10** *Epilobium angustifolium* (Onagraceae), **11** *Ipomopsis aggregata* (Polemoniaceae), **12** *Potentilla glandulosa* (Rosaceae), **13** *Castilleja Applegatei* (Scrophulariaceae), **14** *Castilleja Payneae* (Scrophulariaceae), **15** *Pedicularis racemosa* (Scrophulariaceae), **16** *Viola purpurea* (Violaceae).

Habenaria dilatata, **white bog orchid.** Flowers small, white, with projecting spur. Plant ½-2' tall. In boggy areas, up to 7000'. **Plate 4:7.** *H. saccata,* **slender bog orchid,** is similar, but has green flowers. Habitat similar.

Polemoniaceae (Phlox Family)

Collomia mazama, **Mazama collomia.** Half-inch flowers tubular, blue-violet. Leaves bright-green, the upper ones entire, the lower ones toothed near tip. Plant 4-10" tall. Uncommon, in wet places 5000-7000'. **Plate 5:6.**

Ipomopsis aggregata, **scarlet gilia.** Flowers trumpetlike, 1" long, scarlet. Leaves 1-2½' tall. In moist-to-dry places, up to 7500'. **Plate 3:11.**

I. congesta, **ballhead ipomopsis.** Flowers white, tiny, in 1" sphere. Leaves few, highly cleft. Plant small, prostrate. In gravelly or rocky places, 6000-8500'. **Plate 7:6.**

Phlox diffusa, **spreading phlox.** Flowers trumpetlike (look closely) and white, pink, pale-blue or lavender. Leaves needle-like. Plant matted, 2-12" tall. Common in gravelly or sometimes in rocky places, up to 8500'. **Plate 7:7.** *Leptodactylon pungens,* **granite gilia,** is similar, but flowers are funnel-like and often yellowish, and plant is shrubby. Habitat similar.

Polemonium pulcherrimum, **skunk-leaved polemonium.** Flowers ⅓" long, pale-blue with yellow throat. Leaves with many pairs of tiny leaflets, mostly less than ¼" long, these dull-green, slightly sticky, and with skunk odor. Plant 2-12" tall. In rocky places, 6500-9000'. **Plate 7:8.** *P. californicum,* **California Jacob's ladder,** is similar, but leaflets are about 1" long. Plant low, spreading. In shady forests, 5500-7500'.

Polygonaceae (Buckwheat Family)

Eriogonum marifolium, **marum-leaved buckwheat.** Flowers tiny, yellow-to-rust, in clusters on several stalks. Several leafy bracts at base of these stalks. Oval leaves ¼-½" long, hairy, gray-green. Plant matted, 2-8" tall. Very common in dry, gravelly places, 5000-8500'. **Plate 6:11.** *E. ovalifolium,* **oval-leaved buckwheat,** is similar, but its flowers may be yellow, white or pink, and it lacks the leafy bracts. Habitat similar.

E. pyrolifolium, **pyrola-leaved buckwheat.** Superficially quite similar to the very common pussy paws, in the following family, but the buckwheat's leaves are wide and smooth. Plant prostrate. On rocky or gravelly slopes, 6500-9000'. **Plate 6:12.**

E. umbellatum, **sulfur flower.** Similar to marum-leaved buckwheat, but flowers generally bright yellow and clusters are larger, each about 1" across. Plant 4-12" tall. Usually in rocky places, up to 7500'. **Plate 6:13.**

Oxyria digyna, **alpine sorrel.** Flowers tiny, brownish red. Leaves round to kidney-shaped. Plant 2-10" tall. In rocky, sometimes shady and moist, places, 7500-9000'. **Plate 6:14.**

Polygonum bistortoides, **western bistort.** Flowers tiny, creamy, in dense clusters. Leaves lancelike, mostly basal, and having stalks. Plant ½-2' tall. In wet places, up to 7000'. **Plate 4:8.**

P. Newberryi, **Newberry's knotweed.** Stems fleshy, crooked. Whole plant dull-green, turning later to bright-red. Plant prostrate. In gravelly places, 5500-8500'. **Plate 6:15.**

Portulacaceae (Purslane Family)

Calyptridium umbellatum (Spraguea umbellata), **pussy paws.** Flowers tiny, pinkish white, in tufted clusters ("pussy paws"). Stems red. Plant prostrate, 2-8" across. Common in dry gravelly places, up to 8000'. **Plate 6:16.**

Claytonia lanceolata, **western spring beauty.** Petals 5, whitish, each with 3 main pink veins. Leaves 2. Plants delicate, ephemeral, 2-4" tall, fading from green to yellow to orange. Often around melting snow in hemlock forests, from 5500-8000'. **Plate 5:7.**

Primulaceae (Primrose Family)

Dodecatheon alpinum, **apline shooting star.** Petals 4, reflexed, pink-to-magenta, though yellow at base. Plant 4-10" tall. In wet places, from 5500-8000'. **Plate 5:8.**

Trientalis latifolia, **Pacific starflower.** Flowers one-to-several, each white-to-pink, with usually 5-7 petals. Leaves usually 3-6, in a whorl. Plant 2-8" tall. In shady forests, up to 5500'. **Plate 1:9.**

Pyrolaceae (Wintergreen Family)

Allotropa virgata, **sugarstick.** Plant red-and-white striped, like a candy cane. No green. Plant ½-1½' tall. In dry-to-moist forests, up to 6500'. **Plate 1:10.**

Chimaphila umbellata, **western prince's pine.** Flowers drooping, white-to-pink. Leaves shiny, evergreen. Plant 4-10" tall. Common in shady forests, up to 7500'. **Plate 1:11.**

Hypopithys monotropa, **pine sap.** Plant waxy, dull-white to dull-orange and 2-8" tall. In shady forests, up to 8000'. **Plate 1:12.**

Pterospora andromedea, **pinedrops.** Plant orange-to-rust, 1-3' tall. In fairly open forests, up to 7000'. **Plate 1:13.**

Pyrola picta, **white-veined wintergreen.** Flowers similar to those of western prince's pine, above. Leaves dark-green, basal, with white veins. Flower stalk 4-10" tall. On shady forest floors, up to 8000'. **Plate 1:14.**

P. secunda, **one-sided wintergreen.** Flowers whitish, small, on drooping stem. Inch-long leaves basal, bright emerald-green. Flower stalk 2-6" tall. On moist forest floors, up to 7500'. **Plate 1:15.**

Ranunculaceae (Buttercup Family)

Aconitum columbianum, **monk's hood.** Flowers purple to blue-violet, shaped like a monk's hood. Plant 2-6' tall. In wet places, from 4000-7500'. **Plate 5:9.**

Anemone deltoidea, **Columbia windflower.** Sepals petal-like, white, 5 or 6. Flower center yellow or green. Leaflets 3, toothed, in a whorl. Plant 2-10" tall. In shady forests, up to 5500'. **Plate 1:16.**

A. occidentalis, **western pasque flower.** Bowl-shaped flowers creamy to pale-yellow, with yellow and green centers. Later, flowers yield to dense ball of feathery seeds. Leaves in 3s, highly dissected. Stem hairy, rather thick, ½-1½' tall. Plant in gravelly or rocky places, 6500-8500'. **Plate 7:9.**

Aquilegia formosa, **crimson columbine.** Flowers nodding, composed of 5 united, petallike sepals, each with a red, upright spur and a yellow throat. Plant 1-3' tall. In shady, wet places, up to 8000'. **Plate 5:10.**

Caltha biflora, **white marsh marigold.** Flowers white, yellow centers. Leaves round to kidney-shaped. Plants 4-12" tall. In bogs or marshes, 4500-6500'. **Plate 4:9.**

Delphinium depauperatum, **dwarf larkspur.** Flowers spurred, blue-violet. Lower leaves fanlike, deeply cleft. Plants ½-1½' tall. Usually in wet meadows, up to 7500'. **Plate 5:11.** *D. glaucum,* **tall larkspur,** is similar, but usually is 3-8' tall. In wet places, 5000-7500'.

Ranunculus Gormanii, **Gorman's buttercup.** Flowers shiny yellow, ⅓-½" across, with 5 or 6 petallike sepals. Leaves ½" long, on slender stalks. Plants 2-6" tall. Common in wet, grassy places, up to 7500'. **Plate 4:10.**

Rosaceae (Rose Family)

Fragaria virginiana var. *platypetala,* **broad-petaled strawberry.** Flowers white. Leaves of 3 leaflets. Plant prostrate. In moist, sandy places, up to 7000'. **Plate 2:12.**

Horkelia fusca, **dusky horkelia.** Petals 5, white, slightly notched. Basal leaves long, composed of many pairs of deeply lobed leaflets. Stems hairy. Plant ½-2' tall. In gravelly to rocky openings, up to 6000'. **Plate 2:13.**

Plate 4. Wet areas; flowers white, greenish white, yellow or partly yellow.

1 *Arnica mollis* (Compositae), **2** *Erigeron peregrinus* (Compositae), **3** *Rudbeckia californica* (Compositae), **4** *Senecio triangularis* (Compositae), **5** *Veratrum viride* (Liliaceae), **6** *Nuphar polysepalum* (Nymphaceae), **7** *Habenaria dilatata* (Orchidaceae), **8** *Polygonum bistortoides* (Polygonaceae), **9** *Caltha biflora* (Ranunculaceae), **10** *Ranunculus Gormanii* (Ranunculaceae), **11** *Tiarella unifoliata* (Saxifragaceae), **12** *Mimulus guttatus* (Scrophulariaceae), **13** *Heracleum lanatum* (Umbelliferae), **14** *Ligusticum Grayi* (Umbelliferae), **15** *Viola glabella* (Violaceae), **16** *Viola Macloskeyi* (Violaceae).

Luetkea pectinata, **partridge foot.** Flowers creamy, on 2-4" stalk. Leaves deeply cleft, bright-green, fading to red. Plant small, matted. In rocky, often snowy, areas, 6500-9000'. **Plate 7:10.**

Potentilla glandulosa, **sticky cinquefoil.** Flowers creamy-to-yellow. Leaves composed of toothed leaflets, usually 3 at top, 5 or 7 near base. Stems sticky. Plant 4-30" tall. From forest openings to alpine slopes, up to 8500'. **Plate 3:12.**

Saxifragaceae (Saxifrage Family)

Mitella trifida, **Pacific mitella.** Petals 5, 3-lobed, about 1/16" long. Inch-long leaves heart-shaped, basal, with hairy stalks. Slender flower stalk ½-1' tall. In forests, up to 6500'. **Plate 2:14.**

Saxifraga Tolmiei, **alpine saxifrage.** Flowers white, with yellow center, clustered on reddish flower stalk. Leaves basal, thick, fleshy. Plant 1-8" tall. In moist, rocky places, 6000-9000'. **Plate 7:11.**

Tiarella unifoliata, **coolwort.** Flowers white, tiny. Petals 5, 1/16" long. Leaves maplelike. Plant ½-1½' tall. In wet, shady places, up to 7000'. **Plate 4:11.**

Scrophulariaceae (Figwort Family)

Castilleja Applegatei, **Applegate's paintbrush.** Flowers scarlet, somewhat leaflike. Leaves dull-green, with wavy margins. Plant ½-2' tall. Common in dry, open places, from 4000-9000'. **Plate 3:13.** *C. miniata,* **giant red paintbrush,** is similar, but leaves are bright-green and have smooth margins. Plant 1-3' tall. In open, moist places, up to 8000'.

C. Payneae, **pumice paintbrush.** Flowers somewhat leaf-like, dull-yellow to dull-scarlet. Plant 4-8" tall. Fairly common in pumice or gravel, particularly on dry lodgepole-forest floors, 5500-8200'. **Plate 3:14.**

Mimulus guttatus, **common large monkey flower.** Inch-long flowers yellow, with red dots on throat. Leaves opposite. Plant highly variable, 2-24" tall. Usually common in very wet places, up to 7000'. **Plate 4:12.** *M. primuloides,* **primrose monkey flower,** has similar ½" long flowers, but its leaves are in a basal whorl. One flower per plant, atop a 2" stalk. In wet places, particularly lakeshores.

M. Lewisii, **Lewis monkey flower.** Flowers pink-to-rose, 1-2" long. Leaves opposite, elliptical, pointed. Plant 1-2' tall. In very wet places, 4000-7000'. **Plate 5:12**

M. nanus, **dwarf monkey flower.** Flowers ½" long, pink-to-magenta, with yellow centers. Leaves dull-green, fading to rusty-brown. Plant 1-6" tall. Usually growing in masses in gravel or pumice, up to 7500'. **Plate 7:12.** *M. Breweri,* **Brewer's monkey flower,** is similar, but has ¼" long flowers and prefers grass and rock to pumice.

Pedicularis attolens, **baby elephant heads.** Flowers pink, with 3 red stripes. Flowers' trunks about ¼" long. Leaves long, fernlike. Plant ½-1½' tall. In boggy places, 4000-7000'. **Plate 5:13.** *P. groenlandica,* **elephant heads,** is similar, but pink-to-magenta flowers lack red stripes and trunks are about ½" long. Plant 1-2½' tall. Habitat similar.

P. racemosa, **parrot's beak.** Flowers beaked, pink-to-magenta. Leaves lancelike, finely toothed, reddish green. Stems reddish, several to many, 1-2' long. On moist-to-dry forest floors, up to 6500'. **Plate 3:15.**

Penstemon Davidsonii, **Davidson's penstemon.** Flowers tubular, 1" long, magenta-to-purplish blue. Leaves small. Plant matted. In rocky places, 6000-9000'. **Plate 7:13.**

P. Rydbergii, **meadow penstemon.** Flowers tubular, ½" long, magenta-to-purple, in dense whorls on stem. Leaves opposite, lancelike, ascending. Plant ½-1½' tall. In dry-to-wet meadows, 4000-7000'. **Plate 5:14.**

P. rupicola, **cliff penstemon.** Similar to, and hybridizes with, Davidson's penstemon, above. Flowers pink-to-

magenta. Leaves yellow-green, toothed. Plant 2-12" tall. In rocky places, 6000-9000'. **Plate 7:14.**

P. speciosus, **showy penstemon.** Flowers tubular, 1" long, often bulging in middle, mostly blue-violet, but with pink to red-violet at base. Stems many. Leaves narrow, dull-green. Plant ½-2' tall. In dry, open places, up to 8000'. Plate 7:15.

Verbascum Thapsus, **common mullein.** Flower stalk dense with small, yellow flowers. Mature plant 4-8' tall. In dry, open places, often roadsides, up to 6500'. **Plate 3:5.**

Veronica alpina var. *Wormskjoldii,* **alpine brooklime.** Petals violet, with dark veins. Flowers tiny, 4-lobed, in small, terminal cluster. Plant ½-1' tall. In or near water, 5500-7500'. **Plate 5:15.**

V. americana, **American brooklime.** Flowers small, violet, 4-lobed, growing in paired clusters, each pair rising from a pair of leaves. Stems horizontal to ascending, ½-2' long. In or near water, up to 7000'. **Plate 5:16.**

Solanaceae (Nightshade Family)

Chamaesaracha nana, **dwarf chamaesaracha.** Flowers ¾-1" across, white, with yellow at center. Leaves dull-green, lancelike to arrowhead-shaped. Plant 2-4" tall. In dry, open forests, up to 6500'. **Plate 2:15.**

Umbelliferae (Carrot Family)

Heracleum lanatum, **cow parsnip.** Flowers white, in dense clusters that make up a large, umbrellalike cluster. Leaves composed of 3 maplelike leaflets, each up to 1' broad. In moist-to-wet places, up to 6500'. **Plate 4:13.**

Ligusticum Grayi, **Gray's lovage.** Flowers white, in small clusters that make up a larger, umbrellalike cluster. Leaves highly dissected, carrotlike. Plant ½-2' tall. Fairly common in moist, open places, 4000-7000'. **Plate 4:14.**

Lomatium Martindalei, **Martindale's lomatium.** Flowers white, in several small clusters. Leaves dissected. Plant 1-8" tall. In gravelly or rocky places, 5500-8500'. **Plate 7:16.**

Valerianaceae (Valerian Family)

Valeriana sitchensis, **Sitka valerian (mountain heliotrope).** Flowers small, creamy, in dense clusters. Leaves composed of the top pair each of 3 lancelike leaflets, the lower pairs of 3 or 5 leaflets. Plant 1-3½' tall. In wet places, 4000-7000'. **Plate 2:16.** Alpine variety is similar, but ½-1' tall, and on moist-to-dry slopes, 7000-8500'.

Violaceae (Violet Family)

Viola glabella, **wood violet (johnny jump-up).** Flowers yellow, with purple veins on lower petal. Leaves heart-shaped, slightly toothed. Plant 3-12" tall. In wet, shady places, up to 7000'. **Plate 4:15.** *V. Nuttalli* var. *Bakeri,* **Baker's violet,** is similar, but leaves are lancelike and not toothed. Plant 1-4" tall. Habitat similar. *V. adunca,* **western dog violet,** is very similar to Baker's violet, but flowers are violet. Habitat similar.

V. Macloskeyi, **Macloskey's violet.** Flowers white. Plant 1-2" tall. In boggy places, 3000-7000'. **Plate 4:16.**

V. purpurea, **mountain violet.** Flowers yellow. Leaves toothed. The only violet in dry, fairly open places. Plant 1-2" tall. Common 4000-8000'. **Plate 3:16.**

Shrubs

While a good number of people are interested in the wildflowers or trees of a region, few are interested in its shrubs. Shrubs, while plentiful, typically have inconspicuous and/or short-blooming flowers, making the plants hard to identify and thereby discouraging would-be

Plate 5. Wet areas; flowers pink, red, violet, blue or brown.

1 *Dicentra formosa* (Fumariaceae), **2** *Lupinus latifolius* (Leguminosae), **3** *Fritillaria atropurpurea* (Liliaceae), **4** *Lilium pardalinum* (Liliaceae), **5** *Sidalcea oregana* (Malvaceae), **6** *Collomia mazama* (Polemoniaceae), **7** *Claytonia lanceolata* (Portulacaceae), **8** *Dodecatheon alpinum* (Primulaceae), **9** *Aconitum columbianum* (Ranunculaceae), **10** *Aquilegia formosa* (Ranunculaceae), **11** *Delphinium depauperatum* (Ranunculaceae), **12** *Mimulus Lewisii* (Scrophulariaceae), **13** *Pedicularis attolens* (Scrophulariaceae), **14** *Penstemon Rydbergii* (Scrophulariaceae), **15** *Veronica alpina* (Scrophulariaceae), **16** *Veronica americana* (Scrophulariaceae).

Plate 6. Dry, sunny areas; sunflowers, buckwheats and pussy paws.

1 *Arnica cordifolia* (Compositae), **2** *Arnica viscosa* (Compositae), **3** *Erigeron compositus* (Compositae), **4** *Eriophyllum lanatum* (Compositae), **5** *E. lanatum* var. *integrifolium* (Compositae), **6** *Hieracium horridum* (Compositae), **7** *Hulsea nana* (Compositae), **8** *Microseris alpestris* (Compositae), **9** *Raillardella argentea* (Compositae), **10** *Senecio canus* (Compositae), **11** *Eriogonum marifolium* (Polygonaceae), **12** *Eriogonum pyrolifolium* (Polygonaceae), **13** *Eriogonum umbellatum* (Polygonaceae), **14** *Oxyria digyna* (Polygonaceae), **15** *Polygonum Newberryi* (Polygonaceae), **16** *Calyptridium umbellatum* (Portulacaceae).

Plate 7. Dry, sunny areas; all other kinds of flowers.

1 *Arenaria pumicola* (Caryophyllaceae), 2 *Sedum oregonense* (Crassulaceae), 3 *Arabis platysperma* (Cruciferae), 4 *Phacelia hastata* (Hydrophyllaceae), 5 *Gayophytum diffusum* (Onagraceae), 6 *Ipomopsis congesta* (Polemoniaceae), 7 *Phlox diffusa* (Polemoniaceae), 8 *Polemonium pulcherrimum* (Polemoniaceae), 9 *Anenome occidentalis* (Ranunculaceae), 10 *Luetkea pectinata* (Rosaceae), 11 *Saxifraga Tolmiei* (Saxifragaceae), 12 *Mimulus nanus* (Scrophulariaceae), 13 *Penstemon Davidsonii* (Scrophulariaceae), 14 *Penstemon rupicola* (Scrophulariaceae), 15 *Penstemon speciosus* (Scrophulariaceae), 16 *Lomatium Martindalei* (Umbelliferae).

botanists. Therefore, I'm mentioning only a couple dozen species, 16 of them illustrated on Plate 8. Visitors seriously interested in shrubs should get Yocom's *Shrubs of Crater Lake*—available at the national park—which covers most of the shrubs you'll find in southern Oregon's High Cascades.

Betulaceae (Birch Family)

Alnus tenuifolia, **thinleaf alder (mountain alder).** Leaves dull, elliptical, 1-3" long, with both coarse and fine teeth. Plant 3-20' tall. In wet places, up to 7500'. **Plate 8:1.** *A. sinuata,* **Sitka alder,** is similar, but has shiny leaves. *Corylus cornuta* var. *californica,* **California hazelnut,** is also similar, but has fuzzy leaves (feel them) and filbert nuts.

Caprifoliaceae (Honeysuckle Family)

Lonicera involucrata, **bearberry honeysuckle.** Flowers tubular, yellow, usually in pairs, forming pair of dark-purple berries. Leaves in pairs. Plant 2-10' tall. In moist places, 5500-8000'. **Plate 8:2.** *L. conjugialis,* **purple-flowered honeysuckle,** is similar, but has paired purple flowers, these forming pairs of overlapping, "conjugal" berries. In moist places, 3500-7000'.

Compositae (Sunflower Family)

Haplopappus Bloomeri, **Bloomer's goldenbush.** Late-blooming sunflowers yellow. Leaves about 1-2" long, ⅛" wide. Plant ½-1' tall. Very common in drier rocky and gravelly areas, up to 8500'. **Plate 8:3.**

Ericaceae (Heath Family)

Arctostaphylos nevadensis, **pinemat manzanita.** Flowers pinkish white, tiny, urn-shaped, drooping. Leaves small, leathery and oblong, dark green above and pale yellow-green below. Bark smooth, dark red-brown. Plant spreading, ½-1½' tall. In drier forests and on open slopes, 5000-8500'. **Plate 8:4.** *A. patula,* **greenleaf manzanita,** has very similar flowers and bark, but leaves are roundish and plant is 2-6' tall. In open areas, often with other shrubs, up to 7000'. *Phyllodoce empetriformis,* **pink mountain heather.** Flowers pink-to-rose, tiny, urn-shaped, upright. Leaves small, needlelike. Plant ½-1½' tall. Usually in wet places in hemlock forests, 5500-7500'. **Plate 8:5.** *Kalmia polifolia* var. *microphylla,* **bog kalmia,** is similar, but flowers—of 5 fused petals—are open, not urn-shaped, and leaves are about ¼" broad. Habitat similar. *Vaccinium membranaceum,* **big whortleberry (thinleaf huckleberry).** Berries prominent, reddish black. Leaves thin, bright-green, 1-2½" long. Plant 2-5' tall. On shady, damp forest floors, 3500-6500'. **Plate 8:6.** *V. scoparium,* **grouse whortleberry (broom huckleberry).** Berries small, red. Leaves sparse, light-green, mostly ¼-½" long. Plant ½-1' tall. On shady, damp forest floors, 5000-7000'. **Plate 8:7.** *V. occidentale,* **western blueberry,** is similar, but has bluish black berries, dull blue-green leaves, these mostly ½-¾" long. Densely leaved plant 1-2' tall, in boggy areas. *V. caespitosum,* **mat huckleberry,** also grows in boggy areas, but has 1" leaves and is ½-1' tall.

Fagaceae (Oak Family)

Castanopsis sempervirens, **bush chinquapin.** Fruits are spiny balls, about 1" across. Leaves leathery and oblong, dark green above, pale yellow-green below. Plant 2-8' tall. On dry slopes and in dry woods, up to 8000'. **Plate 8:8.**

Rhamnaceae (Buckthorn Family)

Ceanothus prostratus, **squaw carpet.** Flowers tiny, aromatic, bluish, in dense clusters. Leaves hollylike. Plant a dense mat, 1-4" tall, but up to 3 yards wide. On dry slopes and in dry woods, up to 8000'. **Plate 8:9:** *C. velutinus,* **tobacco brush (snow brush).** Flowers small, aromatic, creamy, in large clusters. Leaves glossy, slightly sticky. Plant 3-10' tall, forming dense brush fields, up to 7000'. **Plate 8:10.**

Rosaceae (Rose Family)

Holodiscus discolor, **cream bush (rock-spiraea).** Flowers white, small, in open sprays. Leaves toothed, spicy scented. Plant 1-4' tall. In dry, rocky places, up to 8000'. **Plate 8:11.** *Rosa gymnocarpa,* **wood rose.** Inch-wide flowers pink-petaled, with yellow centers. Leaves of 3-7 toothed leaflets. Stems thorny. Plant 2-6' tall, in forest openings, up to 5500'. **Plate 8:12.** *Rubus lasiococcus,* **dwarf bramble (creeping raspberry).** Flowers white. Raspberries green-to-red. Leaves toothed, 1-2½" broad, and *almost* cleft into 3 leaflets. Plant prostrate. In shady forests, 4500-7000'. **Plate 8:13.** *R. ursinus,* **Pacific blackberry,** is similar, but usually has 3 separate leaflets. Berries black when mature. Stems long and thorny. *R. parviflorus,* **thimbleberry,** is a giant-size "bramble," 2-6' tall, with 3-6" leaves and pink berries. *Sorbus sitchensis,* **Sitka mountain ash.** Flowers creamy, small, in dense clusters. Berries orange-to-scarlet. Leaves usually alternate, composed of 9-13 toothed, narrow leaflets, each about 2" long. Plant 3-12' tall. In open, moist-to-wet places, up to 7500'. **Plate 8:14.** *Sambucus microbotrys,* **red elderberry (Caprifoliaceae),** is similar, but leaves are opposite, these with 5-7 leaflets, each about 2½-3" long. Plant 1-4' tall. Habitat similar.

Saxifragaceae (Saxifrage Family)

Ribes erythrocarpum, **Crater Lake currant.** Very similar to dwarf bramble, above, but dull leaves mostly 5-lobed. Small, short blooming flowers copper-colored. Berries solitary (unlike raspberries) and red. Plant prostrate. Among conifers, particularly mountain hemlocks, 6000-8000'. **Plate 8:15.** *Ribes viscosissimum,* **sticky currant.** Flowers small, bell-shaped, greenish white to pinkish white. Berries bluish black. Leaves 3- or 5-lobed, dull-green, 1-3" wide, and sticky, with mint odor. Plant 3-5' tall. In forested areas, up to 7500'. **Plate 8:16.** *R. cereum,* **squaw currant,** is very similar, but has small, tubular flowers that yield to reddish berries. Leaves similar, mostly ½-2" wide. Plant ½-4' tall. In dry, rocky places, up to 9000'. *R. lacustre,* **swamp currant,** is somewhat similar, but has glossy, deeply lobed leaves and prickly stems. Common in very wet areas.

Trees

In the Crater Lake area, most of the trees can be identified without printed visual aids. Exceptions to this general rule occur where two or more species hybridize, and then you must chemically analyze the tree's resin, which is hardly practical for the average visitor! I've tried to include all the trees you're likely to see, except willows, which are more often shrubs than trees and can be hard for the average person to differentiate. Fortunately, the area's trees are sufficiently few to be grouped into the eight following divisions:

Needle- or scale-leaved trees

1. Pines: needles in bundles of 2-5, cones hanging.

Plate 8. Shrubs.

1 *Alnus tenuifolia* (Betulaceae), 2 *Lonicera involucrata* (Caprifoliaceae), 3 *Haplopappus Bloomeri* (Compositae), 4 *Arctostaphylos nevadensis* (Ericaceae), 5 *Phyllodoce empetriformis* (Ericaceae), 6 *Vaccinium membranaceum* (Ericaceae), 7 *Vaccinium scoparium* (Ericaceae), 8 *Castanopsis sempervirens* (Fagaceae), 9 *Ceanothus prostratus* (Rhamnaceae), 10 *Ceanothus velutinus* (Rhamnaceae), 11 *Holodiscus discolor* (Rosaceae), 12 *Rosa gymnocarpa* (Rosaceae), 13 *Rubus lasiococcus* (Rosaceae), 14 *Sorbus sitchensis* (Rosaceae), 15 *Ribes erythrocarpum* (Saxifragaceae), 16 *Ribes viscosissimum* (Saxifragaceae).

2. True firs: needles in rows along branches, cones upright.

3. Spruce, Douglas-fir and hemlocks: needles in rows, cones hanging.

4. Yew: needles in rows, fruit berrylike (no cones).

5. Incense-cedar: leaves scalelike, cone small and simple.

Broad-leaved trees

6. Oak: leaves lobed, acorns or spiny fruits.

7. Maple: leaves 5-pointed, fruit winged.

8. All others: leaves round, oval, elliptical or lancelike.

1a. Pines with 2-needles per bundle.

Pinus contorta var. *Murrayana*, **lodgepole pine.** Needles 1-2½" long. Cones 1-2½" long. Bark thin and scaly. Tree up to 120' tall, mostly shorter. Grows in places where ground water is plentiful, 4000-8000'.

1b. Pines with 3 needles per bundle.

P. ponderosa, **ponderosa pine.** Needles 5-10" long. Cones 3-5" long. Bark yellow and platy in mature trees. Tree 120-200' tall. Grows on well-drained flats and gentle slopes on both sides of Cascade divide, up to 6000'. Jeffrey and Washoe pines, along the lower east side, are very similar, but grow mostly outside our area.

1c. Pines with 5 needles per bundle.

P. albicaulis, **whitebark pine.** Needles 1½-3" long. Cones 1½-3" long. Bark thin and scaly, like that of lodgepole pine. Tree up to 50' tall, but a prostrate shrub at highest elevations. Grows from 6500-9200'.

P. Lambertiana, **sugar pine.** Needles 3-4" long. Cones 10-16" long, growing at ends of long, graceful branches. Tree 150-240' tall. Grows on well-drained, somewhat sunny slopes and flats, up to 6500'.

P. monticola, **western white pine.** Similar to preceding. Needles 2-4" long. Cones 4-8" long. Tree 50-150' tall. Grows on well-drained, somewhat sunny slopes, 4000-7500'.

2a. Firs with curved upright needles.

Abies lasiocarpa, **subalpine fir.** Cones 2-4½" long. Tree to 90' tall, but usually much smaller and sometimes shrubby. Lower branches on or just above ground. Grows in cold, exposed places, 6000-8500'.

A. magnifica var. *shastensis*, **Shasta red fir.** Cones 4½-8" long; cone scales with conspicuous bracts. Bark of mature tree reddish brown, deeply furrowed. Tree 100-200' tall. Grows on well-drained slopes, 5000-8000'. Noble fir grows among red fir. Both are very similar, and some researchers consider them 2 varieties of a single species.

2b. Firs with straight, slightly ascending needles.

A. concolor, **white fir.** Each needle has a half twist at its base. Cones 3-5" long. Bark of mature tree grayish brown, deeply furrowed. Tree 150-230' tall. Grows usually to 6000', but some seen at 6700'. Grand fir and Pacific silver fir are very

similar, but the former usually grows below our area, the latter north of it.

3. Spruce, Douglas-fir and hemlocks

Picea Engelmannii, **Engelmann spruce.** Needle tips painfully sharp. Cones like those of mountain hemlock, 1-2½" long. Tree 120-170' tall, usually growing in well-watered canyons, 4000-6000'. *Pseudotsuga Menziesii*, **Douglas-fir.** Superficially resembles its associate, Engelmann spruce, but has soft, pliable needles. Cones 2-4" long, with forked bracts projecting from scales. Bark dull-brown, deeply furrowed. Tree 150-230' tall, forming shady forests, up to 6000'.

Tsuga heterophylla, **western hemlock.** Soft, yellow-green needles, about ½" long, mostly in 2 rows. Cones ½-1¼" long, littering ground around trees. Tree 150-200' tall, forming shady forests. Along lower slopes and canyon bottoms, up to 5500'.

T. Mertensiana, **mountain hemlock.** Soft needles about 1" long, growing all around the branches. Cones 1-3" long. Top of tree droopy. Tree from shrub height up to 120' tall. Grows in areas of deep snowpack, 4500-8000'.

4. *Taxus brevifolia*, **Pacific yew.** Soft, yellow-green needles, about ½-¾" long, pale underneath, growing in two rows. Fruit ¼" across, coral-red when mature. Tree 20-50' tall, growing in western-hemlock forests, up to 5500'.

5. *Calocedrus decurrens*, **incense-cedar.** Scalelike leaves yellow-green, about ⅛-¼" long, and growing in flat, horizontal sprays. Cones about 1" long, with only 2 scales. Bark cinnamon-brown, fibrous. Tree 80-120' tall. Grows in sunnier, drier parts of fir forests, up to 5500'.

6. *Quercus Garryana*, **Oregon white oak.** Leaves lobed, about 3-6" long, and about half as wide as long. Tree 20-60' tall. Grows on dry slopes, mostly below 3000' but locally up to 5500'.

7. *Acer macrophyllum*, **big-leaf maple.** Leaves maplelike, ½-1' broad. Tree 20-80' tall. Grows near water, up to 5000'.

8. Leaves round, oval, elliptical or lancelike.

Arbutus Menziesii, **madrone.** Bark of branches and upper trunk smooth and red-orange to tan. Leaves leathery, finely toothed, dull-green below and about 2 by 4". Tree 20-80' tall, in open parts of west-side forests, up to 4500'.

Castanopsis chrysophylla, **golden chinquapin.** Bark furrowed. Leaves toothless, about 2-5" long and ½-1½" wide, dark-green above, dull-yellow below. Tree 10-50' tall, uncommon, in west-side forests, up to 4500'.

Cornus Nuttallii, **Pacific dogwood.** Bark quite smooth. Leaves thin, toothless, about 3-5" long, 2" wide. Giant early-season "flowers" (white floral leaves surrounding tiny flowers). Tree 10-50' tall, in west-side forests, up to 5000'.

Populus tremuloides, **aspen.** Bark white, smooth, thin. Leaves finely toothed, 1-2" long, roundish with pointed tip; rustle in the wind. Tree 10-60' tall. Grows near water, up to 6000'.

P. trichocarpa, **black cottonwood.** Bark on lower trunk furrowed, gray-brown. Leaves toothed, 2-3" long, about half as wide. Tree 60-120' tall. Grows near water, especially in Klamath Lake basin, up to 6000'.

7 Zoology

Introduction We're all familiar with the adage "All men are brothers." From a biologist's standpoint, a broader generalization can be made: "All the earth's organisms are relatives." You need only look back far enough through geologic time to find a common ancestor. For humans, birds, fish, insects, flowers and all other multicellular organisms, that common ancestor lived about 1½ billion years ago, when nucleated cells, or eukaryotes, first evolved. For the 2 billion or so years preceding that evolutionary advance, life was considerably simpler, being composed of prokaryotes, similar, to some extent, to today's bacteria and cyanobacteria (blue-green algae).

And we share a common ancestry with them too, for all living matter on this planet can be traced back to the spark of life that germinated in a nutrient-rich primordial "soup" about 4 billion years ago. Evidence of this common ancestry appears in life's biochemistry. Rather than use all of the amino acids available on earth, organisms—be they mice or men, birds or bees, shrimp or snakes—all use a basic set of about two dozen amino acids as building blocks for protein synthesis. Furthermore, all the natural amino acids are "left-handed" (molecules can exist as mirror-image twins, like a pair of gloves). If life had multiple origins, then we'd expect to see both right- and left-handed amino acids, for in laboratory synthesis equal amounts of both are produced.

Without these amino acids, we wouldn't have DNA, and without DNA, the continuity of life would be impossible. It is a sobering thought to realize that each time an organism dies without leaving any offspring, its 4-billion-year lineage of DNA replication is terminated. This applies to the *vast majority* of this planet's organisms, which never survive long enough to reach adulthood. About 6900 years ago, Mt. Mazama underwent its climactic eruptions, terminating the lineages of organisms over hundreds of square miles. Fortunately, nature is resilient, and an influx of organisms from bordering areas reestablished life in this devastated area, quickly transforming it into the diverse living assemblage of life we see today.

Invertebrates One tends to think of the recolonization of the lifeless, post-Mazama landscape as consisting of an influx of birds and mammals in conjunction with the dispersal of plant seeds by these animals and by the wind. But all these life forms are possible only with the influx of the lowly organisms. Could a forest survive without its soil bacteria? Could a meadow survive without its insects? Probably not. The lowly organisms of this planet can easily survive without the vertebrates—certainly without man—but the reverse is not true.

In a mountain meadow there can be thousands of invertebrates in every square yard: in the meadow-splotched Mountain Lakes Wilderness, their numbers are countless billions. As in other land environments, insects make up the bulk of the species and are the most important agents in wildflower pollination. The evolutionary record shows a contemporaneous rise in the flowering plants and in the more advanced insects, and in all likelihood this was anything but coincidental: eliminate today's insects and you'd eliminate today's wildflowers.

37

An insect we'd all like to eliminate is the seemingly ubiquitous mosquito, whose presence is greatest in our area's wet, showy wildflower gardens. But this despised creature is one of our area's most prolific pollinators, for honeybees are virtually nonexistent here. Yellowjackets may congregate at campgrounds or picnic tables, but like our area's few other bee species, these are essentially nonpollinators.

Insects are also beneficial in culling forests of old and sickly trees and then reducing the fallen snags to humus, with the aid of other invertebrates and of fungi and bacteria.

Fish From our biased view, fish are regarded as the lowest of the vertebrates, since all other land vertebrates evolved from fishy ancestors. In the Crater Lake area, the predominant kind of fish is trout, and the commonest species are rainbow and eastern brook. While some trout are native to our area's streams, none are really native to its high, mountain lakes—particularly Crater Lake. Yet we see trout in most of them, thanks to past and/or current planting. For information on our area's species and their distributions, see Chapter 4.

Amphibians and Reptiles Ancestral fish gave rise to ancestral amphibians about 350 million years ago, which in turn gave rise to ancestral reptiles about 300 million years ago. This time may seem very remote, but in terms of earth history, it is quite recent. If all of the earth's history could be compressed into one year, then amphibians would appear around December 4 and reptiles around December 8.

Amphibians and reptiles, like fish, are cold-blooded, and hence do rather poorly in mountain environments. In the park proper, only eight species of amphibians and four species of reptiles are known to exist, but more are found lower down, such as around Lake of the Woods, in the deep west-side canyon bottoms, and particularly along the west edge of the Klamath Lake basin.

Park visitors are unlikely to see any amphibians, for the vast majority of park amphibians, which are relatively scarce to begin with, are not along the Crater Lake rim. Rather, they are down on the moist or wet lower slopes and canyon bottoms. In the high mountains, particularly in or around lakes and meadows, the wilderness traveler is likely to see or hear Pacific treefrogs, whose resounding choruses belie their dwarf stature. These come in an assortment of colors, even in a small area, but are readily identified by their dark eye stripe. Also present

is a mute cousin, the tailed frog, which has rough skin and, as its name implies, a stubby tail. Cascades frogs are a bit more robust, lack eye stripes, and have spotted backs and yellowish undersides. The boreal toad, thriving even on desolate lava flows, is the largest of the common amphibians, easily recognized by its drab, warty body. Salamanders, while present, are secretive, and you shouldn't displace logs and rocks in search of them.

In our area proper—above 6000 feet—only one reptile stands a good chance of being seen, the common garter snake. It prefers moist or wet areas, usually meadows, where frogs, salamanders and a cornucopia of invertebrates abound. Like the boreal toad, garter snakes are found on Crater Lake's Wizard Island, both species apparently having migrated to that vicinity before the early lake's waters rose sufficiently to create the island (see Chapter 8, Stops 8 and 17). In the 6000 years of isolation, the Wizard Island garter snakes have evolved into a very distinctive "negroid" race. The population is black, which gives them excellent camouflage from predatory birds. The island lacks the grassy habitat these snakes usually occupy.

One reptile you won't have to worry about is the western rattlesnake, which is virtually absent above 6000 feet—our area's prime hiking terrain. However, they do exist lower down, but only where mammals such as meadow mice or ground squirrels are relatively plentiful. Neither predator nor prey is likely to be met in our area's lower, shady canyons.

Birds Birds appear to have evolved from dainty dinosaurlike ancestors roughly 150 million years ago. They are sketchily represented in the fossil record, this scarcity being due, in large part, to their delicate bones, which are rarely preserved. In terms of species, birds greatly outnumber all the other vertebrates—mammals, reptiles, amphibians and fish. There are about 200 bird species in our area, roughly four times that of their nearest rivals, the mammals. The Park Service provides a handy brochure that lists the Crater Lake birds, and this, by and large, is a suitable list for bird watching in our entire area.

Birds have the distinct advantage over most other animals in being able to escape bad weather by flying away from it. As winter approaches, most species migrate either south or down to lower elevations. A few, however, "dig in" and actually do quite well during the long, cold winter. For example, during this period the chickenlike blue grouse usually stays in the confines of the forest deep, eating conifer needles (lodgepoles are favorites), staghorn lichen or some other paltry food item that most other animals wouldn't consider.

No visitor to the Crater Lake rim avoids being greeted (or scolded) by gregarious, garrulous Clark's nutcrackers—they almost leap at you to snatch food from your hand (don't feed them). These oversized "gray jays," like other members of their family, are omnivorous, and will eat almost anything. During the winter, however, they'll often subsist on pine nuts, particularly those of the high-elevation whitebark pine. But if supplies are insufficient, they'll migrate down eastside slopes and try their luck among ponderosa pines.

Still, most birds make very distinct migrations. One of the commonest and most easily recognized is the dark-eyed junco (Oregon junco), which is a small finch with a black or gray neck and head and with white outer tail feathers. Along the Crater Lake rim, you'll see these demure birds standing in the background, waiting to pick up scraps of food left by the raucous, aggressive nutcrackers.

On mountaintops, the hiker is occasionally rewarded with sightings of mountain bluebirds or violet-green swallows, both species catching insects on the wing, or of gray-crowned rosy finches, which scour the alpine terrain for seeds, insects and spiders. Like the nutcracker, this finch seems reluctant to leave its mountain home in the wintertime.

Because our area is, for the large part, cloaked in a forest of relatively tall conifers, birds are usually hard to observe. Perseverance is a prerequisite for the serious bird watcher. By sitting quietly in a number of different environments, you can observe several dozen species of birds in a day's time. One can't do that with mammals.

Clark's nutcracker takes the spotlight, dark-eyed junco stays behind, and mountain chickadee, often heard, is rarely seen. Golden-mantled ground squirrel competes with nutcrackers, deer visit campgrounds, crayfish lurk on Wizard Island.

Mammals Had it not been for the rise of the dinosaurs, we humans might have evolved on this planet millions of years sooner. More than 200 million years ago, as our reptilian ancestors began to diversify, dinosaurs arose and then dominated the landscape for about 150 million years. They kept our ancestors small and scarce until the last of these "tyrants," many of them small, died out over a relatively short period, totally disappearing about 65 million years ago. After that mass extinction, mammals were free to diversify.

During the Ice Age Oregon had quite a diverse assemblage of large mammals, but by about 10-12,000 years ago stone-age man had driven virtually all of them to extinction. More recently, 20th Century man has continued this unnecessary carnage, eradicating the grizzly from the Crater Lake area as well as from most of the West. And wolverines and fishers, trapped for their pelts, were exterminated over much of their range. It remains to be seen in our area of dwindling forests whether these large members of the weasel family can maintain sufficient numbers to avoid extinction. The mountain lion's future in our area is equally precarious.

Fortunately, the fate of our largest indigenous animal, the Canadian elk, looks a little brighter. The bull elk, which can weigh half a ton, had been hunted almost to extinction by the 1960s. Today's Crater Lake population is derived from animals introduced from Yellowstone National Park. They browse shrubs and graze meadows, such as those along the park's western section of the Pacific Crest Trail. On that lightly used section, the author saw more elk than people, neither plentiful.

Bear and deer are two other large mammals that visitors often hope to see but only occasionally do. Once you learn to recognize animal droppings, you'll note that both often use the hiking trails. The black bear, despite its powerful jaws (which were probably used on flesh in Ice Age times), is largely a vegetarian, eating berries, fruits, nuts, bulbs and grasses. Most of the meat that brother bruin consumes is in the form of insects. You need not fear him, but only respect him. In our area mule deer frequent the eastern slopes while black-tailed deer, a subspecies, frequent the Cascade crest and the western slopes. These animals prefer to browse shrubs, and hence are often seen in brush-choked logged areas.

Campgrounds, picnic areas and the Crater Lake Rim Drive are the most likely places to observe chipmunks and ground squirrels, which are the only mammals to greet you with open (hungry) arms. The Cascades golden-mantled ground squirrel has a white side stripe like its smaller brethren, the chipmunks, but its face is plain, lacking their facial strips. The chipmunk you're most likely to meet is Townsend's chipmunk. Lower down, particularly in ponderosa-pine forests, you're more likely to meet the yellow-pine chipmunk.

On the trail the hiker has a fair chance of spotting marmots or pikas in rocky, high-elevation sites. The marmot is a cat-sized, overstuffed "ground squirrel," while the pika is a pint-sized mouse-eared "rabbit."

The bulk of our mammalian species go unseen, for most are nocturnal and reclusive. Grassy meadows teem with shrews, moles, voles and mice, while drier slopes of lupine and paintbrush attract pocket gophers, hares and rabbits. Common predators are long-tailed weasels, badgers, coyotes and red foxes.

In shady conifer forests, ground vegetation is less, as are rodent populations. Here, the chattering chickarees (Douglas squirrels) and their quiet cousins, the northern flying squirrels, cash in on treetop crops of conifer seeds. These rodents are kept in check by martens and predatory birds.

Finally, there is one group of mammals that mountain visitors can expect to see daily—bats. The little brown myotis is perhaps the commonest species above 6000 feet, the big brown bat below it. In the evening you'll see them darting and flitting among or above the trees, harvesting unfortunate aerial insects. Like shrews, they can, in a few hours, voraciously consume their weight in insects. So rather than squirm at these flying beasties above your campsite, be thankful they're culling the crop of mosquitoes.

8 Crater Lake Rim Drive

Introduction To appreciate the size, beauty and wonder of Crater Lake, you should drive entirely around the lake on the park's Rim Drive. Without stopping, this 31½-mile loop (minus the side trips) takes about an hour. Using this road log, you can expect to take about three hours if you're in a hurry, half a day if you're not. Visitors who are interested in wildflowers or who plan to climb Mt. Scott should allow a full day.

Roughly 18½ of the 31½ basic miles are along a stretch that is one-way: clockwise. Without realizing the implications of this one-way route, too many visitors end up with less-than desirable photos. This is because many of them start near the Rim Village in the morning, shooting into the sun as they start to drive around the lake. If they've made lots of stops, then they end up on the east side in the afternoon, and are still shooting into the sun. Generally, good lighting for photographs is after 10 a.m. on the west rim, before 2 p.m. on the east rim. If you plan to get an early start, then begin this road log at the north-rim junction, Stop 13. If you are starting in late morning or in the afternoon, then begin with Stop 1.

This road log is *not* official, so you won't find numbered posts along the park's Rim Drive. The log's 52 stops are at turnouts that the author thinks are important for visitors who want a complete tour of the lake. Some of these turnouts are small, but most have ample parking. Many visitors may not want to take the time to stop at every one, and they should read ahead to select the ones that appeal to them. The geology in the descriptions below, which is fairly extensive, is based primarily on research by Prof. Howel Williams done before World War II and by Dr. Charles Bacon (U.S. Geological Survey) done in the early 1980s.

Most of the 52 stops are shown as gray half-circles (or, in a few cases, circles) on Maps 8, 9, 10, 13 and 14. Forty-eight of these lie along Rim Drive; the remaining four lie along the Pinnacles road. Each half-circle represents a described turnout, and you can easily see which side of the road each is on (circles represent both sides of the road). Almost all the turnouts are paved; the few that aren't are identified in the text. To prevent unnecessary traffic jams, the author has omitted most of the minor turnouts.

A few words of caution are necessary. The Crater Lake rim is quite precipitous, and one wrong step could be fatal. Most turnouts have low stone walls, and parents should make sure that their children don't go beyond these walls. Before August, some of these walls may be buried under snow, and then the situation is even more dangerous, for some children (and adults) like to walk to the brink of snowfields. *The Crater Lake rim is no place for unsupervised children!* Hazards also can exist along Rim Drive. Minor rockfalls occur almost daily, so be prepared for rocks on the road, especially in the morning. If roadside snowbanks are present, their meltwater sometimes freezes on cold nights. Therefore, if you are driving in the morning, be alert for patches of ice on the road, especially from Kerr Notch to Vidae Falls.

Stops 6, 16, 27, 30 and 44 are picnic areas. Besides having tables and benches, they have toilets, usually portable ones. You'll also have portable toilets at Stop 18, the Cleetwood Cove parking lot and trailhead. Most of the stops, like most of Crater Lake, appear on Map 9. Our route begins at the park headquarters, on the lower left part of that map. The headquarters are immediately northeast of the end of the loop Rim Drive (Stop 48), which in turn is immediately northeast of the park's only gas station. Be sure you have enough fuel.

Crater Lake Rim Drive

Stop 1: Mile 0.0   Crater Lake Park Head-quarters. Here you can get information on weather, road hazards, naturalist programs and wildflower conditions. You can also get wilderness permits, should you wish to camp in the park's backcountry. You can buy books and pamphlets about the park and the Cascade Range, and can mail any letters or packages at its small post office (weekdays only).

During the summer the headquarters parking lot contains a number of identified shrubs and wildflowers. If you are really interested in wildflowers, you should visit the nearby Castle Crest Wildflower Garden (Stop 47). Although you can drive to it, you can also reach it by a 0.3 mile trail, which begins opposite the entrance to the headquarters parking lot. Wildflowers usually bloom from late June through late August.

Go 2.7 miles to

Stop 2: Mile 2.7   Rim Village junction. The Rim Village, which is the park's most popular spot, lies immediately east of this junction. Driving through the village, you pass, on your right, a complex with a gift shop, a small grocery store, a cafeteria and a restaurant. Behind this complex are rustic cabins for rent, usually on a daily basis. Just past this complex is the Rim Center, which has audiovisual presentations about the park, and immediately past it is a picnic area with rest rooms. Opposite the picnic area is a small Visitor Center, where you can get information, wilderness permits, books and pamphlets. From the center's west side, a stairway leads down to the Sinnott Memorial, which provides one of the best views of the lake. It is here that rangers give talks about Crater Lake (the lake's major landmarks are pointed

out at the next stop). Crater Lake Lodge stands at the end of the Rim Village road, and fortunate guests can view the lake from their rooms. This mammoth lodge, open mid-June through mid-September, serves breakfast and dinner in a dining room with lake views.

Immediately past the lodge you'll find the start of the Garfield Peak Trail (all trails starting from your rim route are described in Chapter 9 in precisely the same order that you'll meet them on your drive). In the author's opinion, the Garfield Peak Trail is the park's best trail, for it excels both in views and wildflowers. There are two other trails starting in the Rim Village area. The Discovery Point Trail runs through the Rim Village and connects the Garfield Peak Trail with the Lightning Springs Trail (Stop 5). The Dutton Creek Trail, starting 60 yards south of the Rim Village junction (Stop 2), descends rather steeply 2.4 viewless miles to the tri-state Pacific Crest Trail. From the Rim Village junction

Go 0.2 mile to

Stop 3: Mile 2.9   the last of three small turnouts. The main part of the Discovery Point Trail begins here. As at the Rim Village and other popular areas, here you'll be pestered by golden-mantled ground squirrels and Clark's nutcrackers (large gray "jays"), all looking for handouts. Often joining them at the sidelines are reticent dark-eyed juncoes ("Oregon" juncoes), who are small members of the finch family. Please don't feed any animal.

You could take the Discovery Point Trail, but its views aren't any better than those you'll get here and at Stops 4 and 6. The trail's best viewpoint is near our Stop 3—just 90 yards up the trail. If you are interested in the park's vegetation, then certainly take the trail, which is mostly through a mountain hemlock/whitebark pine forest (Stop 6).

As at the Rim Village, you have very good views of 20½-square-mile Crater Lake. The lake's deepest point, roughly 1932 feet below the water level, is three-fourths of the way across the lake, if you look straight across to the opposite rim. Supposedly only six lakes in the world are deeper than Crater Lake, and in the Western Hemisphere only Canada's Great Slave Lake is deeper—by less than 100 feet. Crater Lake formed some time after a large volcano, Mt. Mazama, self-destructed back around 4900 B.C., creating the Crater Lake caldera. A *caldera* is a large, somewhat circular basin that forms mainly due to collapse of a major volcano after an exceptionally large eruptions (see diagrams on page 44 showing the evolution of Crater Lake.).

As you drive around Crater Lake, you'll learn more about Mt. Mazama, Crater Lake, and all of the park's prominent features, but before you drive on, note six of the area's landmarks. These are seen from most of the turnouts along the rim. Wizard Island, to the north, is the most conspicuous one, and above it rises Llao Rock, dominating the caldera's northwest rim. Just east of Llao Rock rises the pointed summit plug of Mt. Thielsen (pronounced "Teelsen"), 17 miles way. On the steep northwest slopes of the caldera, you can see, especially in the early morning light, the Devils Backbone, which stands out as a prominent ridge beyond the west side of the Wizard Island cinder cone.

Looking east, you'll see the park's highest feature, Mt. Scott, which stands about 2 miles beyond the east rim. Just to its left is Cloudcap, above Redcloud Cliff, which is the highest point on the east rim. These landmarks will be mentioned a number of times in the tour. Except for Mt. Thielsen, these landmarks and many others are shown on the page 45 geologic map.

Go 0.8 mile to

Stop 4: Mile 3.7   Discovery Point   (Stops 4 through 13 are on Map 8). Although the Klamath Indians had known about Crater Lake since its inception, it remained hidden from Oregon settlers until June 12, 1853. On that day, John Wesley Hillman and his fellow prospectors became the first whites to see the lake. These Jacksonville (Medford area) prospectors named it, appropriately, Deep Blue Lake. Early pioneers, however, weren't interested in the Hillman party's tales of the lake, and it became forgotten. The lake was rediscovered by other parties in 1862 and 1865,

but was little known as late as 1885, when William Gladstone Steel made his first visit to the lake. He was so impressed by the lake that he waged a campaign to preserve it (Stop 15). His efforts succeeded on May 22, 1902, when President Theodore Roosevelt signed a bill creating Crater Lake National Park. In 1980 the park was enlarged by 36 square miles, bringing it up to 286 square miles.

Between this saddle and the one at Stop 5, you pass another saddle, with equally good views. It may have been the true Discovery Point of the Hillman party. From Stop 4,

Go 1.2 miles to

Stop 5: Mile 4.9   Lightning Springs Trail, at a gravel turnout. About ¾ mile down this trail, a drop of about 300 feet, is a short spur trail leading to several campsites among the two Lightning Springs. Although some springs are closer to the Rim Drive, these two are the most accessible. A lot more springs lie on lower slopes, particularly below the west and southwest rims of the Crater Lake caldera. Studying Map 8, you might conclude that these lower springs are due to seepage from Crater Lake. Actually, none has been linked to such seepage. Rather, all originate with percolating groundwater that has been derived from melting snow.

Does Crater Lake have considerable seepage? It must, for in an average year, roughly 69 inches of precipitation reach the lake, but only 23 inches of evaporation take place. Since the lake level stays fairly constant from year to year, that means that the remaining 46 inches must be due to seepage. This 46-inch drop translates to a rate of 89 cubic feet per second, which may sound like a large flow, but is miniscule compared to the combined flow of the creeks that originate on the lower slopes of the Crater Lake caldera.

Go 0.1 mile to

Stop 6: Mile 5.0   Discovery Point Picnic Area. To get a view, you'll have to walk north about 100 yards to a *rocky point*. If you were to walk north another 200 yards, you'd reach an abandoned road that predates the current Rim Drive. This abandoned road makes an acceptable footpath over to the west flank of The Watchman, and it provides an alternate route to the lookout at its summit.

From the rocky point you can look down at Wizard Island, which is barely one mile away. You'll note that this island is composed largely

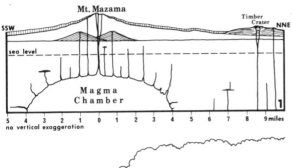

Mt. Mazama to Crater Lake

1 On a fairly level volcanic landscape, Mt. Mazama was born about ½ million years ago, fed by a magma chamber several miles underground. The mountain grew as several overlapping cones, eventually coalescing and reaching 11-12,000 feet elevation fairly late in the Ice Age, perhaps 100,000 years ago. Later, Timber Crater formed, and for a few thousand years, until about 10-12,000 years ago, glaciers lapped against this smaller volcano.

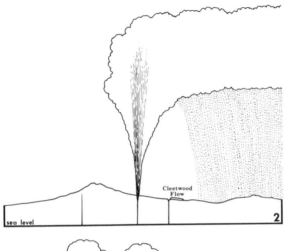

2 About 6900 years ago, a few thousand years after all major glaciers had vanished, Cleetwood Flow, like several slightly older lava flows, was extruded onto the landscape. This latest extrusion was apparently brought to an end when a major vent opened a couple of miles south of the flow. This vent produced a Plinian eruption, that is, it sent molten ejecta tens of thousands of feet into the atmosphere—so high that most of the material had time to solidify before landing on the earth as pumice and ash. Gradually the towering column decreased in height as the vent widened, the column sending destructive molten ash flows down the mountain's north and east slopes (as shown in the right half of 3).

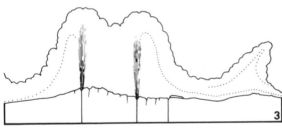

3 The end of the first series of eruptions was brought about by the collapse of Mt. Mazama into the magma chamber. This collapse blew ejecta from a ring of vents down the mountain in all directions not just in the northeast quadrant. These pyroclastic (molten ash) flows, schematically shown by lines of dots, mostly hugged the ground, abrading the nearby landscape while farther away burying much of the low-lying topography.

4 The mountain collapse left a hollow bowl, or caldera, which was enlarged by massive landsliding during and just after the mountain's dying gasps.

5 Perhaps just a few years after Mt. Mazama collapsed, two small cones began to grow—although Merriam Cone may have started a bit before Wizard Island Cone. Lava flows accompanied the growth of Wizard Island Cone. Crater Lake began to fill.

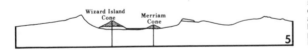

6 Crater Lake today. The top of Wizard Island Cone stands about 760 feet above the lake's surface: the top of Merriam Cone lies about 500 feet beneath it.

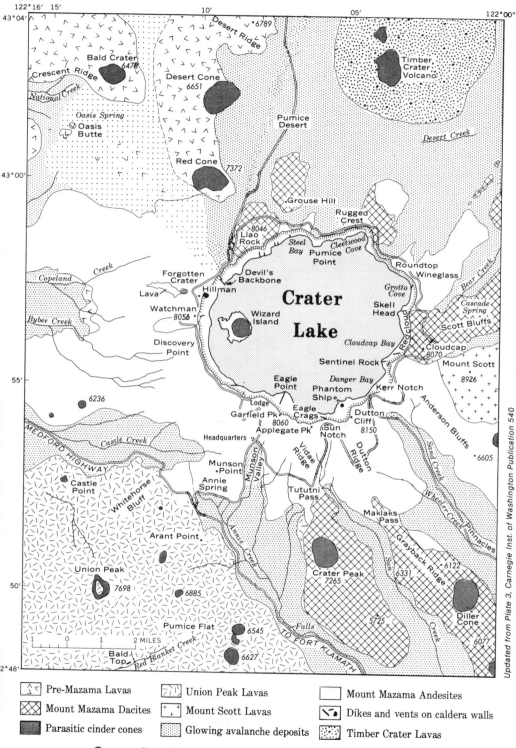

Generalized geologic map of Crater Lake & Vicinity

Updated from Plate 3, Carnegie Inst. of Washington Publication 540

Legend:

- △⌄⌐ Pre-Mazama Lavas
- ⌐⌐⌐ Union Peak Lavas
- ☐ Mount Mazama Andesites
- ⊞ Mount Mazama Dacites
- +₊+ Mount Scott Lavas
- ⌐▼● Dikes and vents on caldera walls
- ■ Parasitic cinder cones
- Glowing avalanche deposits
- Timber Crater Lavas

Top: Mt. Bailey, distant Diamond Peak above Diamond Lake, and Mt. Thielsen. Left: visitors in the precipitous Sinnott Memorial. Center: glacial striations; Mt. Scott and Kerr Notch in background. Lower right: Chaski slide, at base of an extensive talus field that lies between Applegate and Garfield peaks.

of a cinder cone and two lava flows. Tour boats circle the lake counterclockwise, and you just might see one of them pulling into or out of Governors Bay, on the right side of the south (right) flow. If the lake were a couple of hundred feet shallower, tour boats would pass another island, which today lies submerged about ½ mile east of Wizard Island. This "island" appears to be a small dome of thick, pasty rhyodacite lava. Its summit, covered probably with green algae, comes within about 100 feet of the lake's surface and, in proper lighting, you should be able to see it from a tour boat—if it passed over it.

The Discovery Point Picnic Area gets more than its share of snow, so that in some years, snow hangs around into early August. The abundant mountain hemlocks, which block both wind and views, are in part responsible for building up the large snowdrifts. Here as well as south along the Discovery Rim Trail (which starts at the saddle by the Lightning Springs trailhead), you'll also find red firs and whitebark pines. Higher up, such as on The Watchman— the peak just north of you—the whitebark pines become dominant. Lower down, the western white pines, which are scarce along the rim, become a common forest constituent.

Where you find mountain hemlocks, subalpine firs and red firs along the rim, you're likely to also find the Crater Lake currant, an ankle-high shrub with copper-colored flowers and dull, maple-like leaves. The range of this shade-and-snow-loving plant is quite restricted— oughly the area covered by this book. Other shade-loving plants you can expect to see along the rim are western prince's pine, white-veined wintergreen, one-sided wintergreen and Mertens' coralroot.

Go 0.6 mile to

Stop 7: Mile 5.6 Union Peak view. On a clear day, you see three peaks projecting above the southern horizon. Closest is steep-sided Union Peak (7698'), 8 miles away. Behind its east shoulder is younger Mt. McLoughlin (9495'), 35 miles away. Left of both, in northern California, is perennially snow-covered Mt. Shasta (14,162'), a whopping 105 miles away.

Union Peak is only the tip of a large shield volcano, which is a broad, gently sloped volcano that typically is built up by many eruptions of thin, very fluid, basaltic lava flows. Many flows are only several feet thick, though some are more than 10 feet thick. Building this 50-square-mile, 2000-foot-high shield must have taken

quite some time and, judging by the amount of glaciation upon it, the volcanic activity must have ended some time ago. That volcano originated perhaps ½ million years ago and ceased activity by 100,000 years ago. Late in its life, it constructed a cinder cone similar in size to Wizard Island's cone. Not much later, a viscous mass of lava rose from the conduit, congealing as the Union Peak plug.

Union Peak stands alone, and thus attracts more than its share of lightning strikes. The strikes create *fulgurites,* which are small tubes of fused, glassy rock. Mt. Thielsen (Stop 9) has a summit plug that is steeper, due to extensive glaciation on its north and east flanks. Because that isolated peak is almost 1500 feet higher than Union Peak, it attracts substantially more lightning. Indeed, it is known as "the lightning rod of the Cascades."

Steep-sided Mts. McLoughlin and Shasta stand in bold contrast to the Union Peak shield volcano. These two volcanoes are known as composite cones, stratovolcanoes or strato-cones. Such volcanoes consist of layers of lava flows and layers of pyroclastic materials. *Pyroclastics* consist of all matter explosively ejected from the volcano, and may range in size from fine ash to house-sized boulders (pyroclastics are also known as *ejecta* and as *tephra*). When ejected, these pyroclastics may range in temperature from cool to extremely hot, and in phases from solid to liquid (with large amounts of gas). Whereas shield volcanoes are composed mostly of basalt, stratovolcanoes are composed mostly of andesite. Andesite is more viscous than basalt, and the resulting lava flows tend to be shorter and thicker. The result is a volcano with steeper sides.

Mt. Mazama, the stratovolcano whose collapse created the Crater Lake caldera, stood at 11,000-12,000 feet at its prime, roughly midway in bulk and elevation between Mt. McLoughlin and Mt. Shasta. Mazama, however, lacked the symmetry of most of today's stratovolcanoes, at least in its final days, when its flanks had been emaciated by glaciers and bloated with domes and flows.

The Watchman, a peak your stretch of road traverses, is one of these flows. The source of this 1¼-mile-long dacite flow was a vent that lies hidden below the peak's lookout. If you hike to that lookout, you can gaze west and get a good idea of the size and shape of the flow, which descended to about 6500 feet elevation roughly 50,000 years ago. Due to a treacherous cornice on a long-lasting snowfield, the trail to the lookout is the last one in the park to open. If it is still closed, then from just north of this road stop, hike east up the slopes, cross an abandoned road, and soon intersect the safe, upper part of the trail.

Go 0.8 mile to

Stop 8: Mile 6.4   Wizard Island overlook. Wizard Island is one of the youngest volcanoes in Crater Lake National Park. The island's oldest trees germinated less than 1000 years ago; the Crater Lake caldera developed almost 6900 years ago. Wizard Island's age has to lie between the two dates. Until the early 1980s the island's age was considered to be about 1000 years, based on its very fresh appearance. However, the island seems to have been formed *above* water, which means that it had to pre-date Crater Lake. Theoretically, Crater Lake could have filled to its present 4 cubic miles in about 200 years—assuming no loss by evaporation or underground seepage. In actuality, the time was more like 500–1000 years. Therefore, the lake should have stabilized at or at about its present level roughly 6000 years ago, about 4000 B.C. The island, which is composed mainly of an andesitic cinder cone and two lava flows, probably existed by this time. Stop 17 gives a tentative chronology of the lake's underwater features.

From your vantage point you have a pretty good view south of The Watchman's steep east face, which is part of the caldera wall. You may note a dark ridge that starts at the brink of the caldera and descends two thirds of the way to the lake. This is a *dike,* which is a more or less vertical sheet of intrusive rock. Like The Watchman, the dike is dacite, and it extends inward to the vent that gave rise to this massive lava flow.

The caldera's steep slopes are quite unstable, particularly beneath The Watchman. In time, its avalanches may fill Skell Channel, the shallow strait that separates the island's west lava flow from the caldera's slopes.

If you like views, then you'll love the views from the Watchman lookout. From it, you can look down on every rim peak except Hillman, Applegate, Dutton Cliff and the Cloudcap. Allow one hour minimum for the round trip.

From Stop 8, your view north is of Hillman Peak, which happens to be the eroded remnant of Mt. Mazama's westernmost flank volcano. It is really only half an andesite volcano, for the eastern half disappeared with the collapse of Mt. Mazama, and this action exposed the volcano's vent. This vent, about ¼ mile northeast of Hillman Peak's actual summit, is best viewed on a boat tour (Stop 18). The volcano erupted about 70,000 years ago, around the start of the last major Ice Age episode, the Wisconsin glaciation.

Except for a small enclosure with several whitebark pines and mountain hemlocks, your large viewpoint is very open. Soil is poorly developed and water is in short supply. The wildflowers present, therefore, are adapted to droughtlike conditions. In this vicinity you'll find ample populations of Newberry's knotweed, spreading phlox and, especially west of the road, western pasque flower. Davidson's penstemon is also present, though it prefers rocky outcrops to pumice and, when in bloom, it adorns many of the Rim Drive's roadcuts.

Before you leave, note Williams Cone, which lies about ¼ mile west of where the Rim Drive crosses the west ridge of Hillman Peak. It is the *only* cinder cone that lies close to our route. You can inspect it firsthand by making a short hike from the next stop.

Go 0.7 mile to

Stop 9: Mile 7.1   Mt. Thielsen View. At this turnout you have the best roadside view of the landscape lying north of Crater Lake. Red Cone stands in the foreground, the southernmost of a 6-mile-long belt of small volcanoes. Diamond Lake lies 3 miles beyond the northern one, and is flanked by two small stratovolcanoes: Mt. Bailey (8363') left, and Mt. Thielsen (9182'), right. Diamond Peak (8744'), 39 miles north of us, is another one. Mt. Thielsen and Diamond Peak erupted over a period from about 500,000 to 100,000 years ago, and both have been significantly carved away by glaciers. Mt. Bailey is younger, having erupted perhaps from about 200,000 to 20,000 years ago. It is less glaciated, due to its younger age and to its lower height. Of course, during the life span of each volcano, it was dormant far more often than it was active, like Mt. St. Helens today.

On clear days you can see two snowy peaks, the stratovolcanoes seen just right of Diamond Peak. These are Middle Sister (10,047') and South Sister (10,358'), 85 and 82 miles away respectively.

Though few people walk over to Williams Cone, you can do so quite easily by heading west down the south slopes of the ridge your road just crossed. The "cone" is actually composed of five vents and one cinder cone. One of these vents ejected debris that built the prominent basaltic cinder cone, while other vents gave rise to a mile-long flow and to three short flows and/or domes. The eruptions from these four vents contained mixed lava, not just basaltic lava. Some andesite and dacite were present. This implies that some of the *magma* (subterranean lava) beneath Mt. Mazama found its way to this site. All the eruptions took place late in the Ice Age, roughly 25,000 years ago.

Go 0.5 mile to

Stop 10: Mile 7.6 early summer snowfield. Unlike a snowfield that lies 100 yards past Stop 9, this one has ample parking. Both fields typically last until late July in normal years, providing safe winter-style fun until they begin to disappear.

By hiking 0.2 mile east up gentle slopes, you'll reach the Crater Lake rim, which provides a fairly good view of the throat of the Hillman Peak volcano and an excellent view of Devils Backbone (next stop).

On your way to Stop 11 you'll pass several minor turnouts on both sides of the road.

Go 0.5 mile to

Stop 11: Mile 8.1 Devils Backbone. The "pinnacle" you see below you is the lower part of Devils Backbone, which is the largest dike that appears on the slopes of the Crater Lake caldera. There are more than a dozen other andesite dikes, but only the Devils Backbone extends from rim to water. Its maximum thickness is about 50 feet. Dikes appear to form in response to increased pressure from a volcano's rising magma. The pressure fractures adjacent volcanic rock, usually creating outward-radiating fissures. These fissures fill with magma, creating dikes when it solidifies, and if it reaches the surface before solidifying, it gives rise to lava flows, lava domes or explosive eruptions.

Your view north is similar to that from the previous stop, but now Diamond Lake is hidden from view. Red Cone hides Desert Cone, 3 miles to its north. Both of these basaltic cinder cones erupted late in the Ice Age, perhaps about 40,000 years ago. The flat-floored, barren Pumice Desert lies at the base of Desert Cone, and it buries a valley that existed up to about 4895 B.C. Around that year Mt. Mazama experienced its climactic eruptions, which

caused the mountain's collapse. These final eruptions buried much of the Crater Lake landscape under thick deposits of volcanic *ash*, *lapilli* (volcanic ejecta from 4 mm to 32 mm in diameter) and *bombs* (ejecta more than 32 mm in diameter). The Pumice Desert deposits buried the former valley to a depth of about 200 feet. *Pumice* is a kind of volcanic rock that may be either liquid lava or pyroclastic ejecta. In the case of the Pumice Desert, it is definitely pyroclastic. Most of it was deposited when gas-charged, pyroclastic flows of silica-rich ejecta raced down the mountainside.

Go 0.2 mile to

Stop 12: Mile 8.3 glacial striations, at the first of two small turnouts. The rock before you has been polished and striated by the last major glacier to descend north from Mt. Mazama's higher slopes. At its maximum this glacier probably extended north as far as Diamond Lake. There it was joined by glaciers descending from Mts. Bailey and Thielsen, and the combined glacier flowed 9 miles north, terminating a substantial 24 miles from Mazama's summit. Other Mazama glaciers, mostly unaided by feeder glaciers, flowed considerably less far, the largest ones being down the west slopes. These flowed as far west as the Rogue River, about 17 miles from Mazama's summit. Southbound glaciers, exposed to more intense solar radiation, flowed only about 12 miles down through the deep troughs of Annie Creek and Sun Creek (Map 13). In places each glacier became up to 1000 feet thick. Glaciers flowing north, east and west from the summit area occupied shallower troughs and consequently they spread out and were much thinner.

The glacial striations at Stop 12 are among the best in the park. Such striations can be seen at dozens of places along the rim, and the orientation of the striations marks the direction of the ice flow *at that point*. If you were to extrapolate these orientations back up toward the summit, you would discover that they don't meet in any one spot. Rather, they suggest a pattern of glaciers radiating from several summits. Such extrapolations, however, are risky, since glaciers rarely flow in straight lines. For example, if we could take 12,276-foot-high Mt. Adams—a close analogue to Mt. Mazama—and remove every bit of that mountain that is above 7000 feet, would the beheaded canyons point to its singular summit? Definitely not; we would conclude Adams had several summits. Similarly, if we could remove every bit of larger, higher Mt. Shasta that is above 8000 feet, the beheaded canyons would point to a singular summit. We know, however, that Mt. Shasta has two (14,162' and 12,330'). Obviously, geologic sleuthing can be a very tricky business. Other evidence indicates that just before its collapse, Mazama may have been a complex of summits and ridges. Its true configuration may never be worked out.

Go 0.2 mile to

Stop 13: Mile 8.5 north-rim access road junction. Stop just before the first junction or just after the second one, which appears on Map 9.

Mt. Mazama began erupting over 400,000 years ago, and after 100,000 years could have grown high enough to support small glaciers. From then on, major glaciers existed over much, if not most, of the time until roughly 10,000-12,000 years ago. Late in the Ice Age, which is composed of a number of glacial periods, Mt. Mazama underwent a profound change. By 25,000 years ago, Mazama's eruptions had shifted in composition largely from andesite to rhyodacite. Rhyodacite has more silica (silicon dioxide) than andesite, and this makes it more viscous and glassy. Along with increased viscosity comes increased gas pressure. Consequently, rhyodacite flows tend to be shorter and thicker than andesite flows, and eruptions of rhyodacite pyroclastics tend to be more violent. Sometimes the rhyodacite is so viscous that it barely flows, and then it creates rhyodacite domes (Stop 29).

Around 8000 years ago some rhyodacite magma worked its way upward, blew out four craters on the flanks of Mt. Mazama, and extruded thick flows. The four flows are: Llao Rock, immediately northeast of you; Grouse Hill, hidden behind Llao Rock; Cleetwood, above Cleetwood Cove; and Redcloud, the massive upper-rim cliff you see below Mt. Scott. The first eruptions gave rise to Redcloud Cliff and Cloudcap, above it. Perhaps a few dozen to a few hundred years later, at roughly 5065 B.C., the Llao Rock flow was extruded. The period of extrusion may have taken only a few months. The same holds true for the Grouse Hill flow (Maps 5 and 9), which arose perhaps a few years later. The last rhyodacite flow to form was the Cleetwood flow, from a vent near Mazama Rock (Stops 19 and 20). This formed at the same time as Mt. Mazama's climactic eruptions. It was the last of an arc of eruptions, from The Watchman clockwise around the rim to Sentinel Rock.

Go 2.7 mile to

Stop 14: Mile 11.2 Chaski slide. Looking across the lake, you see a stretch of high rim, with a peak at each end. Garfield Peak (8060') is the one on the right; Applegate Peak (8135') is the one on the left. Below this high rim is an extensive talus field, which rests on top of a block of lava flows. For a century geologists from Diller through Cranson have maintained that this block is a giant landslide, though due to its relative inaccessibility no one has studied it thoroughly. If it is a landslide, it is indeed a remarkable one. Unlike southern California's giant Blackhawk landslide, which flowed from high in the San Bernardino Mountains out to the Mojave Desert's edge, the Chaski slide apparently flowed only half way down the steep caldera rim. It does not bulge out into Chaski Bay, nor do the lake's underwater contours signal its presence. In addition, the strata should be somewhat broken, but on closer inspection (from the tour boat) they appear quite intact. Finally, the strata appear to be continuous with the section of rim immediately west of it. If this last observation is correct, then Chaski slide is definitely not a slide.

Whether or not it is really a slide may be determined in the near future by the U.S. Geological Survey. It is possible that the Chaski slide may have been one of the last of a series of giant slides that occurred when the Crater Lake caldera was formed. The current view of this caldera formation is that there was a "nearly instantaneous creation" of a 3-mile-diameter caldera, which was followed immediately or accompanied by massive landsliding that enlarged the caldera to its present 5-mile diameter.

Before driving to the next stop, note two deep gaps in the Crater Lake rim. Sun Notch lies immediately left of Applegate Peak, and the deeper Kerr (pronounced "car") Notch lies to its left. These are glacier-carved canyons that were truncated when Mazama collapsed. The low, nearly flat rim right of Garfield Peak is a remnant of two more large, glaciated canyons.

Go 0.6 mile to

Stop 15: Mile 11.8 Llao Rock view. Your turnout stands high above Steel Bay, which was named for William Gladstone Steel. Steel was the catalytic agent that led to the establishment of Crater Lake National Park in 1902. After visiting the lake in 1885, he urged scientists to study it. In the same year, he accompanied

Rangers accompany boat tours, explaining the caldera's geology and sights, such as the Devils Backbone, center. Right: Shasta red fir and one of its cones, below. Lower left: Grouse Hill, above the Cleetwood Cove rim.

Major Clarence E. Dutton and Professor Joseph LeConte (of the University of California at Berkeley), who made a reconnaissance. Impressed, Dutton returned the following year, and with M.B. Kerr and others made 168 soundings of the lake and surveyed the adjacent terrain. The lake then became widely known, particularly after Dutton's assistant, Joseph S. Diller, published his first accounts of the lake in an 1897 issue of *National Geographic* magazine.

Although trees block most of your view, you still have about the closest view—short of a boat ride—of the massive Llao Rock rhyodacite flow. University of California's Prof. Howel Williams corrected a previously held notion that the ¼-cubic-mile flow originated higher on Mazama's slopes. He was able to identify the flow's conduit, which lies mostly hidden at the flow's pointed base. He stated that the flow erupted in a glacial valley—the lower outline of the flow—then overflowed the valley and spread out in all directions. Detailed study by Dr. Charles R. Bacon in the early 1980s led to another conclusion. The glacial valley wasn't a valley at all; rather, it was an explosion pit created by gas-charged eruptions. Just as Diller had provided the groundwork for Williams' later, more detailed study, Williams provided the groundwork for Bacon. And so it goes: the accepted view of Crater Lake, over time, is increasing in accuracy and complexity.

Go 0.3 mile to

Stop 16: Mile 12.1   Cleetwood Picnic Area, among shady mountain hemlocks. The first of four small turnouts is just past the picnic area. Your next stop will be at the second turnout.

Go 0.1 mile to

Stop 17: Mile 12.2   Crater lake eruptions. Your view due south is of Sun Notch, whose form is that of a glaciated canyon (see Stop 14). To its right is the talus field above Chaski "slide" and below Eagle Crags. If a glacier were to form anywhere within the Crater Lake rim, it would do so here, on the shady, north-facing slopes of this talus field. It's possible that small glaciers may have formed during brief, cold spells in the last several thousand years.

Sun Notch lies about 5½ miles due south. About one fourth of that distance away, roughly 1¼ miles, lies a buried andesitic volcano, Merriam Cone. Its summit, under almost 500 feet of water, rises 1400 feet above its base. It

appears on Map 9 as a very symmetrical, if oversized, cinder cone. Like the slopes of the andesitic Wizard Island cone, this cone's slopes are about 30° steep. Like it, Merriam Cone was probably created above water.

When Mt. Mazama collapsed on itself roughly 6900 years ago, it left a huge, gaping hole in the earth—the Crater Lake caldera. As I've mentioned at Stop 8, the caldera took some time to fill to its present level, perhaps up to 1000 years. What did the caldera floor look like before the lake's development? Its slopes were steep-sided, as Map 9's underwater contours suggest, but its floor was probably relatively flat, though hummocky. Merriam Cone did not exist, nor did the large, west-side platform that juts east to the center of the lake. However, there is reason to suspect that both formed shortly after Mt. Mazama's climactic eruptions. For example, after Mt. St. Helens' major eruption of May 1980, more lava began to well up. In about a year it had produced a lava dome 600 feet high. Krakatau's August 1883 eruption, about 18 times as voluminous as St. Helens' but roughly a third the size of Mazama's, was also followed by substantial buildup, though it began 44 years later.

Merriam Cone probably formed in the first few years after Mazama collapsed. Had it erupted later, say even 50 years after the collapse, it would have erupted in water several hundred feet deep, and therefore would not have resembled a land-based cinder cone.

Wizard Island, also an andesite cone, may have erupted at about the same time as Merriam Cone, though a Klamath Indian legend mentions just one fiery, smoking mountain in the lake, not two. The legend could refer to either cone. If the legend is accurate, then Wizard Island would have to be a later feature, though perhaps by only a couple of hundred years. Apparently the last feature to erupt was the Wizard Island platform, which extends east from the island. The *top* of this platform seems to be younger than the Wizard Island cone, for no ejecta from that cone's eruptions have been found there. If the top of this rhyodacite platform were older, it would have been mantled with a veneer of ejecta. I emphasize "top," because the platform may be a series of flows with the oldest, of course, on the bottom.

Around midsummer the dry pumice along the north and east rims comes alive with drought-adapted wildflowers. In season you'll see many of them from this stop clockwise to

Cloudcap, Stop 32. The more prominent ones are mentioned at Stop 21.

Go 0.8 mile to

Stop 18: Mile 13.0   Cleetwood Cove Trail. The only official trail down the caldera wall leads to the boat landing on the north side of the lake. The 1.1 mile Cleetwood Cove Trail, averaging 11% in steepness, drops about 650 feet to the boat dock. Nonhikers will find this gradient on the steep side.

The tour boats operate from about July through September, and leave on the hour from 9 a.m. to 3 p.m. The tour takes about two hours, so before you go, use the portable outhouses by the trailhead. Bring along water and food, if you wish. Weather can change quickly, so be prepared for burning sun, chilly wind and, when the surface is rough, spray.

The tour is counterclockwise, the boat going past Llao Rock and Devils Backbone and through Skell Channel before docking in Governors Bay, on the south side of Wizard Island. The views from Wizard Island's summit are certainly second rate compared to those from the rim, and most boat passengers don't make that 760-foot climb. Those who do can always catch a later boat (unless they are already on the last tour). Likewise, fishermen can try their sport for a few hours, then take a later boat. From the island the boat continues counterclockwise around the lake and loops around Phantom Ship, which is the high point for most passengers.

Go 0.2 mile to

Stop 19: Mile 13.2   Cleetwood flow, seen at the second of two small turnouts. The precipitous cliffs immediately below your viewpoint are part of the Rugged Crest, which is a huge flow of rhyodacite lava that arcs around Cleetwood Cove. Mazama Rock is this flow's high point. This flow is the most recent of the four large rhyodacite flows mentioned at Stop 13 (oldest to youngest: Redcloud, Llao Rock, Grouse Hill, Cleetwood). Before the Cleetwood's lava completely solidified, Mt. Mazama underwent its climactic eruptions, erupting about 7 cubic miles of magma and initiating the collapse of the mountaintop. This collapse in turn forced out another 5 or more cubic miles of magma and created the caldera. Into this caldera slipped a still-pasty part of the Cleetwood flow. This *backflow* is the jumbled mass of lava you

see tumbling down the slopes immediately east of your viewpoint.

Go 0.6 mile to

Stop 20: Mile 13.8   Cleetwood flow rift gully. Here, about 250 yards northwest of unseen Mazama Rock, the Rim Drive passes by some impressive vertical cliffs that were created when this part of the Cleetwood flow was rifted apart. This rifting was due to the backflow, which drained part of the Cleetwood flow's interior and caused part of the flow to slump toward the Crater Lake caldera. In your vicinity, you can find other more or less parallel gullies that are perpendicular to the general southwest movement of the backflow. These rift gullies are analogous to crevasses, which, under tension, develop across glaciers.

Go 0.6 mile to

Stop 21: Mile 14.4   Grouse Hill view. Here, as at most rim turnouts, you have excellent views of most of the lake. From your vantage point, dark-gray Llao Rock stands out boldly from its surrounding strata. Below and well to the right lies the Cleetwood Cove Trail, descending to the boat dock at the extreme west end of Cleetwood Cove. Above this trail and the lake's rim rests gently domed Grouse Hill, which acted like a giant boulder in a severe sandstorm: the southern side of this flow, which bore the brunt of Mazama's climactic blasts, was severely abraded and denuded, while its northern (lee) side built up a series of dunes.

Turning toward a much closer subject, you might note your turnout's wildflowers. For a brief period, the lake's rim of pumice can flourish with quite a display. Most of the flowering plants tend to be ankle-high or less, which is disappointing to us but is very adaptive for the plants. Below that height—roughly 4 inches—even strong, debilitating winds are greatly reduced. Trees and shrubs that grow in extremely windy locations pay a dear price, as we'll see atop Redcloud Cliff (Stop 32).

For wildflower enthusiasts, the author has compiled a list of two dozen rather common species seen along the rim's sunny, windswept pumice fields. Each plant is described in this book's botany chapter, which is arranged by families (as below). Of the following plants, only the woolly butterweed, scarlet gilia, sticky cinquefoil and showy penstemon typically grow 6 inches or more high. Some species mentioned along the Garfield Peak and Mt. Scott trails are also found along this dry stretch of rim.

Pink Family
pumice sandwort
   Sunflower Family
cut-leaved daisy
alpine microseris
dwarf woolly sunflower
dwarf hulsea
silky raillardella
woolly butterweed
   Mustard Family
pioneer rock cress
woody rock cress
   Waterleaf Family
dwarf silver-leaved phacelia
   Pea Family
elegant lupine
   Evening Primrose Family
spreading gayophytum
   Phlox Family
scarlet gilia
ballhead ipomopsis
spreading phlox
   Buckwheat Family
oval-leaved buckwheat
pyrola-leaved buckwheat
Newberry's knotweed
   Rose Family
sticky cinquefoil
   Figwort Family
dwarf monkey flower
Davidson's penstemon
showy penstemon
   Carrot Family
Martindale's lomatium
   Violet Family
mountain violet

Go 0.3 mile to

Stop 22: Mile 14.7   Palisades view. This stop is at the lowest point on the Crater Lake rim, about 6690 feet. You are barely 500 feet above the lake. Just 2½ miles to the south-southeast, atop Redcloud Cliff, is your route's highest point, 1650 feet above the lake.

For most of its history, Mt. Mazama grew via summit eruptions of layer after layer of usually thin andesite lava flows. Later in its history, mostly in the last 100,000 years, the flows changed both in source and in character. Rather than erupting mostly from the mountain's summit, these flows erupted mostly from its flanks, and they tended to be shorter and

thicker. The mountain's upper magma was shifting in composition, from andesite toward dacite. The Watchman flow (Stop 7), across the lake, was one of the earlier dacite flows. The Roundtop flow, immediately southeast of you, is composed of silicic andesite and is probably about 50,000 years old. Its maximum thickness is at least 500 feet, though where it is exposed along the caldera as the Palisades, it averages about 300 feet.

Beneath the Palisades lies the mountain's greatest accumulation of glacial sediments. Glaciers eroded the mountain's northeast flank, in time creating a broad glacial trough that extended roughly from Cleetwood Cove southeast to Grotto Cove. Today the base of that trough lies below lake level.

At this stop you may see a sign about the story of soil. During the mountain's climactic eruptions, all of the mountain's existing soils were either buried or blown away—along with the vegetation. Consequently, the mountain's present soils are, at most, only about 6900 years old, a very youthful age. All the plant populations found in this soil are equally youthful. Fortunately, nature has its gardeners. For example, conifers are continually being planted by Clark's nutcrackers, who collect conifer seeds and bury them. Ground squirrels, chipmunks, pikas and other rodents harvest seeds of shrubs and wildflowers, distributing them in the process.

Here you'll see the rim's common drought-tolerant shrubs. Bloomer's goldenbush is probably the commonest, recognized by its drab, linear leaves. Wax currant and cream bush both have broad leaves. When in bloom, the plants are distinct, even from a distance. But without flowers, you can still distinguish them, for the wax currant's sticky leaves smell like mint, whereas the cream bush's leaves smell spicy, something like pepper. You'll also see greenleaf manzanita, with smooth red bark and roundish leaves. This shrub typically grows at lower elevations, as does the ponderosa pine, growing just below your turnout. Climatic conditions here are similar to those at lower elevations, for this spot captures a lot of after-noon sun and is one of the first rim spots to shed its winter snow. Before leaving, note the *upright* cones of a nearby fir, which is growing on a steep slope below you. The cones of all the non-fir conifers hang down. This fir is a red fir, and it differs from the park's two other firs in that its cones have conspicuous bracts.

Go 0.9 mile to

Stop 23: Mile 15.6 Roundtop Trail (Map 10), at a graded turnout. If you don't want to take this unmaintained trail (a former gravel road), drive on to the next stop. Starting here you can reach Cascade Spring in 5¾ miles. In the process, you'll first lose about 1000 feet of elevation, then climb about 750 feet up to the spring. Only the ignorant take this route. From Stop 27 you can reach the spring in 1½ miles with only a 600-foot drop. You should, however, be competent at cross-country navigation with map and compass. The spring arises near the brink of a lava flow, and its creek cascades merrily down a trough it has cut through the flow.

Go 0.2 mile to

Stop 24: Mile 15.8 the Wineglass, at a small, graded turnout. You won't see the Wineglass, for this landmark lies below you. From a tour boat, however, it is quite apparent. The cup of the Wineglass is a partly exposed lava flow; the stem is a narrow band of scree (loose rocks). Of more significance are the pumice deposits you're standing on, which are products of Mt. Mazama's final day.

Mt. Mazama had been a relatively quiet volcano from about 50,000 years ago until about 150 years before that climactic day. Evidently, while "sleeping," it was preparing for the Big Event. Its demise may have been brought about partly by the extrusion of the four previously mentioned rhyodacite flows, but more by a tremendous eruption that produced an estimated 1½ cubic miles of ejecta (versus ½ cubic mile of lava for the four flows). For comparison, the 1980 Mt. St. Helens eruption produced only about ¼ cubic mile of ejecta. The eruption evidently took several days, for its ash, carried hundreds of miles, was widely scattered rather than being confined to a narrow belt, as short-lived eruptions are. This tremendous eruption, which immediately preceded the Llao Rock flow, emptied the mountain's magma chamber sufficiently to lower the pressure on the confining magma, possibly setting the stage for more eruptions.

When the mountain blew about 140 years later, it did so in two stages, which were possibly only hours apart. The extrusion of the Cleetwood flow was apparently brought to an end when a major vent opened about 2 or 3 miles to the south. The vent produced a Plinian eruption; that is, it sent molten ejecta tens of thousands of feet into the atmosphere—so high that most of the material had time to solidify before it reached the ground. A lot of pumice fell near the mountain, building up deposits of 60 feet or more. Gradually the towering column decreased in height as the vent widened, the column producing destructive ash flows that raced down valleys of Mazama's north and east slopes. Deposits of those closely spaced ash flows are thick, well preserved, and well exposed at this stop, the Wineglass, and hence Howel Williams named them the Wineglass Welded Tuff.

The end of the first series of eruptions was brought about by the collapse of Mt. Mazama into the subterranean magma chamber. This collapse blew ejecta from a ring of vents down the mountain in all directions, not just in the northeast quadrant. Pyroclastic flows of this second series of eruptions largely abraded Grouse Hill, buried the valley beneath the Pumice Desert, and flooded the mountain's west, south and east canyons. If a Klamath Indian legend is correct, both the first and second series of eruptions occurred within a few hours, for the legend says the mountain was there one evening and gone the next morning.

Go 0.5 mile to

Stop 25: Mile 16.3 the first of two medium-size turnouts. Here, where conifers frame Mt. Thielsen and dwarf wildflowers speckle color on the pumice, we conclude the Mt. Mazama story.

The ash flows from the second series of eruptions were violent enough to remove some of the deposits left by the first series of eruptions. Like that series, this second series also shot ejecta—from fine ash to cabin-size blocks—into the air. The smaller particles shot high into the stratosphere, a layer of high winds and low humidity. Clouds never form in it except over Antarctica during the winter. When volcanic ash gets into the stratosphere, it tends to stay there a long time, for the strong winds tend to keep it aloft, and there are no rainstorms to wash it away.

When Krakatau, an island volcano between Java and Sumatra, erupted and produced a caldera in August 1883, its strato-spheric ash began to have worldwide effects in two weeks. Particularly impressive were months of spectacular sunrises and sunsets: instead of turning red, the sun turned blue! Aside from asthetics, the ash produced some chilling

Upper left: the Palisades, part of a giant lava flow. Upper right: Redcloud Cliff, topped with a thick layer of pumice. Center: toppled whitebark pines, which were undercut by rapid erosion of pumice. Bottom: from the Cloudcap road, Mt. Scott appears to be barely eroded, except for its deep northwest bowl.

effects: during the next three years, temperatures over much of the world were below normal,
because the ash in the stratosphere intercepted
some incoming solar radiation.

Mt. Mazama's climactic eruptions, being
several times larger than Krakatau's, may have
had an even greater effect on the northern-
hemisphere climate, perhaps dropping it by
several degrees for a few years. Though
Mazama charged the stratosphere with a
significant amount of ejecta, only the ash stayed
high for a long time. Other particles settled out

quickly, the heaviest ones very close to the
caldera. Within Crater Lake National Park,
ash-fall and ash-flow deposits locally get up to
over 300 feet thick. The accompanying map
shows the approximate thickness of these
pumice deposits from all the climactic eruptions.
The Newberry caldera, in the map's upper-right
section is about 65-70 miles northeast of
Mazama, yet it received about 2 feet of ash fall.
The ash fall thinned to the northeast, but it was
still a measurable ½ inch thick in southwestern
Saskatchewan, 750 miles away.

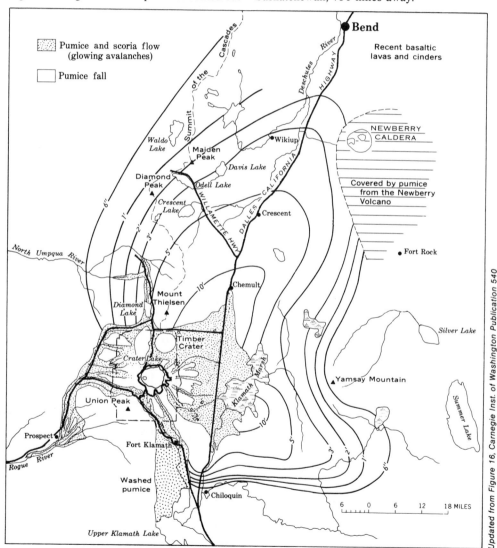

Map showing distribution of pumice deposits

Go 0.1 mile to

Stop 26: Mile 16.4 the second of two medium-sized turnouts. As usual, you have another great view of the lake, but you get an even better one by taking a footpath 90 yards southwest down to the top of a lava cliff. Looking northwest, you have a fine view of the Palisades, which is the vertical edge of a massive late Ice Age lava flow. Note all the pumice overlying the flow: the great bulk of it was derived from Mt. Mazama's climactic eruptions.

Go 0.5 mile to

Stop 27: Mile 16.9 Skell Head Picnic Area. This small, viewless picnic area is the best point to start a cross-country descent to Cascade Spring. The springs lie on an 80° bearing, 1¼ miles away, but you will have to work your way around some steep cliffs. Those expert with map and compass can make the trip to it and back in about two hours. Those with less skill may not find it.

Go 0.2 mile to

Stop 28: Mile 17.1 Skell Head viewpoint. This is one of the Rim Drive's largest turnouts, and rightly so. You have an excellent view of the lake, from Sun Notch, to the southwest, clockwise to Grotto Cove, just below you to the north. Mt. Thielsen rises above and just to the right of Timber Crater, which is a large cinder cone atop a broad shield volcano. Opposite Mt. Thielsen, massive Mt. Bailey rises above partly hidden Cleetwood Cove. Before late morning, the structure of The Watchman and of Hillman Peak show up well.

From your vantage point, you might try to envision what Mt. Mazama looked like. At its prime—perhaps 100,000 years ago—it may have risen as much as 12,000 feet above sea level. The summit stood above a point roughly halfway across the lake, if you look west-southwest toward Discovery Point (the low point midway between Garfield Peak and The Watchman). By the time the peak entered its climactic stage about 6900 years ago, it showed the ravages of time. It may have stood a thousand feet less high, and its north and east slopes had been severely glaciated to form a broad, deep bowl. However, at the time of the climactic eruptions, the glaciers, if they existed at all, were small. If you look across the lake toward Hillman Peak, you can envision the site of Mazama's first series of climactic eruptions, which lay about 2 or 3 miles due west from your

viewpoint (and about ½ mile west of the lake's deepest spot: 1932 feet). Those first eruptions were in part confined by the broad, glaciated bowl, which channeled ash-flow deposits to the north and east to form the Wineglass Welded Tuff.

A sign at this stop repeats a Klamath Indian legend of a fierce battle between Skell and Llao, two great spirits. Ultimately, Llao was defeated, cut into pieces, and thrown into the lake. His head still appears in the lake today: Wizard Island.

Go 1.4 miles to

Stop 29: Mile 18.5 domes and calderas, seen at the first of two small turnouts. Mt. Scott looms large to the southeast, Mt. Thielsen pierces the northern skyline and, on clear days, South Sister, to the east of Thielsen, displays its domed, snowy summit. The Scott Bluffs, across the canyon, are glaciated sides of large dacitic lava flows that date back 50-60,000 years ago.

Your view beyond the bluffs is northeast down a glaciated canyon that is flanked, 4 miles away from you, by two low, conical hills: Bear Butte (left) and Scout Hill (right). These are two of about two dozen dacite domes that lie in a north-south zone near the park's eastern boundary.

Also to the northeast, beyond miles and miles of forest and 7110-foot Walker Mountain, stands a high peak, on the hazy horizon about 65 miles away. This is 7984-foot Paulina Peak which, like Crater Lake's 8060-foot Garfield Peak, makes up the southwest rim of a caldera. This caldera, part of the "Newberry caldera," exists where the summit of a 20-mile-broad volcanic area once stood above the surrounding terrain. This area has been active a long time—more than a half million years—and has seen many eruptions. Over 400 cinder cones dot its surface. The volcano's summit collapsed before Mazama's did, for Newberry's several small, nested calderas are veneered with Mazama ash. The calderas today have two good-size lakes: Paulina and East, separated by recent cinder cones and their associated lava flows. If you're heading north on Highway 97 toward Bend, you just might take a couple hours to explore this area; perhaps you'll become entranced and stay a couple of days.

Go 0.7 mile to

Stop 30: Mile 19.2 Whitebark Pine Picnic Area. Here is the Rim Drive's only open picnic area, nestled among clusters of whitebark pines. From it, you have an excellent view south up the deep, glaciated bowl of Mt. Scott.

The picnic area lies in the lee of Cloudcap, due west, so it develops quite a snowpack. Consequently, you can enjoy safe winter sports in this area through late July in most years.

There is very limited parking at the next stop, the Mt. Scott trailhead, so if you don't plan to hike up the trail, drive on to either Stop 32 or 33 (read ahead). Otherwise,

Go 0.2 mile to

Stop 31: Mile 19.4 Mt. Scott Trail, starting from a graded turnout. For many visitors, the 2½-mile hike in rarefied air up to the park's highest summit is not worth the effort. However, if you're in half-decent shape, and have the time, then it is certainly worth the effort. The trail to the 8926-foot summit is easy to follow even when some snowpatches are present. Since the summit lies 2 miles east of the Crater Lake rim, your summit views encompass the *entire* Crater Lake caldera and surrounding terrain. You can see many slopes sweeping up to the rim, and you'll need little imagination to project them upward to a vanished summit. See Chapter 9's Mt. Scott Trail for more information.

Go 0.1 mile to

Stop 32: Mile 19.5 the Cloudcap road. The highest point on the Crater Lake rim to which you can drive lies at the end of this road. Unfortunately, the Cloudcap road accumulates a great deal of snow, and is the last stretch of park road to open. In some years it may not open until early August, if at all. Taking this road adds 2.0 miles to your basic 31.5-mile loop.

If you find the road closed, you might still walk ¼ mile northwest up it, to a turnout just beyond a road junction (if you're driving, you'll head down the south road from this junction, not the one you came up, to save mileage). At this turnout, you have a revealing view of Mt. Scott: except for its deep northwest bowl, the volcano appears to be barely eroded. From your vantage point you can easily reconstruct the shape of Mt. Scott before its glaciated bowl developed. A similar-sized glaciated bowl cuts into the volcano's southeast slope. During the Ice Age glaciers in each bowl of this miniature Mazama flowed about 4 miles downslope, the one from the northwest bowl joining another one that originated high on the real Mazama.

While the rocks Mt. Scott grew upon may be 300-400,000 years old, the volcano itself may be much younger. Mt. Scott's history may be similar to that of Mt. Bailey (Stop 9). If Mt. Scott was an ancient volcano, it should have been severely eroded by glaciers, particularly on the north slopes. These, however, are only mildly glaciated, in contrast to the southeast and northwest bowls, which appear to be heavily glaciated. Quite likely, the two bowls were excavated in part by volcanic eruptions, much as Mt. St. Helens produced its bowl, and then the bowls were later enlarged by glaciers. With this interpretation, Mt. Scott would be perhaps only 50,000 years old. Geologists who propose an ancient age for Mt. Scott will have to tell why the volcano's largest cirque faces southeast, into the sun.

From the Mt. Scott turnout of the Cloudcap road, continue west to the loop at the road's end. The loop is atop a thick layer of pumice that lies on the Redcloud flow, which was the first of four rhyodacite flows to be extruded just before Mt. Mazama went into its death throes. The views from the loop are excellent, and they now include your first good view of Phantom Ship, a small island just off the base of Dutton Cliff, 3 miles to the southwest.

While the whitebark pines along most of the Rim Drive turnouts are very treelike, those at the Cloudcap road loop are very shrubby. This dwarfed form of trees is called *krummholz,* which is German for "twisted wood." At least one botanist has proposed that this *krummholz* form may be a separate race of whitebark pines. Obviously, he hadn't visited Crater Lake National Park, and here's why:

Just before Mt. Mazama self-destructed, the only krummholz whitebark pines were the ones growing high on the mountain's slopes. When the mountain died, so did this krummholz population. In fact, after Mazama's second series of climactic eruptions, no vegetation existed on the mountain's slopes or for miles around. Over time, Clark's nutcrackers helped to reseed the whitebark pines on Mazama's remaining slopes. The seeds were from treelike pines, which grew on a few peaks in the vicinity. Yet today, we see *krummholz* forms around the Cloudcap loop. Is it possible that a *krummholz* form evolved in about a dozen generations? Extremely unlikely, especially when you consider how little the conifers have evolved in the last 100 million years. Rather, their form is due to winter winds that whip across the lake to this high point and freeze parts of any plant—whitebark pine or whatever—that grows above the safety of snow cover. The *krummholz* forms are due to wind cropping, not to rapid evolution.

If you skip the Cloudcap road, then from its first junction with Rim Drive, Stop 32,

Go 1.3 miles to

Stop 33: Mile 20.8 Redcloud Cliff and Pumice Castle. If you've taken the Cloudcap road, head almost one mile back to that road's junction, turn right and descend briefly to the Rim Drive. Follow it 1.1 miles to Stop 33. Your route has left Map 10 and is now back on Map 9.

At Stop 33 you see familiar landmarks, such as pointed Mt. Thielsen above the lake's Palisades. You also get a fairly close view of Redcloud Cliff, which is part of the previously mentioned Redcloud flow. Pumice from Mazama's climactic eruptions lies atop it. You'll note, just below the south part of Redcloud Cliff, an orangish-tan "castle." Early in the century it was known as Cottage Rock, but then it got upgraded to Castle Rock. Indeed, if you could walk up to it, you'd find it is of castle-size proportions. Today it is called the Pumice Castle, for the term "rock" is misleading. Pumice Castle is the layered remains of several ash-fall deposits. These deposits of dacite pumice may have been laid down at intervals of a few seconds to a few hours. Some deposits were of molten or partly molten pumice, and these formed solid, resistant layers, which you'll note in the castle. Other deposits were mostly solid, so there was less welding of them, and these layers are more erodible.

Pumice Point, beneath broad Grouse Hill across the lake, is composed of similar deposits. More deposits of a similar age are found at various locations in the caldera wall. All these dacitic eruptions (with minor flows) took place roughly 50,000–60,000 years ago, and about 40,000 years elapsed before Mazama began its ultimate series of rhyodacite eruptions.

Go 0.2 mile to

Stop 34: Mile 21.0 Victor View. From the middle of this turnout, a steep trail descends 0.2 mile to Victor View, which is the summit of a massive cliff known as Sentinel Rock. From Victor View you have the feeling that if you pushed off hard enough, you could high-dive 1000 feet down into Crater Lake. You can't.

Although Victor View presents one of the lake's best views, the great majority of visitors should *not* descend to it, for its trail is steep, exposed and potentially deadly. It is much safer to enjoy the views at the turnout. Up there you'll note toppled whitebark pines, which were undercut by erosion. You'll see others with exposed roots, which are likely candidates for toppling. Erosion in this unconsolidated pumice is too rapid for plants to establish an erosion-retardant ground cover with a network of roots.

Go 0.2 mile to

Stop 35: Mile 21.2 Kerr Notch view. Here you have views similar to those of the preceding stop, but not as good. Note Kerr Notch, your next stop, which is a cross section of a deep, glaciated canyon. Just beyond it stands the mighty wall of Dutton Cliff, which is a series of lava flows that were erupted largely over the first half of Mazama's 400,000+-year life.

Go 2.0 miles to

Stop 36: Mile 23.2 Kerr Notch. Through a forest of firs, hemlocks and pines, you have your best *roadside* view of Phantom Ship. While it looks small from here, it is quite impressive from a tour boat, for it rises 160 feet out of the water. This island lies so close to the lakeshore that it is very difficult to spot from most of the Rim Drive's viewpoints—hence the name "Phantom Ship." The "hull" of the ship is largely volcanic ejecta, while its "sails" are part of a massive dike. Most of the dike makes up the steep ridge that rises from the shoreline opposite the island. This andesite dike and the associated andesite flows and ejecta are part of 400,000 year-old Phantom Cone, which was the first major known volcano to form in the Mt. Mazama locality. Mt. Mazama was constructed largely by flows and ejecta from a cluster of overlapping volcanoes. Remnants of Phantom Cone rise only part way up Dutton Cliff; the cliff's upper 1000 feet are composed of products from later volcanoes.

Danger Bay lies below Kerr Notch, extending from Dutton Cliff to Sentinel Rock. The lava flows just above the bay are younger than those above Phantom Cone, and date back about 340,000 years.

If you don't want to make a side trip to The Pinnacles, then skip the next stop and go 0.8 mile to Stop 38. Otherwise,

Go 0.1 mile to

Stop 37: Mile 23.3 Pinnacles road junction. There are four stops along this 6.0-mile-long road. The vast majority of visitors will be

Phantom Ship, with "sails" set, "docks" near the base of Dutton Cliff. View is from Sun Notch. At the end of the Pinnacles road, you see many spires pointing skyward. Mt. Scott is in the background.

interested only in the last one, Stop D, at road's end. This road adds 12.0 miles to the length of your basic 31.5-mile loop. For off-season access to The Pinnacles, see the first paragraph of trail notes in Chapter 10's Godfrey Glen Trail.

Go 1.3 miles to

Stop A: Mile 1.3   Anderson Bluffs Trail, with limited parking by the start of a closed, gravel road. The "trail," along an old road, is viewless and unmaintained. Only diehard naturalists or hiking addicts would consider taking it.

Go 1.8 miles to

Stop B: Mile 3.1   Grayback Ridge Nature Trail (Maps 10 and 14), an old, gravel road with limited parking at Lost Creek Campground. Until 1980 you could drive this road, which provided an early-summer route between Kerr Notch and Vidae Falls. (The part of Rim Drive that lies between these two points is subject to major rockfalls and deep snowfields.)

The nature trail goes 4.5 miles to the Vidae Falls Picnic Area (Stop 44), and is worth taking if you've got someone to pick you up at the picnic area. However, by doing so, you'll miss Sun Notch, and the Rim Drive, being one-way, prevents you from driving back up to it. Take the nature trail on another day, when you have the time.

Go 2.2 miles to

Stop C: Mile 5.3   Maklaks Spring Trail (Map 14), an old gravel road with no parking. Park along Pinnacles road near Wheeler Creek, which is just north of the trailhead. If you know what a seeping spring looks like, then you won't have to hike to Maklaks Spring.

Go 0.7 mile to

Stop D: Miles 6.0   The Pinnacles (Map 14), at the roadend loop. Mt. Mazama's second series of climactic eruptions produced the deposits you see here. There are three main layers. The bottom, buff-colored layer—about 80 feet thick—is composed mostly of rhyodacite pumice and ash. The middle, gray layer—also about 80 feet thick—is composed mostly of andesitic scoria and ash. (Scoria is typically basalt-to-andesite and is less gas-charged than pumice, which is typically dacite-to-rhyolite.) The Pinnacles occur only in this middle layer. The top layer—about 10 feet thick—is

composed of gray ash. The lower half of this layer is reddish.

Now that you've met the "actors," we can get on with the "play." As mentioned at Stop 24, Mt. Mazama experienced two series of climactic eruptions. The first series was from a large vent on the mountain's northeast flank. Basically, it consisted of an ash fall that was immediately followed by ash flows. The *ash fall* is just that, ash raining down from the sky. If *sufficient* ash falls under the proper conditions (such as high temperatures), then when it hits a sloping surface, it rushes downslope as an *ash flow.*

The second series of climactic eruptions was similar to the first, except that they came from several vents that were created by a collapsing mountaintop. The mountain's magma chamber was zoned, with rhyodacite magma on top, andesitic magma below. As the mountain was collapsing, it expelled the last of the rhyodacite magma, which was hurled miles into the air, cooling to a solid form before it hit the ground to form ash flows. Such ash made up the bottom layer.

But then the mountain ran out of rhyodacite magma and began expelling tremendous quantities of basaltic magma. This magma wasn't hurled as far into the air, and it collapsed onto the mountain's slopes and raced down them as glowing ash flows. Although these flows radiated considerably less from their source than the ash falls, they left behind a more dramatic deposit: The Pinnacles. This semi-molten deposit furiously steamed away immediately upon settling, releasing superheated water vapor and other gases. These rising fumes hardened their escape vents, making them more resistant to erosion. Over the last few thousand years, erosion has stripped away much of this deposit, but the escape vents, or *fumaroles,* being more resistant, stand before you as needlelike spires.

As the ash flows were coming to an end, the fine ash that had been blown high into the atmosphere began to settle atop the fuming flows. The superheated gases rising from those flows were hot enough to oxidize the lower part of the ash layer, converting its iron-bearing minerals into rust-colored iron oxide.

The ash falls and ash flows weathered to produce a nutrient-rich soil. Although this area's soil didn't begin to form until less than 6900 years ago, it has yielded a bountiful forest of lodgepole pines. You'll also see a few large ponderosa pines, which grow in abundance on the east slopes of the Cascade Range.

Go 6.0 miles back to Stop 37, then

Go 0.7 mile to

Stop 38: Mile 24.0   two cascading creeklets. These are fed from snowfields on the upper slopes of Dutton Cliff.

Go 0.1 mile to

Stop 39: Mile 24.1 another cascading creeklet for folks who enjoy such cascades.

Go 1.0 mile to

Stop 40: Mile 25.1 Klamath Lake basin view at a gravel turnout. You have an excellent view of sprawling Upper Klamath Lake, which sits in a *structural basin*. By that I mean the basin was formed not by erosion but rather by sinking, relative to the adjacent topography, along faults. The faulting is complex, not just a single fault on each side of the basin, but several. These faults are oriented north-northwest, but they turn north where or just after they intersect the southern Cascades.

Your view due south is along the basin's west edge, beneath which lies a hidden fault. Up to about 10,000 years ago, glaciers in the mountains west of the basin were dumping prodigious amounts of sediments into the basin. But, as you can see, the basin shows no such accumulations. The reason for this is twofold. First, late in the Ice Age, Upper Klamath Lake's water level was a bit higher, and it lapped against the base of the mountains. Consequently, some sediments got dispersed by lake currents. Second, the basin's west side is sinking, taking the glacial sediments down with it. Unless a major lava flow erupts across the outlet of Upper Klamath Lake, which is not too likely, the lake will continue to remain shallow, for as the lake deepens by subsidence, new sediments are deposited on the lake's floor.

Go 0.7 mile to

Stop 41: Mile 25.8 pumice ridge with a gravel turnout. Although the ridge obstructs your views, it provides the botanically inclined with a garden of delights. Here you can identify plants *sans* people. To the south, the ridge arcs for ¾ mile before giving way to shrubby slopes. To the north, this ridge—Dutton Ridge—climbs 1¼ miles to the brink of Crater Lake. Besides providing unexcelled views of Crater Lake, the Dutton Ridge-Dutton Cliff summit area

provides one of the best assemblages of wild-flowers. This cross-country hike certainly surpasses the Garfield Peak Trail because, lake scenery and wildflowers being roughly equal on the two, the Dutton hike rewards you with excellent views down the glaciated Sun Creek and Sand Creek canyons.

Go 0.3 mile to

Stop 42: Mile 26.1   Sun Notch view. Here, at the first of several minor turnouts, you've got a fine view of Sun Notch and the Sun Creek canyon. It's not hard to imagine a large glacier slowly flowing down this canyon. And indeed the glacier was *large,* for in its prime it was about 1000 feet deep at your vicinity, and it would have buried your turnout!

Why are the deep, glaciated canyons found only on the caldera's southern and south-western flanks? The answer to this is quite simple. Most of the eruptions in the mountain's later history were on its northwest, north and east flanks, and the resulting flows buried the canyons that glaciers had cut into those flanks.

Go 1.0 mile to

Stop 43: Mile 27.1   Sun Notch Trail. Short of taking a boat ride, the best view you'll get of Phantom Ship is from Sun Notch. Snowfields linger well into summer near this notch, for it is confined between the steep, shady, glaciated walls of Dutton Ridge and those of Applegate Peak. If the ¼-mile-long trail is still under snow when you arrive, just hike cross-country up to the notch. Actually, you won't see Phantom Ship from the lowest point of the notch. From that point go briefly west (or east) along the precipitous rim. If you bring children up to the notch, be sure they are carefully supervised.

Go 1.3 miles to

Stop 44: Mile 28.4   Vidae Falls Picnic Area junction. The picnic area lies ¼ mile down this road, beside wildflower-and-willow-lined Sun Creek. The Grayback Ridge Nature Trail (Stop 37B) ends at a gate by the picnic area.

Late-summer visitors may find white-crowned sparrows among willows. If they are extremely lucky, they may also see golden-crowned sparrows, though these usually forage at lower elevations. Except for the color patterns on their heads, the two species are virtually identical. They are so much alike that on rare occasions members of the two species mate and produce healthy hybrids. In short, they haven't yet evolved enough to form distinctly separate species.

Another evolutionary problem, one which plagues botanists rather than zoologists, is the status of a dwarf lupine that grows around the Vidae Falls Picnic Area. This is the pretentious-named elegant lupine (*Lupinus lepidus*—see the chapter "Botany"). In the Pacific Northwest there are five varieties of this species—or are there? Its varieties have also been classified as 12 *separate* species! In the Crater Lake area, the plant varies so much with elevation that you'd swear it was at least two species. Again, it is a species in evolution—as *all* species are—and we just happen to see it at an awkward time, at least from the viewpoint of one who has to classify it.

Go 0.1 mile (actually, 90 yards) to

Stop 45: Mile 28.5   Vidae Falls. This is the park's highest cascade, the bulk of it about 100 feet high. Nestled in a deep, glaciated canyon, it presents a problem for photographers. Lighting is poor in early morning and late afternoon; it is best in late morning.

Go 0.6 mile to

Stop 46: Mile 29.1   Crater Peak Trail, starting from a small, gravel turnout at a cut

through a ridge (the only stop shown on Map 13). This trail—an old road—goes 1¾ miles to a junction from which an overly steep trail climbs ¾ mile to the cinder cone's summit. The summit views north from it are quite revealing and, during midsummer, the cone's rim and crater are adorned with wildflowers. A well-used elk route cuts east-west across Tututni Pass, about ½ mile from the Crater Peak trailhead.

Go 2.0 miles to

Stop 47: Mile 31.1   Castle Crest Wildflower Garden. This was mentioned at Stop 1, and is a must for wildflower enthusiasts. In midsummer, when the spring-fed flowers are at their prime, be prepared for mud and mosquitoes.

Go 0.3 mile to

Stop 48: Mile 31.4   south-rim access road junction. For more botanizing, you can head south down this road to the Annie Creek Trail and the Godfrey Glen Trail. You'll find their descriptions at the end of Chapter 10.

To complete your Rim Drive loop, turn right and

Go 0.1 mile to

Stop 1: Mile 31.5   Crater Lake Park Headquarters.

9 Crater Lake's Rim Trails

Introduction Crater Lake National Park and vicinity, as defined by this book, covers an area of about 1200 square miles—roughly the size of Yosemite National Park. Most of that park's use is confined to a very small part of its area, Yosemite Valley, and likewise most of our area's visitation is confined to a similarly small area, the Crater Lake environs. Trailwise, however, the valley and the lake differ. Yosemite Valley's floor is laced with trails, and seven more climb the valley's walls. In contrast, Crater Lake has only four rim trails, one trail down to the lake, and one maintained trail on Wizard Island. For generations, scientists and visitors alike have lamented this dearth of trails.

The 15 trails described in this chapter all start from Rim Drive or from its branch, the Pinnacles road. The trails are listed in the same order you would encounter them if you started near Park Headquarters and drove clockwise around the lake. There are four highly recommended trails, all providing lake views: Garfield Peak, Watchman Lookout, Mt. Scott and Sun Notch. The Discovery Point Trail also provides views, but these are similar to those from Rim Drive and hence the trail is redundant. For additional, unique views, hikers can go cross-country to the summits of Llao Rock, Dutton Cliff and Applegate Peak. The "trailheads" are, respectively, Chapter 8's Stops 13, 41 and 46.

Of the remaining ten trails, three are recommended—if you have the time. Castle Crest Wildflower Garden, when in bloom, is a must for wildflower lovers. The lightly used Grayback Ridge Nature Trail is a pleasant experience, though if you don't have anyone to pick you up at its end, you'll have to retrace its 4½-mile length. The Crater Peak Trail, also lightly used, provides good views and seasonally abundant wildflowers. Finally, the Cleetwood Cove and Wizard Island trails are conditionally recommended. The first is a necessity to reach the tour boats; the second, for some, is quite rewarding.

1 Castle Crest Wildflower Garden

Trailhead Along Crater Lake's Rim Drive, ⅓ mile south of this road's junction near Park Headquarters. Alternate trailhead: Park Headquarters. **Map 9.**

Distance Variable—0.3 mile for complete loop.

Low/High Elevations 6400'/6480'

Trail Notes For most of the summer, Crater Lake's Rim Drive is *one way* from the Cleetwood Cove trailhead, on the north rim, to the road's junction 140 yards south of the Park Headquarters. Therefore, if you start at the headquarters and *drive* to the trailhead, you'll spend an hour driving the 31 miles around the lake. Unless you plan to drive Rim Drive anyway, you'd be far better off to start at the headquarters lot and take a 0.3-mile-long trail that goes south to the Castle Crest Wildflower Garden Trail. This almost level spur trail starts opposite the parking-lot entrance. Before taking this spur trail, first get acquainted with the signed vegetation that grows around the parking lot.

The Castle Crest Wildflower Garden Trail is a loop trail that visits lush displays of wildflowers fed by a number of springs. You may get muddy, wet shoes or be set upon by hordes of mosquitoes, so be prepared. The major wildflowers are identified by signs or in a park pamphlet. In addition, a self-guiding leaflet is available to provide habitat information and wildflower identification for some of the major species. Dozens more can be identified by consulting the botany chapter in this book. Nowhere else in Crater Lake National Park can you see so many species of wildflowers for so little effort. This trail is a must for every wildflower enthusiast.

2   Dutton Creek Trail

Trailhead Near the Rim Village junction on Crater Lake's southwest rim. Park close to that junction and from it walk 60 yards south to the trailhead, on your right. **Maps 8 and 9.**

Distance 2.4 miles, one way.

Low/High Elevations 6080'/7080'

Trail Notes This trail provides a relatively short route down to the Pacific Crest Trail. Because the route is well-forested, wildflowers are few, views are nonexistent and, until mid-July, snow can be quite a problem on the trail's steep upper section. This upper ¾ mile is annoyingly steep for most hikers. The grade abates where the trail crosses Dutton Creek, and you can camp nearby (permits required for all camping). The route recrosses the creek near the trail's end. From where this trail meets the Pacific Crest Trail, a spur trail heads 150 yards down along Dutton Creek to two campsites. The Pacific Crest Trail is described in Chapter 16, route 3.

3   Garfield Peak Trail

Trailhead At east end of Rim Village, beside Crater Lake Lodge. **Map 9.**

Distance 1.7 miles, one way.

Low/High Elevations 7076'/8060'

Trail Notes Garfield Peak, The Watchman and Mt. Scott all provide excellent views of Crater Lake. For the photographer, Garfield Peak is better than the other two because one can take good pictures from it at almost any time of day. Not so for the other two. From The Watchman, you shoot into the sun in the morning; from Mt. Scott, in mid- and late afternoon. Furthermore, Garfield's wildflowers are more abundant than either of the others' in both numbers and species.

The trail, which is mostly snow-free by early July, makes a slight descent east to a forested saddle that nevertheless presents an excellent view of the lake. Beyond it, the trail keeps at a remarkably constant, moderate grade as it switchbacks up to the summit. You'll have a number of views along this ascent, each giving you an excuse to rest and catch your breath.

As elevation increases, the whitebark pines, mountain hemlocks and subalpine firs diminish in size, and they become almost shrublike. This dwarfed form is known as krummholz (see Chapter 8's Stop 32). Roughly ¼ mile before trail's end, when you reach the base of the summit block, you cross a "flat" that can be snowbound well into summer. When it is, the route may not be clear, and those who venture east across the snowfield will meet a precipitous, deadly dropoff. The trail, which ventures up the west side of the summit block, is quite safe, even with snow, but if you are uncertain about the route, turn back.

Your "top of the world" views are hard to beat, and with Maps 8-10 in hand, you should be able to identify every major landmark on the lake's rim. Dark, spreading Llao Rock caps the northwest rim, opposite you, and it is flanked in the distance by two massive volcanoes. Mt. Bailey (Map 1), rises above its west shoulder, while Diamond Peak, a lengthy 45 miles away, rises above its east shoulder. East of that peak stands spirelike Mt. Thielsen (Map 2). Of the far-ranging peaks, Mt. Shasta, about 103 miles due south, is the most identifiable one. This stratovolcano rises above symmetrical, gentle-sloped Pelican Butte (Map 23), which lies near the southeast corner of the *de facto* Sky Lakes wilderness. West of it is a larger, steeper volcano, Mt. McLoughlin (Map 21), which lies near the wilderness' southwest corner. Only 7 miles to your southwest stands monolithic Union Peak, the plug of an ancient volcano.

The most abundant, colorful flowers on the trail tend to be Davidson's penstemon, Applegate's paintbrush and spreading phlox. However, the sunflower family has the most species: expect to see about a dozen of them. One plant of note is the squaw carpet, a matted, prostrate, holly-leaved shrub. It usually grows below 6000 feet elevation, but on Garfield's dark, warm, southwest-facing slopes, it grows almost up to 7800 feet. (Also see Chapter 8's Stop 41.)

4   Discovery Point Trail

Trailheads Several along Crater Lake's southwest rim. The three most prominent ones are Rim Village, Discovery Point and Lightning Springs saddle. **Maps 8 and 9.**

Distance 2.8 miles, one way, from Garfield Peak trailhead to Lightning Springs saddle.

Low/High Elevations 7030'/7310'

Trail Notes Most visitors walk only the stretch of trail that extends along the Rim Village. Others start about ¼ mile northwest of

From Garfield's summit, the lower slopes of missing Mt. Mazama are prominent. Applegate Peak is near the center; Mt. Scott is at the far left, above Phantom Ship.

the Rim Village junction, by the last of three small turnouts, and hike a short way up the trail. Few hike the trail's entire length. Indeed, the last half mile appears to be more *de facto* than official trail. Also, in too many places, the trail is too steep, and the views from the trail are no better than those from nearby turnouts. It's a good trail for finding shade-loving, ankle-high plants such as Crater Lake currant, western prince's pine and two species of wintergreens. But if botanizing isn't your bag, you'll probably end up cursing your decision to take this trail in the first place.

5   Lightning Springs Trail

Trailhead   Near a saddle along Crater Lake's Rim Drive, 2¼ miles northwest from the Rim Village junction. **Map 8.**
Distance   4.1 miles, one way
Low/High Elevations   5860'/7150'
Trail Notes   Like this chapter's second hike, the Dutton Creek Trail, this trail descends to the tri-state Pacific Crest Trail. However, our route, being an old road except at its upper end, is better graded than the Dutton Creek Trail, though it is also longer and loses more elevation. Furthermore, once you reach the "PCT," you have to hike it either north or south about a mile to find an adequate campsite.

On the Lightning Springs Trail, you reach a spur trail after a ¾-mile descent. This makes a loop past two Lightning Springs and several campsites, which are the most easily reached official backcountry sites to be found in the park. About ¾ mile beyond the spur trail and just beyond a hairpin turn, you reach a delicate cascade cavorting merrily down a steep boulder pile. Lewis monkey flowers seasonally color the tranquil scene. Beyond it, your route to the PCT is down through a typical pine-fir-hemlock forest.

6   Watchman Lookout Trail

Trailhead   Near a saddle along Crater Lake's Rim Drive, 3.7 miles northwest of the Rim Village junction and 2.1 miles southwest of the north-rim access road junction. **Map 8.**
Distance   0.7 mile, one way.
Low/High Elevations   7600'/8056'
Trail Notes   By the south end of a large Rim Drive turnout, your route—an abandoned road—traverses southwest. Along part of this stretch lies a long-lasting snowfield, whose treacherous cornice stands above a blocky-lava talus field. Until the snow melts, usually in early August, the route remains closed. If you find it closed, then start from an alternate trailhead mentioned in Chapter 8's Stop 7, last paragraph.

After 0.3 mile of road, you branch right on a broad path, which switchbacks east up to the fire lookout, which is manned only in times of high fire danger. Signs at its base describe the park's climatology and identify major landmarks. The lookout sits upon a buried vent that gave rise to the Watchman lava flow roughly 50,000 years ago. This 1¼-mile-long flow of dacite lava descends west to about 6500 feet in elevation, and from the lookout—the high point of the flow—you can discern the size and shape of this flow. For more information on the adjacent geology, read Chapter 8's Stops 7 and 8.

Whitebark pines grow on most of the flow, though near the lookout these trees are reduced to shrubs. As at other high summits you'll find Davidson's penstemon and creambush, but you'll also see alpine saxifrage, with red, dainty flower stalks, growing in damp spots among the rocks.

7   Cleetwood Cove Trail

Trailhead   Along Crater Lake's Rim Drive, 4.5 miles east of the north-rim access road junction. Immediately east of the trailhead's large parking lot, Rim Drive is one-way. **Map 9.**

Distance   1.1 miles, one way.

Low/High Elevations   6176'/6820'

Trail Notes   This is primarily a utility trail, one that people take to reach the tour boats rather than one they take for enjoyment. The trail descends one of the least interesting parts of the caldera wall, with very few good exposures of Mt. Mazama's strata. One that stands out is a "lava flow," about 30 feet thick, past which you descend near the start of the trail. This formation is part of the Wineglass Welded Tuff (see Chapter 8's Stop 24 for more about this ash flow).

Because the broad trail is on sunny, south-facing slopes, it passes vegetation you'd normally see at lower elevations. Near the bottom, above the boat dock, stands a fairly large ponderosa pine at the brink of a thick andesite flow. Note the smooth texture of the flow's bottom 4 feet, the smoothness being due to rapid chilling of the lava near the relatively cold ground. By the lake's water-gaging station, just west of the dock, you could dive into the lake's *cold,* crystal-clear water, but that might turn you as blue as the lake! You can also fish in this vicinity, though few people ever catch any of the lake's trout. Better fishing (but still poor) is from Wizard Island.

8   Wizard Island Trails

Trailhead   Same as for preceding route. **Maps 8 and 9.**

Distances   1.1 miles to island's summit; 1.0 mile to island's west-flow ponds.

Low/High Elevations   6176'/6940'

Trail Notes   See Chapter 8's Stop 18 for information about boat tours out to the island. From the island's boat dock, a trail switchbacks ¼ mile up to the crest of the island's southwest lava flow. Here a vague trail, which very few take, starts west-southwest along the flow before dropping to the lake. It then follows the island's shoreline ¼ mile north and dies out at Fumarole Bay, at the base of the west flow. Ahead lies ⅓ mile of tedious traverse across the broken surface of this lava flow. Working northwest across this flow, you won't have much trouble locating the ponds. Their most interesting inhabitants are crayfish, and just how they got there is somewhat of a mystery. Perhaps crayfish eggs were inadvertently carried there by gulls. The vertebrate populations are easier to explain. Toads, garter snakes and chipmunks likely migrated to this site when Crater Lake was lower and Wizard cone had not yet become an island (see Chapter 8's Stops 8 and 17). You can swim in the west-flow ponds, but the temperature is cold: usually in the low 50s, like Crater Lake.

Of the minority of boat passengers who choose to hike on the island, most of them hike to the island's summit. The crater of the island's cinder cone is interesting, but the author and others thought the panoramic views of the lake were a bit disappointing. Looking west, you'll see extensive talus slopes below The Watchman, and may even witness the daily minor rockfalls down them. In time, Skell Channel, which separates the west flow from the caldera wall, may be filled with rockfall sediments.

Up at the cone's rim, pinemat manzanita and whitebark pines abound, as they do on much of the island. With a bit of searching, you can also find, where snowpatches linger among the rocks, alpine saxifrage. The vegetation indicates that winters are severe on the island, more so than along the Cleetwood Cove Trail.

9   Roundtop Trail

Trailhead   On the left side of Crater Lake's one-way Rim Drive, 2.6 miles beyond the Cleetwood Cove parking lot. **Map 10.**

Distance 5¾ miles to Cascade Spring.

Low/High Elevations 5720'/6730'

Trail Notes For the vast majority of hikers, this abandoned road is not worth taking. Should you wish to visit Cascade Spring, then go cross-country to it, following Chapter 8's Stops 23 and 27. For the geologically inclined, Sharp Peak, near the lower end of the trail, is worth a visit, though you'd be far better off starting near the park's boundary at the junction of Roads 2308 and 040 (see Maps 6 and 10). Sharp Peak, like about two dozen other dacite domes along the park's eastern borderlands, was extruded in the form of viscous, "constipated" lava.

10   Mt. Scott Trail

Trailhead At a small turnout 0.2 mile past the Whitebark Pine Picnic Area. On summer weekends, the turnout may be overflowing, and then you'll have to park a bit farther along the one-way Rim Drive. **Map 10.**

Distance 2.5 miles, one way.

Low/High Elevations 7670'/8926'

Trail Notes At 8926 feet, Mt. Scott is the park's highest summit, and that is reason enough for many people to climb it. However, the air is sufficiently thin to discourage those who are out of shape. If you are, then take it easy, allowing 2-3 hours for the ascent—no need to court a cardiac arrest. The trail starts as an old jeep road, but after ⅓ mile it narrows to a broad trail. Like the Cleetwood Cove Trail, the Mt. Scott Trail maintains an 11% grade over most of its length, which is on the steep side for nonhikers.

Chapter 8's Stop 21 mentions two dozen Rim Drive wildflowers and, if you look closely, you may see most of them along your ascent. You may also see a half dozen more, including, at the trail's lower elevations, alpine microseris, pumice paintbrush, Applegate's paintbrush, vari-leaf phacelia, Sitka valerian and western pasque flower. Where you reach the first switchback, you've covered about two-thirds of the distance but barely half the climb. Switchbacks take you up to lake views and then to the fire lookout. Along this upper half, watch for another half-dozen species, such as heart-leaved arnica, partridge foot, skunk-leaved polemonium, alpine sorrel, shaggy hawkweed and, of course, alpine saxifrage.

The first half of Chapter 8's Stop 32 discusses the age and form of Mt. Scott, which is a pint-sized stratovolcano. Of greater interest to most hikers are the views, which encompass the entire Crater Lake rim plus much of the surrounding terrain. You can see many slopes sweeping up to the rim, and you'll need little imagination to project them up to the vanished summit of Mt. Mazama (see Chapter 8's Stops 24 and 25 for the demise of that large stratovolcano). On clear days you can see other stratovolcanoes, such as Mt. Shasta, 105 miles to the south, Mt. McLoughlin, 36 miles to the south-southwest, South Sister, 82 miles to the north and, if the day is exceptionally clear, Mt. Jefferson, just right of the Three Sisters, and a staggering 121 miles away.

Before mid-July, Mt. Scott's large, north-facing snowfield is usually continuous enough for *experienced* mountaineers to make it down to the trailhead in about 15 minutes. Expert skiers will find this descent the park's best early-summer ski run. Most hikers, however, should avoid the snowfield's allure and return the way they came.

11   Anderson Bluffs Trail

Trailhead On the left, at a bend in the Pinnacles road, 1.3 miles beyond this road's junction with Rim Drive, which is near Kerr Notch. **Maps 9 and 10.**

Distance 4.0 miles to trail's end near east boundary.

Low/High Elevations 6180'/6420'

Trail Notes This "trail," along an old road, is viewless and unmaintained. Only diehard naturalists and hiking addicts would consider taking it. The first ⅓ mile of road is good, going to a pumice quarry, but then the road turns southeast and descends about one mile toward Sand Creek. Where the road becomes overgrown with young pines and firs, another branches east and quickly crosses the creek. This road is more obvious over the next mile, as it rambles across slopes and crosses a Sand Creek tributary before ascending to a junction in a shallow bowl. The road south from here dies out in ⅔ mile; the road east climbs over one ridge saddle and then dies out atop a second one. Road 2308, just beyond the park boundary, lies about 0.4 mile downslope from the route's end.

12   Grayback Ridge Nature Trail

Trailhead On the right, 3.1 miles down the Pinnacles road, which begins near Kerr Notch. **Maps 9, 10, 13 and 14.**

Distance   4.5 miles to Vidae Falls Picnic Area (Chapter 8's Stop 44).

Low/High Elevations   5970'/6770'

Trail Notes   Until 1980 you could drive this route, which was part of pre-World War II Rim Drive. Along this nature trail there are 14 stops, each supposedly marked by a numbered post. Because this route is now abandoned, some posts are missing, and more will be missing in the years ahead. The nature trail starts west through isolated Lost Creek Campground and, just before reaching Lost Creek, it reaches

Post 1.   Lodgepole pines abound here, as they do in other parts of the park below the rim,

particularly where soils are boggy or pumice is deep and dry. Where boggy soils prevail, the lodgepoles are often joined by subalpine firs, with "Christmas tree" silhouettes. Unlike the park's red fir and white fir, the mature subalpine fir has a conical shape and its lowest branches touch or almost touch the ground. Immediately past Lost Creek is

Post 2.   Showy flowers are few and far between on pumice soils, but they flourish at creeks. Two prominent species at Lost Creek are arrowhead butterweed and wandering daisy, both in the sunflower family. Also look for monk's hood and crimson columbine, two com-

Top: super-wide panorama from the Watchman Lookout shows all of Crater Lake plus Hillman Peak, far left. Left center: view south, from wildflowered summit of Crater Peak. Right center: Crater Peak, right, and the southern Cascades, from the Grayback Ridge Nature Trail. Bottom, Crater Lake, from near the summit of Mt. Scott.

mon members of the buttercup family. In about ¼ mile, as the road curves right and starts to climb more steeply, is

Post 3. Where soils are neither boggy nor pumicelike, the lodgepole pine associates with western white pines and red firs. Western white pine has five needles per bundle, versus lodgepole's two. Its cones are considerably longer, and they hang from the ends of the tree's branches. The red firs, being true firs, have solitary needles and upright cones. Where you see these three species of conifers, you're bound to see a foot-high shrub, pinemat manzanita. Its taller, round-leaved cousin, greenleaf manzanita, also grows here, but it generally prefers sunnier slopes, as you'll see. Continue your climb ¼ mile up to Wheeler Creek and

Post 4. Note that the creek flows under the roots of a red fir. Before Mt. Mazama collapsed roughly 6900 years ago (see Chapter 8's Stops 24 and 25), the mountain's slopes had many more streams. Today, *most* of its streams flow beneath several feet of pumice, which are frothy rocks that were deposited during Mazama's climactic eruptions. Where creeks surface at the park's mid-to-lower elevations, you may see a beautiful pink wildflower, the Lewis monkey flower. Now climb for 1⅓ miles, to where the road starts to curve south toward a ridge. On this curve is

Post 5. Here, above a small vale, the vegetation is adapted to dry conditions. You should see marum-leaved buckwheat, Newberry's knotweed, pussy paws, vari-leaf phacelia, pumice paintbrush and pearly everlasting. The narrow-leaved shrubs are the very common Bloomer's goldenbush, which blaze into golden blossoms in late summer. You have your first of many good views south-southeast to the Klamath Lake basin, which is described in Chapter 8's Stop 40. Continue briefly south to where the road bends west,

Post 6. Looking northeast, you have a good view of conical Mt. Scott, a small stratovolcano lording it over the Anderson Bluffs. See the first half of Chapter 8's Stop 32 for more information on this mountain, which is the park's highest summit. Start a brushy traverse west, with a short-lived view of Mt. McLoughlin, and in ⅓ mile reach

Post 7. On these dry, sunny slopes below the south end of Dutton Ridge, thickets of shrubs abound. Tobacco brush (also known as snow brush) and greenleaf manzanita monopolize the

slopes, the former species often identified by its seasonally powerful, sensuous odor. You'll also find Bloomer's goldenbush, wax currant (mintlike aroma) and bitter cherry. All are good browse for deer. As your road begins to round a ridge, you reach

Post 8. Here you have a fine view down deep, glaciated Sun Creek canyon, which in past times was buried under as much as 1000 feet of ice. On clear days you can see Mt. Shasta, a 14,162-foot-high stratovolcano standing 100 miles to the south. Mt. McLoughlin, a 9495-foot-high stratovolcano that is 32 miles away, is now hidden behind nearby, forested Crater Peak. This cone is quite youthful, perhaps less than 20,000 years old, and it has not been abraded by glaciers. The trail to its summit, which is this chapter's last hike, is certainly worth the effort. In about 100 yards, after the road curves northwest, is

Post 9. Look south at the cross section of Sun Creek canyon. Glaciers flowed down this canyon, widening it and giving it a U-shaped cross-section so typical of glaciated canyons. The farthest glacier descended to the north edge of the Klamath Lake basin. In 100 yards is

Post 10, with similar views. About 10 yards past the post, you'll see, on your left, a couple of young white firs. These usually grow at lower elevations, and here they are near the top of their altitudinal limit. Notice that their needles tend to grow in two almost horizontal rows, as opposed to those of red firs and subalpine firs, which curve sharply upward from their twig attachments. After a ¾-mile traverse northwest, you'll find

Post 11, where the road begins to curve north. This locale tends to be shady and cool, and it gets quite a bit of snow. Consequently, mountain hemlocks thrive, which seek out such conditions. Indeed, these droopy-topped conifers prolong the snowpack by growing in dense clusters, which shade the snow from the sun. If you walk about 35 yards west, you'll get a poor view of Vidae Falls. The peak above and right of the falls is Applegate Peak. Descend north almost to a curve in the road,

Post 12. Along the east bank of your road, the vegetation is lush, like that of this chapter's first hike, through the Castle Crest Wildflower Garden. If you're botanically talented, you can identify several dozen species, including western bistort, alpine brooklime, coolwort, Mertens' coralroot, corn lily, Gray's lovage, rein orchid and two wintergreens. Your road makes a hairpin turn south, then quickly bends west at

Post 13. Crater Lake currants, which are ankle-high shrubs with copper-colored flowers, grow near some mountain hemlocks. This species is quite restricted in range, growing only in an area roughly the same as that covered by this book (perhaps insects don't like copper-colored flowers). Growing nearby is the broad-petaled strawberry, which is a variety of the Virginia strawberry. That species has an immense range, growing in forests from California to Alaska and east to the Atlantic states. At willow-lined Sun Creek is

Post 14, just before the Vidae Falls Picnic Area. See Chapter 8's Stop 44 for a look into plant and animal speciation.

13   Maklaks Spring Trail

Trailhead On the right, at a bend in the Pinnacles road, 5.3 miles from Rim Drive junction near Kerr Notch. Park near Wheeler Creek, which is just 50 yards north of the trailhead. **Map 14.**

Distance 3.3 miles to Maklaks Spring.

Low/High Elevations 5450'/5870'

Trail Notes Maklaks Spring is a seeping spring that is poor in wildflowers but rich in sedges, grasses, mosses and mosquitoes. It is of little interest to most hikers, though botanists may find it interesting. Being one of the park's lower trails, this one displays some vegetation usually not found higher up: white fir, ponderosa pine, Scouler's willow, bush chinquapin and the colorful sugarstick. This miniature "barber pole" lacks chlorophyll and therefore must tap its roots either into those of adjacent plants or into soil fungi.

You'll know you are near the spring when your road becomes overgrown with lodgepole pines. Here, look for a spur "road" plowed by a tractor. It ends at the spring, 70 yards away. The unmaintained main road goes about 2 miles to the Sand Ridge area, by the park's southeast corner.

14   Sun Notch Trail

Trailhead Along Rim Drive, just below Sun Notch. **Map 9.**

Distance ¼ mile to Sun Notch.

Low/High Elevations 7060'/7115'

Trail Notes See Chapter 8's Stop 43.

15   Crater Peak Trail

Trailhead Along Rim Drive at a cut through a ridge, which is 2.0 miles past the obvious Sun Notch trailhead. Parking limited to two vehicles. **Map 13.**

Distance 2.5 miles to west rim of Crater Peak.

Low/High Elevations 6490'/7265'

Trail Notes The first 1¾ miles is along an abandoned road to a trail junction. If you were to continue down the main branch of that road, you would reach the park's south boundary in 6¾ miles.

From the trailhead, the old road first switchbacks, then descends to nearby Tututni Pass, which is frequently crossed by elk. At the trail junction, about 1¼ miles beyond the pass, your route's gradient changes from reasonable to unreasonable, especially the last ¼ mile up to the cone's west rim. The trail dies out here, but you should continue up through the shallow crater to the north rim. From it you have an excellent view of Garfield and Applegate peaks, Sun Notch, Dutton Ridge and Mt. Scott. Wildflowers in the crater and along the rim are similar to those along the Crater Lake rim (see Chapter 8's Stop 21), but also include an abundant display of sulfur flower, which is uncommon over much of the area covered by this book.

Once your heart has stopped pounding from the strenuous climb, you can appreciate your crater's isolation and tranquility. You may find that the meadowy crater, carpeted with subtly aromatic wildflowers, invokes images of a pastoral Andrew Wyeth landscape, one that invites you to dally and enjoy an unhurried afternoon picnic.

10 Crater Lake's Other Trails

Introduction Below the slopes of the Crater Lake rim, the trails are typically viewless. In fact, only one trail, the Union Peak Trail, provides views worth the effort, but the summit views are rewarding indeed. To compensate for this dearth of views, the author has thrown in an easy cross-country route to Red Cone.

This chapter's first three hikes visit springs, the third hike (to Boundary Springs) being the most rewarding for the effort expended. All the springs can be reached via park trails, but the shortest routes to all are on trails originating from just beyond the park boundary. Next in the chapter come two cinder-cone hikes, to the summits of Red Cone and Timber Crater, the latter hike being essentially viewless.

Near Mazama Campground, which is just north of Highway 62, are three more hikes. Annie Spring Cutoff Trail provides the shortest route to the Dutton Creek campsites, and little more. Annie Creek Trail rivals the Castle Crest Wildflower Garden Trail in wildflower abundance and may exceed it in wildflower diversity. Godfrey Glen Trail presents a canyon landscape similar to the Park's east-side Pinnacles (Chapter 8, Stop 37D).

South of Highway 62 are trails to Union Peak and Stuart Falls. The first is this chapter's most scenic hike. The second, while interesting, is about a mile longer than two west-side routes to the same place. Finally, the author has added a short cross-country jaunt to Thousand Springs, which is the park's most extensive "pumper station."

Some of the park's unmaintained trails (abandoned roads) are mentioned only in passing. Most of these branch west from the Pacific Crest Trail, and are mentioned in that trail's description in Chapter 16.

1 Crater Springs and Sphagnum Bog

Trailhead From the junction of Highways 62 and 230 west of Crater Lake National Park, drive 6.0 miles north on 230 to Road 6530, which branches east along the Jackson/Douglas county line. You bridge the Rogue River in 1.0 mile, pass the southeast-heading end of Road 6535 just 0.2 mile later and then, 0.1 mile beyond that, fork right on the start of Road 6535, a loop road. Drive 4.9 miles up it to where it angles right. Take Road 660, straight ahead, to its end at the edge of a clearcut, in 0.9 mile. **Maps 3, 4, 7 and 8.**

Distance 2.3 miles to Crater Springs.

Low/High Elevations 5360'/5700'

Trail Notes The first ½ mile may be hard to follow, but that is the price you pay for taking this shortcut route. If you had started west from the park's north-rim access road (top of Map 9), you'd hike 7.9 miles, not 2.3. From the fence just past Road 660's end, continue east on an old road about 200 yards. It dies away, and you head south about 35 yards to a trail that curves counterclockwise up to the signed park bound-

73

ary. Eastward, you follow an obvious old road 1.2 miles down to a junction. This chapter's following hike climbs east from it. Since camping is not allowed within 0.5 mile of Sphagnum Bog, this junction is the closest northern site, should you plan to camp on this hike.

Start southwest from the junction, descending just over ½ mile to a spur road, which goes 120 yards south to a roadend loop. The major Crater Spring is obvious, for it gushes noisily from the ground. A smaller, quieter Crater Spring flows from the south side of the loop. If you plan to explore Sphagnum Bog—something only serious naturalists will do—be sure you've brought along wading boots and plenty of mosquito repellent. Among the bog's more interesting plants are four carnivorous ones: common and mountain bladderworts and round-leaf and linearleaf sundews.

2   Oasis Spring

Trailhead   Same as for preceding route. **Maps 3 and 4.**

Distance   3.9 miles to Oasis Spring.

Low/High Elevations   5410'/5700'

Trail Notes   See the preceding route's trail notes, first paragraph, for the first 1.7 miles to a junction. From it, you make an easy climb northeast, descend easily in that direction, and then descend moderately past 200-foot-high Oasis Butte. You can easily miss it, since it is largely obscured by dense forest. Soon the trail turns north and goes an almost level ½ mile to Oasis Spring. By late summer this small pool can dry up. Before then, underground water surges into the pool, disturbing the fine volcanic sand as it produces miniature eruptions—a rather fascinating display, but hardly worth the effort of the hike. The spring is the source of Middle Fork National Creek.

From the spring the trail continues 3.2 miles to a junction northeast of and below Bald Crater. This cinder cone, like Oasis Butte, is largely obscured by a dense forest. Just ¼ mile past Oasis Spring, this trail enters a shallow gully and makes an abrupt turn from north to east. Here you'll find an abandoned road that starts west before curving ⅔ mile down to a wet meadow, the source of North Fork National Creek. You could camp nearby, preferably in a tent you've brought along, for the tune hummed by the zillions of mosquitoes is hardly one's idea of a mountain lullaby.

3   Boundary Springs Trail

Trailhead   From the junction of Highways 138 and 230 near the southeast shore of Diamond Lake, drive 3.3 miles southwest on 230 to a road branching left. This minor road is just ¼ mile past South Umpqua Road 3703, a major road branching right. Take the minor road 0.3 mile southeast to its end at Road 760. Follow this road 2.9 miles to the west bank of the Rogue River. Rogue River Trail 1034 crosses the road here, but you continue 0.2 mile up to a flat and Boundary Springs Trail 1057. Shallow Lake West lies 0.4 mile farther on Road 760, with fairly warm swimming but no fishing. **Map 4.**

Distance   1.3 miles, one way.

Low/High Elevations   5080'/5260'

Trail Notes   The Boundary Springs Trail goes but 110 yards to a gully, from which the Rogue River Trail begins its very lengthy, ill-maintained route down-river to the town of Prospect. From the gully junction you climb south almost ½ mile to Crater Lake National Park's 1980 boundary. Soon the trail levels, and then it descends to the river and follows it to the 1902 boundary, beyond which it immediately ends at the turnaround loop of an old road. From the loop's east end, a trail of sorts goes over to several large, noisy Boundary Springs—the source of the Rogue River. The springs are so voluminous that you could start, immediately below them, a raft trip down the mighty Rogue (though fallen trees make such a trip impractical). Dozens of water-loving shrub-and-wildflower species flourish here, as do hordes of mosquitoes. No camping is allowed within ½ mile of these springs.

Should you head up the old road, you'll reach a junction in 1.9 miles. Southwest, one road rambles 3.2 miles to Oasis Spring (preceding route), while another road climbs a monotonous 4.1 miles south past lodgepoles to the Pacific Crest Trail (Chapter 16).

4   Red Cone

Trailhead   At a turnout on the park's north-rim access road, roughly 1½ miles south of the westbound Pacific Crest trailhead and 1 mile north of the road's junction with Rim Drive. **Map 8.**

Distance   1.4 miles, one way by shortest route.

Low/High Elevations 6770'/7372'

Trail Notes This route is strictly cross-country; no trail exists. Your objective, however, is perfectly obvious, and you just cross a barren drainage divide to reach it. The first 200 feet of elevation gain is moderate, but the remaining 400 feet is steep, though safe. The sparsely forested subalpine summit provides views in all directions, though you're not quite high enough to see Crater Lake through the Hillman Peak-Llao Rock gap. To the north you see broad Mt. Bailey and pointed Mt. Thielsen. Between them lie, from west to east, Diamond Peak (above partly hidden Diamond Lake), Middle, North and South Sisters (all very distant) and asymmetrical Cowhorn Mountain.

5   Timber Crater

Trailhead Along the park's north-rim access road, just ¼ mile south of the Pumice Desert turnout. Limited parking at the start of a closed road heading east. **Map 5.**

Distances 4.1 miles to saddle north of Timber Crater; another 0.5+ mile cross-country up to north rim of crater.

Low/High Elevations 5980'/7403'

Trail Notes Once all the snow melts, this route lacks water, for all the streams flow underground, beneath a deep mantle of pumice. This route also lacks views, even along the crater's rim, which is well-forested.

The route, an abandoned road east, goes ¾ mile to the south-climbing Pacific Crest Trail. Continuing east, you quickly reach a road fork near the southeast tip of the Pumice Desert. You can take either fork and make a 12.6-mile loop—with moderate climbing—and end up back at this fork. Some of the eastern part of the loop (Map 6) is through a stately ponderosa-pine forest, though it does have some burned sections.

To reach Timber Crater, fork left, as the northbound Pacific Crest Trail does. After 1.3 miles of easy climbing, this trail branches left, and your road's gradient becomes moderate, staying that way for almost 2 miles up to a broad saddle. Beyond it, the road is vague for about 150 yards and can be especially hard to follow before mid-July, when lots of snow patches prevail.

To reach the rim of Timber Crater, just head steeply upslope. About 360 feet up, you reach a shallow bowl, which is the northernmost, and oldest, of this volcano's vents. From the bowl's southeast corner, you climb another 160 feet, pushing your way up through dense clusters of mountain hemlocks before you reach the low north rim of the summit crater. The crater, composed of two or three vents, is remarkably flat. This flatness is due to air-fall deposits of pumice from Mt. Mazama's final eruptions (see Chapter 8's Stops 24 and 25). The flat floor makes a fine, secluded spot for dry camping. Early season hikers will find ample snow for water; bring along Hawaiian punch or some other liquid concentrate and treat yourself to some "home-made" snow cones.

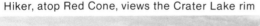
Hiker, atop Red Cone, views the Crater Lake rim

6   Annie Spring Cutoff Trail

Trailhead   Immediately north of the Mazama Campground entrance road, opposite a ranger residence. **Map 12.**

Distance   0.6 mile to Pacific Crest Trail.

Low/High Elevations   6020'/6330'

Trail Notes   This trail provides the shortest route to the Dutton Creek campsites, 2.0 miles away. The trailhead is vague. You can start by a road near a ranger residence, but it really doesn't matter. Just traverse across a flat to its north end and follow a road that climbs briefly up an obvious fault-line gully. The road ends at a water tank, which is fed by a subterranean creek that lies beneath the gully's pumice. From the tank, a trail climbs moderately up the gully to a divide, where it joins the Pacific Crest Trail (see Chapter 16, route 3).

7   Annie Creek Trail

Trailhead   Anywhere along the east side of Mazama Campground between Loops C and G. **Map 12.** (A trailhead is being established behind the Mazama Amphitheater, between loops D and E. A new self-guiding leaflet will be available in 1983, keyed to a counterclockwise flow on the trail, descending by loop G and ascending by loop C.)

Distance   1.7 miles for complete loop.

Low/High Elevations   5775'/6005'

Trail Notes   Like Chapter 9's first route, the Castle Crest Wildflower Garden, this one teems with creekside wildflowers. Unlike that trail, this one also has lavish displays of dry-slope wildflowers. Using this book's botany chapter, you should be able to identify many species. Also, use park pamphlets, if available.

The trail runs along the east side of Mazama Campground, which is perched at the brink of Annie Creek canyon. This nature trail descends near loop G and ascends near loop C. In the canyon, you'll cross Annie Creek four times. The canyon's pumice walls are similar to those of Sand Creek canyon, which are described at Chapter 8's Stop 37D.

8   Godfrey Glen Trail

Trailhead   Along major curve in south-rim access road, 2.2 miles south of Park Headquarters and 0.4 mile east of Goodbye Creek Picnic Area. **Maps 12 and 13.**

Distance   1.0 mile for complete loop.

Low/High Elevations   5980'/6080'

Trail Notes   The Godfrey Glen Trail shows you a geologic setting similar to that of The Pinnacles, along the park's east border. The trail, however, becomes mostly snow-free about two weeks before the road to The Pinnacles opens. Actually, since The Pinnacles are at a fairly low elevation, they are accessible from about Memorial Day onward—but from a route outside the park. To visit them out of season, begin north on State Route 232, which leaves Highway 62 about one mile east of Fort Klamath. Drive 11 miles north on 232 to Road 2304 and follow that road 4 miles northwest to where it dead-ends. Along an abandoned roadbed, walk ½ mile west to The Pinnacles viewpoint.

The geology of the Godfrey Glen area is essentially the same as that at The Pinnacles (see Chapter 8's Stop 37D). In brief, a series of massive ash flows swept down the glaciated canyon, burying the Godfrey Glen area under about 200 feet of poorly consolidated volcanic ejecta. The first of these flows was composed of rhyodacite pumice, the last of basaltic scoria (see Chapter 8's Stop 37D). A layer of ash then settled on these deposits. In the ensuing 6900 years since those flows, erosive processes have cut the canyons you see today. Ground water, seeping out at the base of these flows, undercuts their cliffs, and this action has maintained the vertical-walled nature of the canyons: the cliffs are back-wasting, not down-wasting, just like the ones you see in Utah's red-rock country. At Godfrey Glen, however, the erosion is occurring at a prodigious rate.

Because loose ash lies above a vertical cliff, you put your life in peril when you try a little off-trail exploration. This trail is a very poor one for undisciplined children. Along the rim, stay on the trail!

The trail loops through a mostly fir-and-hemlock forest, whose shade harbors summer snow patches that in turn provide suitable environments for snow mosquitoes. Before August, carry insect repellent. The shady forest floor, littered with needles and cones, is a poor environment for most shrubs and flowers, but a few species are suited to such conditions, such as the knee-high grouse whortleberry and the ankle-high Crater Lake currant, dwarf bramble, western prince's pine and two species of wintergreens. None are particularly showy, even when in bloom. However, you may see two showy species, both lacking green stems and leaves: Mertens' coralroot and sugar stick. Lacking chlorophyll, these colorful, delicate plants get sustenance by tapping their roots into the hyphae of soil fungi and/or roots of adjacent plants. Without this ingenious adaptation, these plants would have a hard time surviving on the dimly lit forest floor, and our walk along it would lack these sunbursts of color. Along the forest's edge, wildflowers and shrubs are more diverse and abundant.

9 Union Peak, via Pacific Crest Trail

Trailhead On south side of Highway 62, 0.8 mile west of the south-rim road junction. **Map 12.**

Distance 5.5 miles, one way.

Low/High Elevations 6190'/7698'

Trail Notes Until about 6900 years ago, Union Peak was dwarfed by its massive neighbor to the northeast, Mt. Mazama. While that stratovolcano existed, perhaps no one would have cared to climb Union Peak. Today, however, Mt. Mazama is gone, and Union Peak dominates its local terrain. No summit on Crater Lake's rim can make this claim, though all are higher than Union Peak. As Mt. Mazama collapsed to form the Crater Lake caldera, its violent eruptions destroyed all vegetation on the mountain's slopes. But today, you see many subalpine species growing high on Crater Lake's summits—where did these subalpine species come from? Perhaps many came from Union Peak, whose diverse population of subalpine species stood a good chance of surviving Mazama's death throes. Climbing up Union Peak's many switchbacks, botanists will find many occasions to stop, rest and examine the flora.

The first 2.9 miles of route are south along an old road that is now a link of the Pacific Crest Trail (Chapter 16, route 2). Most of it is through a mountain-hemlock forest. Except for a small stretch on the Watchman Lookout trail, no other stretch of park trail remains so persistently snowbound. In early July of an average year, snow blankets more than half of the route, and even in early August a few snow patches still remain. Since the entire route is otherwise waterless, the abundant snow cover may serve some purpose.

After you emerge from the forest deep, you traverse ¼ mile across a narrow pumice flat, reaching a junction by its south end. Ahead, the Pacific Crest Trail goes 2.2 viewless miles to a junction with the Pumice Flat Trail (next route), but you take the old road that winds 1⅔ miles west to the base of Union Peak. If you are on horseback, dismount there, or else you'll make an ass of yourself. From it, a footpath climbs to the remnants of a cinder cone, then traverses

Crater Lake rim, from Union Peak. See page 8 for view south.

north across talus to the start of three dozen switchbacks. Traversing the talus, you'll see, and perhaps smell, many sticky-leaved, bushy herbs. These are gummy arnica, which is common here, though rare over most of the park.

Your views improve as you struggle up the switchbacks. The trail is well-engineered, given the limited possibilities of the steep slopes, but still you must be careful. At one spot in particular a slip could be fatal. A final scramble puts you on the summit—one too small to hold a restless troop of Boy Scouts. The summit views certainly justify the effort. Glaciers have dissected part of the Union Peak volcano, and its many-layered nature lies plainly visible below you to the west (see Chapter 8's Stop 7 for more on the volcano's geology). To the north and northeast you see all the major peaks on the Crater Lake rim plus Mt. Bailey, Mt. Thielsen and Diamond Peak. Mt. McLoughlin stands to the south.

Steep-sided Union Peak may offer the park's best technical climbing routes. Being volcanic, however, they can be dangerous, so if you plan to do some roped climbing, check first with park rangers.

10   Stuart Falls, via Pumice Flat Trail

Trailhead   No parking at trailhead, so park at the Cold Spring picnic loop. This is along Highway 62, about 2½ miles southeast of the south-rim access road junction and 7¼ miles northwest of the park's southernmost boundary. From the loop's south end, walk 140 yards south to trailhead. **Maps 12 and 13.**

Distance   5.4 miles, one way.

Low/High Elevations   5430'/6290'

Trail Notes   There are four obvious routes to Stuart Falls: Upper Red Blanket Trail, Lucky Camp Trail, Pacific Crest Trail and Pumice Flat Trail. The first two, at 4.2 and 4.6 miles, are the shortest and are described as the first two routes of Chapter 12. The Pacific Crest Trail, at 7.6 miles, is easily the longest. You wouldn't take that route unless you planned to climb Union Peak, and then the length of the entire hike, round trip, would be 20.4 miles—a good two-day hike.

The Pumice Flat Trail is a suitable day hike for east-side visitors. The two west-side trails are shorter and more scenic, but in the time an east-side visitor drives to either one, he could have been half way to Stuart Falls via the Pumice Flat Trail. This route is strictly for day-hikers, for there is no overnight parking. Going to the falls is easy, for you climb only about 500 feet to the Cascade divide. Returning east from the falls is a moderate effort, for you gain almost 1000 feet to reach the divide.

The trail's namesake, Pumice Flat, is interesting because of its monotony. The floor of this valley was buried in pumice, thanks to Mt. Mazama's final eruptions (see Chapter 8's Stops 24 and 25). Today you see only a pure stand of lodgepoles (seventh heaven for lodgepole needleminer moths) growing on the flat, discounting minor herbs such as the misnamed elegant lupine. On the slopes surrounding the flat, the forest composition is well-diversified. See Chapter 12's first hike for a description of the Stuart Falls environs.

11   Thousand Springs

Trailhead   On Highway 62 drive to Rogue River N.F. Highway 60. This road is 5.9 miles east of Highway 62's junction with Highway 230, and 2.4 miles west of Crater Lake N.P.'s west boundary. On 60, go 0.5 mile, fork left on Road 6000-900, and follow it 2.6 miles to a spur road immediately south of the Thousand Springs gorge, and park. **Map 7.**

Distance   Variable—about 0.2 mile to nearest springs.

Low/High Elevations   Variable and negligible

Trail Notes   In 1980 the Thousand Springs area was judiciously incorporated into Crater Lake National Park. These springs are only a few minutes' walk east from a short spur road that ends at the park's new boundary. The springs lie along a ⅔-mile-long swath, emerging from a layer of porous rock. Though they comprise the park's largest spring complex, they do not produce the most volume—that honor goes to Boundary Springs. Thousand Springs will appeal only to serious naturalists who are willing to brave the muck and mosquitoes. No official trail exists as yet.

11 Diamond Lake Basin and the Upper Rogue River Basin

Introduction   This chapter's first eight hikes are located in and around the Diamond Lake Recreation Area. The trails are described in a clockwise sequence around Diamond Lake, starting with the Horse N' Teal Lakes Trail, whose northern trailhead is by the lake's south shore. Of the eight hikes, only two are exceptionally scenic: the Mt. Bailey and Mt. Thielsen trails. The latter is strenuous, and both get quite exposed near the top—no place for acrophobics. While not particularly scenic, the Howlock Mountain and Thielsen Creek trails do get you up to the high-altitude (relatively speaking) Pacific Crest Trail. And from it you can make cross-country forays up to the eight scenic, 8000'+ summits of the Sawtooth Ridge or to equally scenic 8031-foot Tipsoo Peak, just north of the ridge. This chapter's section of the Pacific Crest Trail is described in detail as Chapter 16's last hike.

The chapter's last four hikes, though peripheral to the scope of this book, are all worth taking. All are very short: a half-hour per trail is sufficient. National Creek Falls lies a linear mile east of Highway 230, while the Rogue River Gorge, Natural Bridge (lava tube) and Mammoth Pines trails lie just west of Highway 62. Between these highways and Crater Lake N.P.'s west border, you can find other trails, though most of them have been supplanted by newer roads. One that persists is the "Rogue River Trail." This extends from Boundary Springs, in Crater Lake National Park's northwest corner, all the way downstream to Prospect. Some parts of the trail are well-maintained; others are essentially cross-country. This composite of trail segments, about 45 miles long, is left to those with a keen sense of adventure.

1   Horse N' Teal Lakes Trail (1482)

Trailheads   Both are along the south part of Road 271, which loops around Diamond Lake. From Diamond Lake Road 4795, drive 0.4 mile west on Road 271 to the South Shore Picnic Ground entrance. One trailhead is nearby, between the entrance and the boat dock. A second trailhead is 0.8 mile farther along Road 271, immediately beyond Horse Lake. **Map 1.**

Distance   1.0 mile from South Shore Picnic Ground to Road 271 by Horse Lake.

Low/High Elevations   5185'/5205'

Trail Notes   For most of the summer, the Horse N' Teal Lakes Trail is a good one for trail-bike riders, for they can drive fast enough to escape hordes of pursuing mosquitoes. The same applies to joggers. Most of the trail, you see, is along or near Diamond Lake's south-shore bog. By late summer, the mosquitoes wane and the huckleberries develop their fruit; this is the time to take the trail.

The boggy, huckleberried stretch of trail receives little use since the few hikers that visit the two lakes start from the Horse Lake trailhead. For most of the summer, Horse Lake is two lobed, the southern lobe being a lily-pad pond. The slightly deeper northern lobe is stocked with rainbow trout. Teal Lake is usually barren.

2   Silent Creek Trail (1479)

Trailheads   One is the same as for the Mt. Bailey Trail (the next hike), but the more popular one is at Road 271's bridge across Silent Creek. This bridge is 1.0 mile southwest of Diamond Lake's Broken Arrow Campground entrance. **Map 1.**

Distance   2.0 miles from Mt. Bailey trailhead to Teal Lake.

Low/High Elevations   5190'/5260'

Trail Notes   From Road 271 the Silent Creek Trail heads downstream from the east side of the bridge and upstream from its west side. Few people follow either stretch all the way. Downstream, the trail goes a worthy ⅓ mile, then heads east through a logged area before ending at Horse N' Teal Lakes Trail, by the northwest corner of Teal Lake. Upstream, the trail goes a very rewarding mile to the headwater springs that feed Silent Creek. You'll find most of the springs along the creek's uppermost ¼ mile, and it's fascinating to watch the creek grow over this short distance from a trickle to a broad, swift stream.

Silent Creek is blessed with a profusion of wildflowers, and is accordingly cursed with a greater profusion of mosquitoes. Before August bring lots of repellent.

3   Mt. Bailey Trail (1451)

Trailheads Starting on Road 271 near the southeast corner of Diamond Lake, drive 1.8 miles west to Road 4795-300, branching left. Take it 0.4 mile south to a parking area for both the Mt. Bailey and Silent Creek trails. To shave 2.2 miles off your 5.4-mile trail, start from another trailhead. From the junction of Highways 138 and 230 near the southeast corner of Diamond Lake, drive 3.1 miles southwest on 230 to South Umpqua Road 3703, branching right. Drive 2.0 miles up this major road to Road 4795-300 and follow it 250 yards east down to a minor road. From the west side of a low crest, this road climbs 1.4 miles northeast to the Mt. Bailey Trail. Not everyone will want to drive up this one-lane road. **Map 1.**

Distance 5.4 miles, one way.

Low/High Elevations 5230'/8363'

Trail Notes After an initial jog north, the Mt. Bailey Trail climbs west up glaciated slopes that are mantled with pumice from Mt. Mazama's climactic eruptions (see Chapter 8's Stops 24 and 25). Where trees are uprooted, you can examine fresh pumice. The trail climbs moderately to Hemlock Butte (two cinder cones), then levels off at a low, hemlock-covered ridge. From a low knoll at the north end of the ridge, you have a fair view of Diamond Lake. Next, your waterless route traverses ⅓ mile northwest across a flat before making a momentary climb to an old road, this hike's second trailhead. If you start here, you cut 2.2 miles and 830 feet elevation gain off your ascent, reducing your overall energy expenditure by about one third.

From the road, you have an unrelenting, moderate-to-steep climb to the south end of Mt. Bailey's summit ridge. Just below it, you'll arc past a crater, which is an explosion pit left by Mt. Bailey's last eruption, near the end of the Ice Age. This mountain, a moderate-sized volcano of basaltic andesite, has been erupting on and off for perhaps the last 200,000 years, and it may erupt again in the future.

The summit ridge is as far as some people get, for the route ahead, up along the west base of a bedrock fin, is quite intimidating. If you fell, you probably wouldn't slide more than a few yards, but the potential for a major accident is there. By the north end of the fin, you climb (literally) back to the ridge, then scamper up to the naked summit. (After your perspiring climb, you'll probably be ready to strip to your shorts, and this summit's a good one for viewful sunbathing.) The few wildflowers that grow nearby are definitely alpine or subalpine in character.

On clear days you can see for miles, from Mt. Jefferson, 107 miles to the north, to Mt. Shasta, 120 miles to the south. Mt. Jefferson pokes above the lower east slopes of "nearby" Diamond Peak. East from both are Three Fingered Jack, Mt. Washington, Middle, North and South Sisters, Broken Top, Bachelor Butte and, closer to us, Cowhorn Mountain. South, you can identify all of the Crater Lake summits, though the lake is just out of view. To their west is Union Peak, flanked by two distant, usually snowy volcanoes: Mt. Shasta, immediately left of the peak, and Mt. McLoughlin, a bit to its right.

4   Rodley Butte Trail (1452)

Trailhead On Road 271 at the west side of Diamond Lake's outlet. **Map 1.**

Distance 3.5 miles to Rodley Butte summit.

Low/High Elevations 5190'/6838'

Trail Notes The Rodley Butte trail is a little-used utility trail that once linked Diamond Lake to Old Man Camp. Subsequent roads have made the trail obsolete. It's the kind of trail a Scout leader would take to punish his troop. This overly steep trail climbs 3¼ miles almost to the south rim of the butte. To attain its moderately forested summit, hike cross-country ¼ mile north along the rim of this cinder cone. You'll be hard pressed to get a good photo of Diamond Lake, Mt. Thielsen and Howlock Mountain. Rodley Butte and the cinder cone at its north base are fairly youthful volcanoes, having erupted late in the Ice Age, perhaps 20,000 years ago.

If you continue south on your viewless, waterless trail, you'll find it becomes vague in about one mile, just after it angles northwest to start a descent toward Road 2735 (off the map). The Rodley Butte Trail does not provide access to a good cross-country route up to the Mt. Bailey summit.

Left: to reach the Mt. Bailey summit, you must veer left around its obstructing ridge. From the summit you have fine views, including this one of the Crater Lake rim, Mt. Scott (far left) and Mt. McLoughlin (far right).

Ken Ng climbing the summit pinnacle; a large near-summit pinnacle with dipping strata; a smaller pinnacle with a view toward the Crater Lake rim.

5   Diamond Lake Loop Trail (1460)

Trailheads   On Road 271, 100 yards east of Diamond Lake's outlet, or at west grounds of Diamond Lake Resort. **Map 1.**

Distances   1.7 miles to Diamond Lake Resort; 5.2 miles to South Shore Picnic Ground boat dock (by start of Horse N' Teal Lakes Trail).

Low/High Elevations   5185'/5240'

Trail Notes   This is not a loop trail at all, but a path along Diamond Lake's north shore. Its chief users are fishermen and resort guests. Nevertheless, some people do like to hike entirely around the lake. Trail 1460 is the northernmost part of this loop, taking you from the lake's outlet to Diamond Lake Resort.

From the resort you walk south to a public boat ramp, from which a short trail parallels the Diamond Lake road ¼ mile southeast to the tip of Diamond Lake Campground. This giant campground runs 2 miles along the lake's east shore, and from the campground's south end you walk over to adjacent South Store, operated by Diamond Lake Resort. Just past it is a parking area for the Mt. Thielsen Trail. Here you head west through the South Shore Picnic Ground. At its west end is the start of the Horse N' Teal Lakes Trail, this chapter's first hike.

The west half of Diamond Lake's south shore, like the lake's west shore, lacks an official trail, though with some effort you can complete the lake circuit on fishermen's trails. By August the lake has dropped a few inches, exposing a gravelly shoreline that can serve as a trail.

6   Howlock Mountain and Thielsen Creek Trails (1448 and 1449)

Trailhead   By a paved parking lot opposite the junction of Roads 271 and 4795. Road 271 starts west on a loop around Diamond Lake, while Road 4795 immediately passes Diamond Lake Corrals, then descends ½ mile to the Diamond Lake Resort entrance. Northeast, Road 4795 terminates at Highway 138 in ⅓ mile. **Maps 1 and 2.**

Distances   3.6 miles to Thielsen Creek; 5.9 miles to Pacific Crest Trail via Thielsen Creek Trail; 7.2 miles to PCT via Howlock Mountain Trail.

Low/High Elevations   5330'/6960' (Tr. 1449), 7320' (Tr. 1448)

Trail Notes   From the east side of the trailhead parking lot, two trails start north. Take the right (east) one, even though both reunite near a horse tunnel under Highway 138. From the far side of the tunnel, a minor trail heads northward, but you climb southeast up the slopes of a lateral moraine. Immediately beyond the crest of that moraine, you meet a second minor trail, which heads north down a gully. You switchback to the crest of a higher moraine and then, from a second gully, you roll ½ mile across slopes to the seasonal west fork of Thielsen Creek. Beyond it you wind 1 mile east to Timothy Meadow, then ½ mile past it up to a Thielsen Creek trail junction.

Thielsen Creek Trail 1449 climbs 2.3 rather steep miles southeast to the Pacific Crest Trail. About 100 yards before that junction, a spur trail west heads down to nearby Thielsen Creek Camp. The Pacific Crest Trail goes 3.1 miles northeast to the Howlock Mountain Trail and 2.5 miles southwest to the Mt. Thielsen Trail. Along these two stretches of trail, particularly the one to the northeast, mountaineers have access to eight 8000'+ summits of the Sawtooth Ridge, including those of Howlock Mountain.

Back at the Thielsen Creek junction, Howlock Mountain Trail 1448 climbs 3.6 mostly forested miles east to the Pacific Crest Trail. near that junction you'll see Howlock Mountain, rising 1000 feet above you. If you are not up to rigorous mountaineering, you can tackle a lower summit. Take the Pacific Crest Trail 1.7 miles north to a broad divide (beyond Map 2) at the base of reddish-black Tipsoo Peak. The divide is the trail's highest point (7560') in Oregon. You scramble north up the cinder slopes of Tipsoo Peak (8031') for views as far north as Mt. Jefferson.

7   Mt. Thielsen Trail (1456)

Trailhead   By parking lot at southeast corner of Diamond Lake. **Maps 1 and 2.**

Distance   4.4 miles, one way.

Low/High Elevations   5190'/9182'

Trail Notes   Because of its pointed summit pinnacle, Mt. Thielsen attracts a lot of lightning and is rightly called "the lightning rod of the Cascades." Needless to say, stay off the mountain's upper, barren slopes when foul

View upstream of myriad springs spawning Silent Creek. National Creek Falls sprays the local environment with mist. Clouds brush across Mt. Thielsen, here viewed from near the Howlock Mountain/Pacific Crest trails junction.

weather threatens. The summit pinnacle is scarred with fulgurites—small tubes of glassy rock fused by lightning strikes.

In height Mt. Thielsen is second only to this book's Mt. McLoughlin. In energy expended, your ascent is equal to that up McLoughlin. In mountaineering skills required, it is second to none—the faint-hearted need not apply.

The Mt. Thielsen Trail begins immediately south of the Diamond Lake Trailer Park entrance road and parallels it east. Just after that road curves north, you intersect the North Crater Trail (next route). Occasional logging operations can add some confusion, but generally it's not too hard to follow the route the remaining ⅓ mile to Highway 138. About 200 yards past it you cross seasonal Camp Creek, then start a moderate, sometimes steep 2⅔-mile climb to the Pacific Crest Trail. At it you are three fourths of the distance to Thielsen's summit but barely halfway elevationwise.

Now you confront the real grind. The trail quickly exits above treeline and then climbs up increasingly loose pumice slopes toward a cleaver, and it appears to veer right (south) around the cleaver. This scree slope is the *descent* route. Rather than fight your way up this unstable slope of Mt. Mazama pumice, climb up solid rock along the left (north) side of the cleaver and continue up toward the 80-foot-high summit pinnacle, which can be climbed unroped only from its southeast ridge. The nearly vertical north and east faces make these last few feet off limits to acrophobiacs.

The view from the summit area is both spectacular and didactic. You can see north 107 miles to Mt. Jefferson (10,497'), south 120 miles to Mt. Shasta (14,162'), and you are even high enough to see a bit of Crater Lake. Amid the beetles, flies and butterflies carried here by the updrafts, gleeful violet-green swallows swoop and dive at their insect harvest while we contemplate the internal structure of a volcano. We can see from the dips, or inclinations, of the strata that Mt. Thielsen's summit once lay to the east, and about 1000 feet higher, above what is now a deeply glaciated canyon. Here is a volcanologist's natural observatory, for the mountain's anatomy is stripped bare.

Mt. Thielsen's broad cone was topped with a tuff cone, which in turn was intruded by swarms of narrow dikes and two large plugs, one of them remaining as your summit. Howlock Mountain (8351'), the prominent peak 3 miles north-northeast, is also a resistant plug.

After downclimbing the summit pinnacle, head south a short way along the ridge and past some enormous pinnacles clinging to the east wall. Soon you come to an obvious spot, not too far from an isolated scrubby whitebark pine, where nearly everyone begins to descend the scree slope to the trail.

8   North Crater Trail (1410)

Trailheads   The north trailhead, about ½ mile north of the Diamond Lake Resort entrance, is the same one as for the Howlock Mountain Trail. The south trailhead, near Highway 138's crossing of the Cascades, also serves the Pacific Crest Trail (Chapter 16). The short road northeast to that trailhead begins 0.5 mile west of the Cascade divide and 0.8 mile east of Crater Lake's north-rim access road. **Maps 1 and 5.**

Distance   9.3 miles, one way.

Low/High Elevations   5210'/5840'

Trail Notes   When snowbound, this route can be a good one for cross-country skiers. During the summer, few people use it. Basically, it is a utility trail that connects Diamond Lake Corrals, at its north end, with the Pacific Crest Trail, at its south end. The route is largely viewless, is deficient in wildflowers, and is always within earshot of either Highway 138 or Diamond Lake's east-shore road—both noisy.

There is access to Trail 1410 in several places, the two most important ones being from Mt. Thielsen Trail 1456 and at the Diamond Lake Information Center. From that center, which is opposite the Diamond Lake Campground entrance, one spur trail goes 0.1 mile north to Trail 1410, another goes ¼ mile south to it.

Trail 1410 can be confusing along its southern part. From the southern trailhead, the trail winds ¼ mile southeast to its end at the Pacific Crest Trail. That part is obvious after the snow melts away. Westward, however, the route is more complex. First it goes about 60 yards to an old southwest descending road that dies out in both directions. Go just 200 yards down this road, then fork right onto a broad path that descends to a gully. Here a snowmobile route climbs northeast, leading eastbound hikers astray. Westward, you cross an old road in 0.5 mile, then join it 0.6 mile later. After that road levels off, in ¾ mile, you leave it, taking a ridge trail that descends north. From that junction, 2⅔ miles past the southern trailhead, the route north is quite obvious.

9   National Creek Falls Trail (1053)

Trailhead   From the junction of Highways 62 and 230 west of Crater Lake National Park, drive 6.0 miles north on 230 to Road 6530, branching east along the Jackson/Douglas county line. Take this paved road 3.7 miles to a poor, 200-yard-long spur road, Road 300, branching right. **Map 3.**

Distance   0.3 mile, one way.

Low/High Elevations   3770'/3990'

Trail Notes   Though out of the way, this short trail from the end of Road 300 is worth taking if you happen to like discovering an "off the beaten track" cascade. National Creek Falls, about 70 feet high, sprays the local environment with its mist; consequently, the vegetation in this predominantly Douglas-fir forest is very lush—a plus for botanists.

10   Rogue River Gorge

Trailhead   Along the west side of Highway 62, 1.0 mile below its junction with Highway 230 and 0.3 mile above the Union Creek settlement. **No map.**

Distance   0.1 mile, one way.

Low/High Elevations   3340'/3360'

Trail Notes   This exceedingly short trail runs along the brink of a Rogue River gorge. From the trail's start beside Highway 62 you can trace the river briefly downstream. It cascades into the narrow gorge, then froths and churns its way to the gorge exit, about 100 yards later. A safety fence prevents you from falling into this 40-60 foot deep, vertical-walled gorge.

11   Natural Bridge Geologic Site

Trailheads   Drive to the Natural Bridge Campground road. This road leaves Highway 62 just 1.1 miles south of the Union Creek settlement and 3.5 miles north of the Forest Highways 60/68 junction. Drive west on the campground road, then in 0.5 mile fork south (left) and drive 0.2 mile to road's end. **No map.**

Distance   70 yards.

Low/High Elevations   Both about 3200'

Trail Notes   From the road's end, head 70 yards west across a flood plain to a lava tube ("natural bridge"). What makes it interesting is that the river flows through it. Note that the amount of water emerging from the lava tube is less than that entering it. The rest of the water emerges from some downstream springs, the most conspicuous one being immediately past an excellent swimming hole that lies 20 yards past the lava tube. Swimming above the lava tube can be very dangerous—you could be carried underground. Swimming below the tube can be safe if you are careful.

12   Mammoth Pines Nature Trail

Trailhead   Along the west side of Highway 62, 0.8 mile south of the Forest Highways 60/68 junction and 1.4 miles north of Kiter Creek (River Bridge Campground) Road. **No map.**

Distance   0.2 mile loop.

Low/High Elevations   Both about 2900'

Trail Notes   At the trailhead you may see a bulletin board with brochures or at least with one on display. If none is found, here is what you will see along the trail's 20 posts: 1) tobacco brush (also called snow brush); 2) western hemlock; 3) California hazel (feel its fuzzy leaves); 4) fallen sugar pine; 5) Douglas-fir; 6) grand fir; 7) ponderosa pine (smell the cracks in its bark); 8) Oregon grape; 9) mixed-conifer forest (including white fir, which hybridizes with its look-alike, grand fir); 10) serviceberry; 11) thimbleberry; 12) mountain ash; 13) succession of plants in logged-over area from sun-loving shrubs to shade-loving conifers; 14) bracken fern; 15) Pacific yew (needles like those of western hemlock); 16) decomposition of logs by insects and fungi; 17) sugar pine; 18) Pacific dogwood; 19) golden chinquapin; and 20) Scouler's willow. This assemblage of species is quite different from one you'd see above 6000 feet. Most of this book's trails are above that elevation, and up there the dominant trees are lodgepole pine, western white pine, whitebark pine, red fir and mountain hemlock.

12   Sky Lakes Proposed Wilderness, west of the Pacific Crest Trail

Introduction   Roughly half of the trails described in this book lie in the proposed Sky Lakes wilderness. The Pacific Crest Trail (Chapter 16), adhering closely to the Cascade crest, bisects the wilderness into a west half and an east half. This chapter deals with two dozen routes in the west half: the next chapter, with those in the east half. Of the western routes, only the Mt. McLoughlin Trail (route 24) is really popular. It is popular in part because the mountain is southern Oregon's highest summit and in part because it is close to Highway 140, to several scout camps and to very popular Lake of the Woods Recreation Area. None of the other routes is close to a state highway, and none goes to a mountaintop with superlative views. Consequently, the west side of the proposed wilderness is lightly used. Two "exceptions" are Seven Lakes Trail (10) and Blue Canyon Trail (20), both visiting lake-blessed basins, and both having perhaps several cars at their trailheads on a typical summer weekend.

Of the remaining routes, three climb up luxuriantly forested, deep, glaciated canyons. Western hemlocks and associated species grow along the lower part of each canyon, giving way higher up to mountain hemlocks and their associates. Along each route, a competent botanist should be able to identify about 100 plant species. The routes are the Upper Red Blanket (1), Middle Fork (7) and South Fork (18) trails. The Upper Red Blanket Trail passes two-stage Red Blanket Falls before ending at a large camp (popular with equestrians) by Stuart Falls. The Lucky Camp Trail (2) also visits these sights, and it deserves to be more popular. The Middle Fork Trail has some fine camping near the base of the Halifax Trail (8), and at least a half dozen secluded sites farther upstream. The Halifax Trail, like the upper Middle Fork Trail, is a real struggle that most hikers will want to avoid. Botanists, however, will find that its steep ascent contains one of the most interesting vegetation assemblages to be found anywhere. The South Fork Trail lacks campsites and waterfalls, and it certainly provides the long way in to a lake basin. It nevertheless appeals to plant lovers, and to equestrians—who of course don't have to expend the energy.

Most of the remaining routes climb into the wilderness on somewhat poorer and steeper but followable trails. These trails, which may attract equestrians but not many hikers, are the Tom and Jerry (4), Mudjekeewis (5), Alta Lake (9), King Spruce (11), Hemlock Lake (14) and Wickiup (16) trails. Routes 4 and 5 go to McKie Camp, an equestrian site with shelter and pasturage, while routes 9 and 11 take long routes to Alta Lake. Trail 14, to Hemlock Lake and vicinity, has some merit, though for most people the 5½-mile hike to that relatively isolated lake may not be worth the effort. Route 16 is lakeless and viewless, but oh, those huckleberries! Perhaps no other trail in this book's area goes through such an extensive huckleberry field. Another route, Cat Hill Way (21), skirts the wilderness over most of its length and is of marginal interest.

Four more routes, in various stages of abandonment, climb into the wilderness: the Onion Springs (15), Red Lake (17), Twin Ponds (22) and Crater (23) trails. Avoid these, and you'll save yourself a lot of frustration. One trail should have been built, but hasn't: to lake-dotted McKee Basin. Hence, a cross-country route to it (19) has been added.

Of the remaining four routes, routes 3 and 6 link the Stuart Falls, McKie and Solace horse camps to each other and to the Pacific Crest Trail, and all are strictly utilitarian in function. Route 13 links the Seven Lakes Trail to the Pacific Crest Trail, providing the quickest access to 7582-foot Devils Peak, in the center of the wilderness. Finally, the Lake Ivern Trail (12) provides bonuses for equestrians, swimmers and sightseers, and it gives rise to an excellent, time-saving, cross-country route north to the nearby Middle Fork Trail (7).

1   Upper Red Blanket Trail (1090)

Trailhead   In Prospect, at a bend in the town's main road, start east on Forest Route 37 (Red Blanket Road), then in 1.1 miles, where it curves south, branch left on Road 6205. When this road forks in ⅓ mile, keep left as you drive 12¼ miles to road's end. (At mile 10.5 you pass Varmint Creek Trail 1070, which climbs 1700 feet in 4 miles to Varmint Camp. Road 830 also goes to this camp, making the trail expendable.) **Maps 11 and 12.**

Distances   3.0 miles to Red Blanket Falls, 4.1 miles to Lucky Camp, 4.2 miles to Stuart Falls.

Low/High Elevations   3940'/5430'

Trail Notes   For a relatively easy hike to Stuart Falls, you have two choices: this trail and the Lucky Camp Trail (route 2). They are quite different. The Upper Red Blanket Trail, starting low, makes a usually steady climb east along the lower north slopes of the canyon. Because you start low and are on north slopes, the first 3 miles of trail are typically snow-free by Memorial Day. In contrast, the Lucky Camp Trail, along south slopes, can have a lot of snow patches even in mid-July. However, with about a 300-foot difference between its high and low points, this trail is certainly the easier way to go once the snow has disappeared.

The Upper Red Blanket Trail starts a level course through a stately forest, quickly passing two seasonally noisy, cascading creeks. In a couple of minutes you reach the southwest corner of Crater Lake National Park, parallel the boundary east, and then switchback. You now face a moderate, 2⅓-mile haul past numerous gullies (some with creeklets) to the brink of two-tiered Red Blanket Falls, which collectively drop about 100 feet, roughly twice the height of Stuart Falls. Close to the brink of the upper fall, the Red Blanket Falls Trail immediately log-crosses swift Red Blanket Creek on its 0.6-mile climb to the Lucky Camp Trail. The lackluster camp lies about 0.6 mile west on that trail. For another perspective of your canyon's scenery, you can, after visiting Stuart Falls, return to your trailhead via the Lucky Camp and Red Blanket Falls trails. The total length of this semiloop venture is 9.8 miles,

Beyond Red Blanket Falls, the Upper Red Blanket Trail climbs at a slackening pace to a junction with the Stuart Falls Trail (route 3). Hikers from the Lucky Camp Trail join us here for a leisurely walk upstream to Stuart Falls Camp, a large, flat area near the base of the falls. Equestrians are requested to picket their horses immediately north of the Stuart Falls Trail, not down at the camp. Stuart Falls provides rhapsodic music for campers, a feature that few other southern Cascade campsites have. At the base of the falls, water-loving shrubs and herbs grow in local abundance.

Note: The botanically inclined will be particularly interested in the vegetation of the lower part of the Upper Red Blanket Trail and of the lower part of trails 7 and 18. The vegetation of the Red Blanket, Middle Fork and South Fork canyon bottoms is quite distinct from that found along most of this book's trails. The forest is predominantly Douglas-fir and western hemlock. You may also see smatterings of other conifers that are growing near their upper-elevation limits: white fir, grand fir, incense-cedar and sugar pine. Mingling with these are two conifers that are growing near their lower-elevation limits: Engelmann spruce and western white pine. At these lower elevations, many of the trails' wildflowers go to seed before the halcyon hiking days of summer, late July through late August. Some hikers then may anguish over the identification of the flowerless forest-floor flora. Some of the more common shrubs are thimbleberry, raspberry, big whortleberry, creek dogwood and California hazelnut—all with edible fruit. Where the forest floor is carpeted in green, you can expect bunchberry, clintonia, starflower, twinflower, vanilla leaf, wild ginger and windflower. Where the ground cover isn't so pervasive, you may see, foremost, Oregon grape, western prince's pine, strawberry and bracken fern. Inside-out flower, parrot's beak, Solomon seal, trail plant, trillium and white hawkweed appear in lesser amounts. In very shady places, look for wintergreens. Near water, many more species appear.

2   Lucky Camp Trail (1083)

Trailhead   In Prospect, at a bend in the town's main road, start east on Forest Route 37 (Red Blanket Road). Follow it 6.0 miles to Road 3795, which branches left 0.4 mile before Route 37 bridges Middle Fork Rogue River. Drive 11.6 miles up Road 3795 to its end. **Maps 11 and 12.**

Distances   1.9 miles to Lucky Camp, 4.1 miles to Red Blanket Falls, 4.6 miles to Stuart Falls.

Low/High Elevations   5200'/5490'

Trail Notes   Before late July, mosquitoes and/or snow patches may be too prevalent for most hikers, and then the Upper Red Blanket Trail is more desirable. Your trail starts with a brief drop, then traverses the fairly flat floor of a glaciated bowl. Late in the Ice Age, this bowl was occupied by a 200-foot-thick glacier, which spilled into Red Blanket canyon, feeding its 1600-foot-thick glacier. Midway across the bowl, you make a noticeable climb over a low

Stuart Falls provides rhapsodic music for nearby campers.

ridge, and from either side of it could make a classic cross-country plunge down to the Upper Red Blanket Canyon Trail. Such a descent, so steep that you'd almost slide uncontrollably down it, really would test your nerve besides giving you an appreciation for the enormity of the glacier that occupied this canyon.

From the ridge you descend moderately for ¾ mile, then ramble across huckleberried slopes for another ¾ mile to medium-size Lucky Camp. Two spring-fed creeklets lie immediately east of it, providing an abundant supply of water—and mosquitoes. More of each lies ahead. Beyond the creeklets you soon embark on a traverse across a hemlock flat, meeting the Red Blanket Falls Trail at the east end. This trail makes a moderate 0.6-mile descent to the Upper Red Blanket Trail, meeting it at the brink of the falls. These falls should not be missed. You can make a semiloop trip to Stuart Falls by descending here, then following the Upper Red Blanket Trail to Stuart Falls and finally returning via the Lucky Camp Trail back to its trailhead. The total length of this easy, rewarding semiloop route is 8.9 miles.

Beyond the Red Blanket Falls Trail, the Lucky Camp Trail passes at least a half dozen springs as it rolls in and out of gullies over to the Stuart Falls Trail (next route). On it you traverse ¾ mile north past seasonal creeks and across huckleberried slopes to the Upper Red Blanket Trail junction, then you climb ⅓ mile northeast to the large Stuart Falls Camp.

3   Stuart Falls and McKie Camp Trails (1078 and 1089)

Trailhead None. Links the Upper Red Blanket Trail to the Lucky Camp Trail, and links both to McKie Camp and the Pacific Crest Trail. **Maps 12 and 16.**

Distances Southbound: 0.7 mile to Lucky Camp Trail, 3.5 miles to Pacific Crest Trail, 4.5 miles to Cedar Springs/Dry Creek trails junction, 4.9 miles to McKie Camp.

Low/High Elevations 5330'/6080' (saddle by Pacific Crest Trail junction)

Trail Notes From the Upper Red Blanket Trail junction, immediately bridge Red Blanket Creek, then make a traverse past three creeks, the middle one flowing all summer in some years. By the third is a small camp, from which you climb 90 yards to a junction with the Lucky

Camp Trail. Like your route, this one abounds in huckleberries. You now make a usually moderate one-mile climb up huckleberried slopes, then have an easy 1¼-mile stroll to the McKie Camp Trail, at its start on a lodgepole flat. Ahead, your route goes ½ mile to a low divide. You'll find the northbound Pacific Crest Trail starting just north of this divide, the southbound "PCT" starting just south of it. Beyond that junction, the Dry Creek Trail traverses the Oregon Desert—a lodgepole-pine flat—and at its east end meets the Cedar Springs Trail. Both trails are abandoned—see Chapter 13, routes 1 and 2.

From the lodgepole flat north of the "PCT," the McKie Camp Trail drops about 510 feet along its well-graded 1.9-mile course to the McKie Camp shelter. You'll find the shelter just 60 yards beyond a junction with the Tom and Jerry Trail (next route) and just 30 yards before a junction with the Mudjekeewis Trail and the southbound McKie Camp Trail (routes 5 and 6). You'll find a nice campsite near the shelter, just beyond the south bank of Halifax Creek.

4   Tom and Jerry Trail (1084)

Trailhead In Prospect, at a bend in the town's main road, start east on Forest Route 37 (Red Blanket Road). Follow it 6.0 miles to Road 3795, which branches left 0.4 mile before 37 bridges Middle Fork Rogue River. Drive 5.9 miles up Road 3795 to where it switchbacks. Here, continue straight ahead (on Road 600) 0.8 mile to road's end. Limited parking. **Maps 15 and 16.**

Distance 5.3 miles, one way.

Low/High Elevations 5000'/6340'

Trail Notes Both this hike and the next go to McKie Camp. Which should you choose? Unless you've got a horse to do your walking, choose this one. The Mudjekeewis Trail is 0.8 mile longer and has a significant, additional 600 feet of elevation gain. Furthermore, its trailhead is more remote.

The Tom and Jerry Trail is a totally viewless, moderately graded, utilitarian trail that seeks out the lowest pass to reach McKie Camp. This no-nonsense trail climbs ⅓ mile to a bowl with a seasonal creeklet, then climbs ⅔ mile to a broad mountain-hemlock flat. From its south side, you switchback ¼ mile up to a junction with the Kerby Hill Way Trail, which climbs moderately-to-steeply 1.1 miles south to the Mudjekeewis Trail. Should you decide to take this route, then look forward to an unremitting 930-foot climb almost to the top of Kerby Hill. Also add an extra 1.1 miles. The Kerby Hill views don't justify the effort.

Climbing east on the Tom and Jerry Trail, you climb almost 2 miles to a shallow pass. Here, an old trail starts northwest, leading unsuspecting *westbound* hikers astray. Your pass, like your route, is viewless, but if you hike cross-country ½ mile north up the divide, you'll reach 6865-foot Tom Mountain (Map 12), with very rewarding views. From it you can trace the entire course of Red Blanket canyon and, to the east and southeast, can identify a string of inactive volcanoes, from the Goose Nest (a crater) and Goose Egg (a dome) south to Big Bunchgrass. To the north and northeast rise Union Peak and the summits of the Crater Lake rim.

Leaving the shallow pass, you face an 810-foot drop to the camp. When snow patches are present, the route can be a bit cryptic, so bear in mind that you first descend 0.5 mile northeast before turning southeast. That 1.2-mile descent is aided, on steeper slopes, by short switchbacks. Your descent ends at the McKie Camp Trail junction, which is just 60 yards northeast of the McKie Camp shelter. Pasturage lies in the rather extensive meadow east of the junction.

Although I didn't recommend taking the Mudjekeewis Trail in to McKie Camp, I do recommend taking it out. Your pack should be lighter and the climb to Kerby Hill involves only about 200 more feet of elevation gain than you'd face if you returned the way you came. The views from the hill, while not super, are certainly worth this additional work. From that hill, descend a ridge to its base, where you'll find the Kerby Hill Way Trail, and it takes you quickly north down to the Tom and Jerry Trail. This semiloop route is 11.7 miles long, versus 10.6 miles if you just go in and back out on the Tom and Jerry Trail.

5 Mudjekeewis Trail (1085)

Trailhead In Prospect, at a bend in the town's main road, start east on Forest Route 37 (Red Blanket Road). Follow it 6.0 miles to Road 3795, which branches left 0.4 mile before 37 bridges Middle Fork Rogue River. Drive 4.3 miles up Road 3795 to a junction with Road

500, branching right. Drive 1.5 miles up Road 500 to a fork, keep left there and park at trailhead in 0.1 mile. Limited parking. **Maps 15 and 16.**

Distance 6.1 miles, one way.

Low/High Elevations 4650'/5670'

Trail Notes Before taking this trail, read the preceding route's description. The only advantage to the Mudjekeewis Trail is its views, but if you make the semiloop route described in the preceding route's last paragraph, you'll get the same views and will save yourself 0.5 mile of walking and about 600 feet of climbing.

Your route begins as a closed jeep road that climbs a steep ¼ mile up to the real start of the trail. The trail, actually, is well engineered, and it is too bad it climbs so high. This is done to avoid the steep, brushy slopes on the north wall of the Middle Fork canyon.

About 2½ miles along your route, you meet the Kerby Hill Way Trail, and then continue 1 mile east to the open, upper slopes of Kerby Hill. Just as you start your descent via many short switchbacks, you have a very revealing view south-southeast through the Middle Fork canyon to its Seven Lakes Basin and Devils Peak. To the northeast you see the summits of the Crater Lake rim. Your 2⅔-mile descent to McKie Camp is in stages: very short switchbacks down a ridge; longer ones from it down to a meadowy bowl; a gradually descending, mile-long descent to a gully (which has an abandoned trail climbing north); a short, steep descent south; and a final rolling traverse past huckleberries and brush to the camp. Just 30 yards before the camp you'll meet the southbound McKie Camp Trail (next route).

6 McKie Camp and Big Bunchgrass Trails (1089 and 1089A)

Trailhead None. Links McKie Camp to Solace Cow Camp and both to the Pacific Crest Trail. **Map 16.**

Distances Southbound: 1.6 miles to Solace Cow Camp, 4.7 miles to Pacific Crest Trail via McKie Camp Trail, 6.0 miles to it via Big Bunchgrass Trail.

Low/High Elevations 5520'/6340' (along McKie Camp Trail)

Trail Notes The McKie Camp Trail, which descends 1.9 miles southwest from the Stuart

Alta Lake lies in a narrow trough eroded along a possibly active fault.

Falls Trail (route 3), makes an abrupt turn south only 30 yards past the camp. You drop to the camp's nearby, usually flowing creek, then quickly find a good campsite. If you camp in this vicinity, remember that horses grazing in the adjacent meadow may pollute the creek. The author also experienced noise pollution, for born-again Christian equestrians had packed in a portable stereo, which was blaring the Good News to man and beast alike. (Is this a new method to keep the bears away?) Your route south passes at least three more seasonal creeks as it rollercoasters over to a junction with the Halifax Trail (route 8). This junction is just 25 yards past a semipermanent creek, which in turn is just 40 yards past a hikers' campsite. From the junction, equestrians usually make the 90-yard wet slog southwest down the Halifax Trail to the Solace Cow Camp cabin. Meadows for grazing are found both east of the trail junction and west of the camp.

Leaving the junction, the McKie Camp Trail climbs east through a meadow before resuming its southward, moderately climbing course up to the Big Bunchgrass Trail junction. The Big Bunchgrass Trail climbs unnecessarily high on its course around the Big Bunchgrass, which is an old, flattened volcano, taking 2.0 miles to reach the Pacific Crest Trail. To reach

that junction via the McKie Camp and Pacific Crest trails, you go only 1.7 miles and climb 120 feet less, so the latter of these two essentially viewless routes is preferable. The Big Bunchgrass Trail, however, is not all that bad, and from grassy slopes ½ mile south along the route, the cross-country adventurer can descend ⅓ mile southwest to Bareface Butte.

7   Middle Fork Trail (978)

Trailhead   In Prospect, at a bend in the town's main road, start east on Forest Route 37 (Red Blanket Road). Follow it 10.2 miles to Road 3790, starting east (this junction is 0.9 mile northwest of a junction with Road 937, which goes ¼ mile southeast to Imnaha Campground and Guard Station). Drive 3.0 miles on Road 3790 to its end. **Maps 15 and 16.**

Distances   3.2 miles to Halifax Trail, 7.8 miles to Alta Lake Trail.

Low/High Elevations   3595'/6205'

Trail Notes   The Middle Fork canyon rivals the Red Blanket canyon in length and depth and in the diversity of plant species found in its stately, mixed-conifer forest (see route 1, last paragraph). Late in the Ice Age, an extensive ice cap grew at the head of each canyon, feeding glaciers to the east as well as to the west. Back then, you could have started at the snout of each canyon glacier (both about 4 miles east of Prospect), hiked up-canyon to the divide, then descended to the west edge of the Klamath Lake basin without once touching solid ground. Roads and trails mimic the icy route up Red Blanket canyon, across the Oregon Desert and down the Dry Creek canyon. Unfortunately, for the Middle Fork canyon, there is a serious gap. Where the Middle Fork Trail begins its final climb to the Alta Lake Trail, another trail should climb 3½ miles east to Ranger Springs divide, but to reach this divide from the Middle Fork Trail today, you have to hike a grueling 9.8 miles. Few people, however, will want to tackle the very direct cross-country route, which is an uphill battle through some incredibly dense stands of vegetation.

With this protest aired, I can say that, once the mosquitoes abate, you'll thoroughly enjoy the 5 easy miles up the Middle Fork Trail. Along this stretch, you are never more than ¼ mile away from the boisterous Middle Fork Rogue River and, with a bit of hunting, can find many small, private campsites, particularly along the first 3 miles of the route. From the Halifax Trail junction south, the campsites—at least a half dozen of them—are less secluded, for the trail stays closer to the river. Two of the best, though certainly the least secluded, are on a west-bank bench immediately south of where the Halifax Trail crosses the river.

After 5 easy trail miles, you veer slightly away from the river and begin an increasingly steep one-mile climb to a switchback near the base of Boston Bluff, which towers ominously above you. Your trail will end at an elevation 500 feet above the bluff. A mile of switchbacks gets you to a minor ridge and well into the mountain-hemlock zone. You now have a very welcome easier climb ⅓ mile up a small side canyon to the start of a second set of switch-backs. If your goal is Alta Lake, prepare yourself for a 2.5-mile, 1200-foot climb to its north shore, which is 9¾ miles from your trail-head. But if the Seven Lakes Basin is your goal, leave the Middle Fork Trail at the start of the second series of switchbacks and traverse briefly south into a second small side canyon. Near its head, veer southeast, up a shallow gully to a nearby gap. Immediately beyond it you'll meet the Lake Ivern Trail and its splinter, the Bigfoot Spring Trail (see route 12).

8   Halifax Trail (1088)

Trailhead   None. Links the Middle Fork Trail to the McKie Camp Trail (routes 7 and 6). **Map 16.**

Distance   3.2 miles, one way.

Low/High Elevations   3910'/5520'

Trail Notes   Combined with the first part of the Middle Fork Trail (route 7), the Halifax Trail provides the shortest route to Solace Cow Camp: 6.3 miles. Due to low elevation of the first trail and to the western exposure of the second, all but the last 1½ miles of route are usually snow-free by Memorial Day. However, those last 1½ miles can still have considerable snow problems even after the Fourth of July. Most of the Halifax Trail's 1600+ feet of ascent is done over a 1⅓-mile stretch with an average grade of 23%. That is enough to discourage hikers, but not equestrians, who are the trail's main users.

From the Middle Fork Trail, the Halifax Trail makes a short, steep drop to the river. On the west bank you'll find a four-man camp and a larger one just upstream. Omnipresent logs get hikers across the swift river, then the wilderness traveler winds over to a murmuring creeklet before climbing to a frolicksome creek. Tank up here, at the start of the 1⅓-mile climb. About halfway up your exhausting ascent you can get additional water at one or two trailside springs. Because your route is up west-facing slopes, an afternoon ascent can be a real sweat. The slopes' vegetation reflects the higher temperature. You'll encounter an ample amount of shadeless tobacco brush and greenleaf manzanita, which do, however, allow you to have views down the impressive Middle Fork canyon. In this vicinity the canyon was buried at times under about 1800 feet of glacier ice. High on your ascent, you may see Oregon oak and incense-cedar, both being far more common down in Prospect than in the wilderness.

Where your climb finally abates, you start a 1½-mile ascent through a fir-hemlock forest. You'll know you're approaching Solace Cow Camp when you reach a sloping meadow. You'll find solace knowing there are no cows. The trail can get lost along this muddy stretch, but as long as you climb northeast along the meadow's edge, you are bound to reach the nearby cabin. The McKie Camp Trail is 90 yards northeast above it.

9   Alta Lake Trail (979)

Trailhead   In Prospect, at a bend in the town's main road, start east on Forest Route 37 (Red Blanket Road). Follow it 13.5 miles southeast to Road 3785, starting east. (This junction is 0.8 mile south of a road that descends 0.3 mile west to Sumpter Creek Campground; the junction is 1.8 miles north of the Road 3780 junction—see next hike.) Drive 3.6 miles on Road 3785 to a trailhead in North Fork Wallowa Creek canyon. **Maps 15 and 16.**

Distances   3.4 miles to Middle Fork Rogue River Trail; 5.3 miles to Alta Lake north shore; 6.4 miles to Seven Lakes Trail.

Low/High Elevations   4860'/6825'

Trail Notes   Since this trail involves 1.2 miles of additional hiking and 300 feet more climbing than the route via the Seven Lakes Trail, there is little incentive for anyone to take it. Perhaps it is a route for seekers of solitude. It starts in a Douglas-fir/white-fir forest that has many of the plants found at lower elevations (see route 1, last paragraph). Your climb is gentle for the first ¾ mile, and in late season huckleberries are waiting to be picked.

As you leave the floor of your glacial canyon to climb its slopes to Gopher Ridge, the trail steepens and becomes annoyingly boulder-filled. Being a minimal-use trail, it receives a minimum of maintenance. Boulders are not a problem along the grassy, wildflowered slopes below Gopher Ridge, which lives up to its name, having a prolific rodent population. Views to the west are pleasant, though not as good as those about ¼ mile after you start a descent. "Gopher" the adjacent crest, which is the brink of the severely glaciated Middle Fork canyon, with a floor about 2000 feet below you. With the proper lighting, the view can be breathtaking. In addition to viewing the avalanche-scarred canyon, you'll see a string of small volcanoes along the Cascade divide: from lowly Big Bunchgrass north to isolated Lone Wolf. During the Ice Age, only summits such as these protruded from a sea of glacier ice. North of the volcanoes stand pointed Union Peak and the summits of the Crater Lake rim.

A few minutes past your viewpoint you reach the upper end of the Middle Fork Trail. From it you make a moderate ascent almost ½ mile south to the upper end of the King Spruce Trail (route 11), on your right. Continuing uneventfully south, you reach well-named

Boulder Pond (when it has water in it). Ahead, a steep half-mile route to Alta Lake's outlet is very bouldery—not a good route for those with weak knees. Tightly confined Alta Lake is short on camps, though some folks have camped near the outlet. A better site lies just beyond the lake's south shore. Before leaving the lake's outlet, walk about 100 yards north to the brink of a ridge for a panoramic view.

10   Seven Lakes Trail (981)

Trailhead   In Prospect, at a bend in the town's main road, start east on Forest Route 37 (Red Blanket Road). Follow it 15.3 miles southeast to Road 3780, climbing east. To reach this junction from *Butte Falls,* drive about 0.9 mile east past the town's ranger station, branch left on Road 992, and follow it 8.9 miles to a junction with Forest Route 34 (Lodgepole Road). Drive 8.2 miles northeast up 34 to a junction with southbound 37, which is 0.6 mile past the South Fork Campground entrance. Go 0.5 mile east on 37 to where it angles north and Road 3780 starts a climb east. Follow Road 3780 4.2 miles up to the crest of a large lateral moraine. **Maps 15 and 16.**

Distances   2.1 miles to Frog Lake; 4.1 miles to Alta Lake, south shore; 4.6 miles to South Lake; 5.0 miles to Cliff Lake; 5.6 miles to Middle Lake (Lake Ivern Trail); 6.1 miles to Grass Lake.

Low/High Elevations   5240'/6900'

Trail Notes   Middle Lake, in the center of the Seven Lakes Basin, lies roughly equidistant from the Seven Lakes trailhead, to the west, and the Sevenmile trailhead, to the east. However, on the Seven Lakes Trail you climb about 1700 feet before dropping 800 feet to that lake, but on the Sevenmile Trail (Chapter 13, route 3), you climb only 600 feet to the lake. Obviously, if you have a choice, begin your hike to Seven Lakes Basin via the Sevenmile Trail.

If you don't have a choice, start up the Seven Lakes Trail. Just ⅔ mile up the crest of a forested lateral moraine, you meet the lower end of the King Spruce Trail (next route). This trail, in combination with the Alta Lake Trail (previous route), climbs 4.0 miles to the north shore of Alta Lake. Both trails tend to be narrow and bouldery.

From the junction, the well-manicured Seven Lakes Trail maintains its moderate grade for over a mile before leveling near a seasonal pond, on your right. Not far beyond it you reach Frog Lake, barely deep enough for swimming, and lacking campsites. From it you make a shady, 1¼-mile climb to a divide, on which the Devils Peak Trail (route 13) begins a quest for its namesake. About 0.2 mile down from the divide, we meet the upper end of the Alta Lake Trail. The lake, nestled in a fault-formed trough, lies an easy 0.6 mile north. Just before it, you'll pass a campsite, on your right. You can also camp on the ridge just above the lake's south part.

Continuing down from the Alta Lake Trail junction, you get several views of the Seven Lakes Basin and Devils Peak before you reach the sloping floor of a glaciated bowl. Your trail winds down to the bowl's lower end, which contains South Lake. Because much of the lake is extremely shallow, it is barren of fish, though you'll find its deeper west half suitable for swimming. Look for a secluded campsite along the lake's north shore.

From the lake's outlet, you drop just ¼ mile to Cliff Lake's outlet. This highly popular lake is ringed with campsites, the best ones above its southeast shore. Reach them on an east-shore trail that passes a fenced-in spring. At the west end of this camping zone, by the edge of a large talus slope, you'll find a small, bedrock cliff that makes a perfect platform for high diving into the lake. No other lake in this book can boast of such a feature.

Just beyond Cliff Lake your trail forks, one branch traversing 0.3 mile northeast to the Pacific Crest Trail (Chapter 16, route 1), the other dropping 0.5 mile to the outlet of hemmed-in Middle Lake. You can camp on a ridge above its northwest shore. The Lake Ivern Trail (route 12) begins at the outlet. For information east of Middle Lake, consult Chapter 13, route 3.

11   King Spruce Trail (980)

Trailhead   None. Connects Seven Lakes Trail (previous route) with Alta Lake Trail (route 9). **Map 16.**

Distance   3.0 miles, one way.

Low/High Elevations   5560'/6340'

Trail Notes   This trail provides yet another route to Alta Lake. It first traverses ¾ mile east through a mountain-hemlock forest to a meadow with a seasonal creek, both immediately north of the trail. You could camp here. The route then climbs briefly northeast before it angles north-

west where the King Spruce Camp once existed. Your climb out of a glaciated canyon is an interesting one, with lots of springs, spruces and wildflowers. Your trail deteriorates in ⅔ mile, as it enters a shallow bowl. Ahead, the trail is very rocky, and higher up the solid rocks give way to loose ones. This is a very tiring route for hikers to descend. Beyond a low divide you climb east up an easier, softer tread to a junction with the Alta Lake Trail. See the last paragraph of that bouldery route up to Alta Lake (route 9). If, after visiting the lake, you descend by the easier Seven Lakes Trail, the total length of your semiloop trip will be 9.7 miles.

12   Lake Ivern Trail (994)

Trailhead   None. Begins 5.6 trail miles east of the Seven Lakes trailhead, 5.2 trail miles west of the Sevenmile trailhead (Chapter 13, route 3). **Map 16.**

Distance   2.0 miles, one way.

Low/High Elevations   5695'/6130'

Trail Notes   This fairly popular, well-graded trail offers you camping, swimming, fishing and scenery, and serves as a vital link between the Seven Lakes Basin and the Rogue River's Middle Fork canyon (route 7). From Middle Lake's outlet, your trail arcs above this scenic lake's north shore, then crosses a low ridge. This ridge, which separates Middle Lake from North Lake, makes a suitable, pollution-free zone for camping (camping at the shoreline sites at hemmed-in Middle Lake is environmentally damaging). From the ridge your trail descends to a wildflower-lined, grassy marsh. For a good campsite, walk up its east side to the far end of North Lake. The lake is very shallow, barely deep enough for swimming, though this shallowness makes it a warmer swimming hole than its trout-stocked neighbor, Middle Lake.

Beyond North Lake the trail makes a verdant descent past babbling Jahn and Buckley springs, then crosses some impressive talus slopes before almost crossing a divide. Here the trail turns from northwest to northeast, and you immediately encounter a spur trail that drops a steep ¼ mile east to Bigfoot Spring horse camp, which is a suitable place to spin your Bigfoot tales to terrified tenderfoots. Also at the bend in the trail, you could start a cross-country hike, just over ½ mile long, to the Middle Fork Trail: Cross the nearby ridge, descend north through a small canyon and, where it turns northeast and drops sharply, continue north over another low ridge to a second small canyon, which holds the trail.

Past the Bigfoot Spring spur trail, the main trail traverses ¼ mile to a ridge, then makes a moderate descent to the north shore of lovely, rockbound Lake Ivern. Hemmed in, the lake is unsuitable for camping, though it is fine for fishing and swimming. It even has rock slabs (with views down the Middle Fork canyon) that are suitable for sunbathing.

From the lake's northeast shore, you can walk ¼ mile north on a narrow ridge to point 5727, at the north end of Boston Bluff. The point, intruding into Middle Fork canyon, gives you an impressive view—it is as if you were flying an airplane down-canyon toward Kerby Hill, at its far end. In past times, this canyon was filled with an 1800-foot-thick glacier, and all but the peaks and ridges lay under an extensive field of ice. This glacier lapped up to the base of Bare-face Butte, on the northeast skyline, atop the canyon's wall.

13   Devils Peak Trail (984)

Trailhead   None. Begins on a ridge 3⅓ miles up the Seven Lakes trail (route 10), and climbs to Devils Peak. **Maps 16 and 19.**

Distance   2.2 miles to top.

Low/High Elevations   6900'/7582'

Trail Notes   Peak baggers can have a field day along this trail, "capturing," in a few hours' time, the summits of Venus, Jupiter, Lucifer, Devils and Lee peaks. A short detour south on the Pacific Crest Trail also nabs Shale Butte. Because the first 1.5 miles are along high-elevation, usually shady slopes, snow persists there—and presents problems—well into July.

From the Seven Lakes Trail your trail climbs south toward nearby Venus peak, then begins to curve southeast and descends just a bit. At this point, you can climb cross-country directly up to the peak. The viewless trail then traverses beneath Jupiter peak's talus slopes before climbing almost to a saddle. From that

Devils Peak summit views. Top: view north shows Middle Fork Canyon, Union Peak and the Crater Lake rim. Bottom: view south shows Cascade crest snaking toward lofty Mt. McLoughlin.

saddle you have a 10-minute climb to that peak. Next, the trail quickly reaches an extensive talus field, presenting us with views of South, Middle and Grass lakes, the Crater Lake rim and Mt. Thielsen. Where the trail comes to within 30 feet of the ridge, you can make another 10-minute foray southeast up to Lucifer Peak, from where you could descend south to the Pacific Crest Trail and "nab" Shale Butte.

Beyond the talus field you quickly reach a ridge and the Pacific Crest Trail. On that trail you cross the ridge and, 100 yards past it, leave it for a ½-mile, no-nonsense climb to the summit of Devils Peak. Just 100 yards before it, you reach a junction, from which a trail descends steeply 300 yards east to the Devils Peak/Lee Peak saddle. The route to Lee Peak is obvious. Being the highest summit, Devils Peak provides the best views. North, you see some of the Seven Lakes plus a good chunk of the Middle Fork canyon, including Boston Bluff. On the northern horizon is pointed Union Peak, the summit plug of a broad shield volcano. A few hundred thousand years ago, the Devils Peak shield volcano and the Luther Mountain shield volcano (2½ miles south of us) may have had similar, broad forms. Immediately west of Union Peak you see Mt. Bailey, which, like Mt. Thielsen, is a distant 36 miles away. Mt. Scott is the easternmost and highest of the Crater Lake peaks. On most days you also see Mt. Shasta, 85 miles due south. Mt. McLoughlin (route 24) is the dominating stratovolcano 15 miles to the south-southwest. Try to imagine this landscape, say, 20,000 years ago, when all but the major summits and ridges lay buried under ice, and the glaciers extended east down canyons to the edge of the Klamath Lake basin. Back in those Paleolithic times, you could have perhaps skied down to your trailhead, ski-jumping crevasses, of course.

14   Hemlock Lake Trail (985)

Trailhead As in route 10, drive 8.2 miles northeast up Forest Route 34 (Lodgepole Road) to a junction with southbound Forest Route 37. Drive 0.9 mile southeast on it to Big Ben Campground. **Maps 18 and 19.**

Distances 5.4 miles to Finch Lake, 5.5 miles to Hemlock Lake, 5.8 miles to Holst Lake, 6.4 miles to Pacific Crest Trail.

Low/High Elevations 4072'/6595'

Trail Notes This lightly used route starts at a low elevation, one that supports golden chinquapins plus a broad array of Red Blanket canyon plants (route 1, last paragraph). In about ½ mile, your closed road reaches the toe of a glacial moraine and then soon crosses Fantail Creek. You climb up the broad ridge of another moraine and, just before climbing up to a better-defined one, pass Aspen Spring, lined with serviceberries and frequented by cattle. For 1¾ miles your ridge road climbs through brush, at times giving you glimpses of the Mt. McLoughlin summit. This stretch is one of the few places in the proposed wilderness where you'll see Klamath weed (one of the trail's features, which says something about this route). Near the upper end, the gradient increases, you enter forest shade, and you climb ¾ mile to the road's end. From it a trail continues an unnecessary climb, then drops abruptly. Where it bottoms out, at a seasonal creeklet just past some "shaly" lava, you can start a ¾-mile, cross-country, huckleberried climb northeast to isolated Finch Lake.

You next make a pleasant traverse past huckleberries, bracken ferns and wildflowers before climbing briefly to Hemlock Lake, which has a horse camp by its northeast corner. You could also camp along the broad, low ridge above the lake's south shore. Holst Lake lies just beyond it and offers additional camping, fishing and swimming. From the Hemlock Lake horse camp, the trail concludes with a sustained climb through a snow-sheltering hemlock forest, ending on a saddle at the Pacific Crest Trail.

15   Onion Springs Trail (977)

Trailhead As in route 10, drive 8.2 miles northeast up Forest Route 34 (Lodgepole Road) to a junction with southbound Forest Route 37. Drive 1.6 miles southeast on it to a trailhead, which is about 20 yards south of Mile Post 17. No parking at trailhead. **Maps 18 and 19.**

Distance 3.9 miles to Wickiup Trail (next route).

Low/High Elevations 4150'/5580'

Trail Notes This trail, well-signed in 1982, is actually in poor shape (cross-country in some places), and it provides the long way in to Wickiup Shelter. Avoid this abandoned route.

16   Wickiup Trail (986)

Trailhead As in route 10, drive 8.2 miles northeast up Forest Route 34 (Lodgepole Road) to a junction with southbound Forest Route 37. Drive 4.1 miles southeast on it to a junction with two roads. Road 755 curves south, but you take Road 760, which curves north. Follow it 0.4 mile up to a ridge. **Maps 18 and 19.**

Distances   2.0 miles to Wickiup Shelter, 5.2 miles to Pacific Crest Trail.

Low/High Elevations   4700'/6585'

Trail Notes   In the author's opinion, this trail visits the best huckleberry hunting grounds in this book other than those of Huckleberry Mountain (Map 11), to which the Klamath Indians made annual pilgrimages long before the pioneers ever set eyes on it. Both areas abound with waist-high big whortleberries. The berries ripen to a blue-black color in September, and the leaves begin to turn color. In late September you'll find much of the Wickiup Trail climbing through a sea of red.

The well-maintained trail climbs moderately, staying just below the crest of a large moraine. After 1¼ miles you reach a junction, from which the rarely used Red Lake Trail (next route) labors 5½ miles south to Red Lake. You branch left, cross the moraine's crest, and descend to a junction just above the floor of a glaciated canyon. Here a trail starts a 0.2-mile descent northwest past potential campsites to Wickiup Shelter, by the edge of Wickiup Meadow. The site is an equestrian favorite.

About 70 yards past the junction the Wickiup Trail crosses a seasonal creek, curves just above Wickiup Spring, then in 250 yards reaches a trail intersection. Ahead (northeast) the Onion Springs Trail passes a fine meadow before climbing to extinction atop a ridge. Left, a minor trail descends to Wickiup campsites. Right, the Wickiup Trail, often crowded with whortleberries, climbs 3.1 miles to a crest intersection with the Pacific Crest Trail (Chapter 16, route 1). Knee-high grouse whortleberries replace big whortleberries on the upper part of your climb, and these have smaller, fewer, less desirable berries. From the crest, the Wickiup Trail, now labeled 3728, descends 2.0 pond-dotted miles to the Sky Lakes Trail (Chapter 13, route 9).

17   Red Lake Trail (987)

Trailhead   Same as for preceding route. **Maps 18 and 19.**

Distances   6.3 miles to Red Lake, 8.4 miles to Lost Creek Trail.

Low/High Elevations   4700'/6320'

Trail Notes   Red Lake, large in area but scant in depth, is in itself not a worthy goal. The Red Lake Trail is the hardest of more than a half-dozen routes to it. The trail's first 1¼ miles coincide with the Wickiup Trail; the next 4½ miles are essentially abandoned and aren't worth taking, even in an emergency. The trail's southern 2⅔ miles are well-maintained, and are described in Chapter 13's route 13.

18   South Fork Trail (988)

Trailhead   As in route 10, drive 8.2 miles northeast up Forest Route 34 (Lodgepole Road) to a junction with southbound Forest Route 37. Drive 5.3 miles southeast on it to a junction with Road 720, which you follow 1.0 mile to its end. *Alternatively,* you can reach this trailhead from Highway 140 or from Butte Falls. From Highway 140, about 1¾ miles west of its Fish Lake Campground/Resort road junction, drive 8.9 miles north on 37 to where it forks east. Ahead, the Forest Route is signed "30," and it goes 9 miles to a junction with Road 992 (mentioned in the route 10 trailhead). That junction is 0.9 mile east of the Butte Falls Ranger Station. From the 30/37 junction, drive 11.4 miles on 37 up to the Parker Meadows Campground spur road, forking left, then 1.9 miles past it down to Road 720. **Maps 18, 19, and 21.**

Distances   4.5 miles to Beal Lake, 5.3 miles to Blue Lake.

Low/High Elevations   4605'/5640'

Trail Notes   The South Fork Trail to Blue Lake is so much longer than the Blue Canyon Trail (route 20) that it will appeal only to those who like a journey through a primal, stately forest. The few takers are usually equestrians, and this is unfortunate since the myriad wild-flowers are too small and delicate to appreciate from the saddle. The first 3¼ miles of trail, up to the South Fork crossing, have the same floristic heritage as in Red Blanket canyon (route 1, last paragraph). Along this stretch, the path is often bouldery and winding.

From the crossing—the second permanent stream—the trail climbs moderately at first, relaxing its grade as it approaches shallow Beal Lake. You'll find an adequate campsite along its southwest shore. Ahead, you climb a few minutes to Mud Lake, which in late summer lives up to its name. In ¼ mile, where the trail curves west, you find, perhaps with your nose, a spacious horse camp. Just beyond it lies Meadow Lake, more meadow than lake, and home to frogs, skeeters and snakes. Your trail slithers just above it, ending at popular Blue Lake, whose overused campsites are now closed to camping. However, if you follow the Blue Canyon Trail southeast just past a spring, you'll find, by the south edge of a spreading meadow, a second spacious camp.

19   McKee Basin

Trailhead See route 18's trailhead for the 30/37 junction. From that junction drive 10.9 miles up 37 to a junction with Road 3770. Park about 3.3 miles up this road. **Map 18.**

Distance 0.9 mile, one way by shortest route.

Low/High Elevations about 5620'/6020'

Trail Notes If no one is parked at your "trailhead," then the odds are that you've got the whole McKee Basin to yourself. Trout-stocked McKee Lake is the only sizable body of water; most of the smaller ones become grassy meadows late in summer. The variable cross-country routes into the basin will appeal to lovers of solitude, but before August bring lots of repellent.

20   Blue Canyon Trail (982)

Trailhead See route 18's trailhead for the 30/37 junction. From that junction, drive 10.9 miles up 37 to a junction with Road 3770. Drive 5.6 miles up this road to a saddle, which is 1.0 mile before road's end atop Blue Rock. **Maps 18, 19, 21 and 22.**

Distances 0.9 mile to Round Lake, 2.0 miles to Blue Lake, 2.7 miles to Horseshoe Lake, 3.3 miles to Pear Lake, 5.1 miles to Island Lake, 5.5 miles to Red Lake Trail.

Low/High Elevations 5640'/6250'

Trail Notes This route to Blue Lake is not only short, it is downhill. The well-graded trail is smooth as a cycle path, and brings you, with little effort, to campless Round Lake, which is pleasantly backdropped by Cat Hill's lava cliff. In several minutes we skirt a seasonal pond, with a larger neighbor that can provide some warm summer swimming. After a pleasant traverse we reach deep, cold Blue Lake, which is dramatically backdropped by a massive, exfoliating cliff. To find suitable camping, head east from the lake's outlet to a large horse camp just past Meadow Lake, or southeast on the Blue Canyon Trail to an equally large site at the meadow's south edge. Get water from a trailside spring, which is fortunately fenced (I don't know why

Top: A peninsula juts into Horseshoe Lake
Bottom: Pear Lake lies just off the beaten track

some horses just have to tinkle whenever they approach water).

Just beyond this second camp, you pass the Meadow Lake Trail, which climbs 1.1 steep miles to the Cat Hill Way Trail (next route). Near the top of the climb, where this trail turns from southwest to northwest, you can descend cross-country to secluded camping at Blue Canyon Lake and its lower companion.

Past the Meadow Lake Trail, the Blue Canyon Trail leisurely winds over to Horseshoe Lake. The trailside camps are closed to camping, but, by plowing through the huckleberries, you can reach a site or two along the lake's peninsula. From the lake's northeast corner, an abandoned trail skirts up through the huckleberries to the southern lobe of Pear Lake, with additional sites. Both lakes offer good fishing and fine swimming.

The Blue Canyon Trail avoids Pear Lake, saving it from packer pressure, though it does send an offshoot down to an adequate campsite at the lake's north end. The trail then climbs east to a seasonal pond, from which you could climb ¼ mile up steep slopes to isolated Carey Lake. Ahead, your trail climbs northeast on a slackening grade, then makes a slight descent to a switchback on a ridge above unseen Dee Lake. Then the trail descends southeast to a shady flat, from which you could head north, cross-country, to that pleasant lake.

After nearly ⅓ mile of forest-floor traverse, you'll meet a spur trail that goes 130 yards north to Island Lake's most abundant campsites. Secluded ones lie above the lake's west shore. Just 0.4 mile past the spur trail, the Blue Canyon Trail ends at the Red Lake Trail. One-half mile down it, you'll reach the northeast corner of Island Lake, with a campsite, from which a trail leads west to more camps above both Island and Dee lakes.

21   Cat Hill Way Trail (992)

Trailhead   Same as for preceding hike. **Maps 18 and 21.**

Distances   2.0 miles to Meadow Lake Trail, 3.6 miles to Pacific Crest Trail.

Low/High Elevations   6100'/6530'

Trail Notes   This trail is a relict of older times and really serves no purpose today. A fence runs along the trailhead crest and, just 30 yards past it, this trail branches south from the Blue Canyon Trail. The viewless trail unnecessarily climbs almost to the summit of Cat Hill, which

got its name back in the days when the big cats— mountain lions—roamed the area. Your trail stays high, traversing through a fir-and-hemlock forest that protects your eyes from logging scars to the west. After the trail reaches the crest, it wanders ⅓ mile south past big whortleberries (a late-season bonus) to a junction with the Meadow Lake Trail. You can descend 250 yards southeast on it to a sharp bend, then continue cross-country down to Blue Canyon Lake.

Beyond the junction, our viewless route climbs almost to the top of a ridge in order to skirt a logged area, then descends through one mile of mature forest to the Pacific Crest Trail. Beyond, the trail is abandoned but followable as it descends 1.9 miles to a trail junction at the south tip of Squaw Lake (see Chapter 13, route 17).

22   Twin Ponds Trail (993)

Trailhead   See route 18's trailhead for the 30/37 junction. From that junction drive 1.5 miles east on 37 to where it bends north, at a junction with Road 3760. Drive 2.6 miles east up Road 3760 to where it curves south at a junction with Road 700. Drive 0.9 mile up this road to the start of an old jeep trail. **Map 21.**

Distances   1.0 mile to Twin Ponds, 3.0 miles to Summit Lake, 3.5 miles to Pacific Crest Trail.

Low/High Elevations   4520'/5840'

Trail Notes   This abandoned though followable route, the first ½ mile up a deteriorating jeep trail, provides a poor way in to waist-deep Summit Lake. It is a good route to avoid, particularly since it is partly overgrown with brush. For Summit Lake, use Chapter 13's route 17.

23   Crater Trail (975)

Trailhead   See preceding route's trailhead for directions to Road 3760. Drive 3.8 miles up this road to a trailhead, which is 0.3 mile past Road 800. **Map 21.**

Distance   Highly variable.

Low/High Elevations   4540'/9495'

Trail Notes   Like the preceding route, this trail is abandoned, but it has far more brush. Only serious mountaineers, aiming for Mt. McLoughlin's summit, try this route. The trail dies out midway up to the summit. Be forewarned: all too often, kids on the summit toss rocks (some of them large) down your route.

24 Mt. McLoughlin Trail (3716)

Trailhead *Fish Lake:* From the Fish Lake Campground/Resort road junction, continue east 2.1 miles on Highway 140 to Road 3650, and 2.4 miles up it to the trailhead. *Lake of the Woods:* From Highway 140 between the lake's east- and west-shore roads, start up Road 3661 and climb 3.0 miles to Road 3650 and the Cascade Canal. Follow both ¼ mile southwest down to the trailhead. **Map 21.**

Distances   1.4 miles to Freye Lake, 4.9 miles to summit.

Low/High Elevations   5580'/9495'

Trail Notes As the highest peak in Oregon's southern Cascades, Mt. McLoughlin is a magnet for all would-be mountaineers. On many summer afternoons, its summit is crowded with achievers, many of them kids from Lake of the Woods' camps. If you're in shape, you can make the ascent in 3 hours, though most people take

Left: north, a sea of trees extends all the way to the Crater Lake rim. Upper right: Mt. McLoughlin's abandoned fire lookout—what's left of it. Lower right: scouts admire a summit view of the Mountain Lakes Wilderness.

about twice as long. Be prepared for a deficit of oxygen and a surplus of ultraviolet radiation. Don't attempt this route if the weather is threatening—why risk a lightning strike at a summit when its views are obscured by clouds?

The trail immediately crosses seasonal Cascade Canal, then climbs, in 0.2 mile, just above a seeping spring. Other than snow, which can last through July, this will be your only supply of fresh water (snow is usually not much of a problem by early July). Climb moderately ¾ mile up to the Pacific Crest Trail, and follow it ¼ mile west at an easier pace to the Freye Lake spur trail, just 50 yards past a gully. The ill-defined trail goes ¼ mile over to the waist-deep lake (lower in late summer). There is ample camp space for those attracted to such lakes.

After you hike another ¼ mile stint west on the Pacific Crest Trail, that trail branches northwest (Chapter 16, route 1). Your trail winds over a mile west to about the 6500-foot level, from where it finally makes a serious attempt to tackle the summit. Over halfway to the summit, trailwise, you'll discover that you've climbed but 1000 of the route's 4000 feet of elevation gain. With that depressing fact, you start up the steep trail, which stays that way, except for stretches where it is *very* steep! This slows you down, which may be fortunate, since the route is quite bouldery (bad for those with weak ankles).

Around 7200 feet the tree cover thins enough to provide good views, which improve with elevation. The summit may not look that far away, but at 8100 feet you may realize that what you thought was the summit was only the apex of two converging ridges. At this higher elevation—the apex—you see McLoughlin's large, northeast bowl plus the real summit. At 8450 feet your westbound path turns abruptly north for a 500-foot, agonizing climb to a bedrock ridge. If you make it this far, you can make it to the summit, one rocky step at a time.

If the climb hasn't taken your breath away, the views should. Mt. Bailey, 49 miles distant, lies along a bearing of 5°. Diamond Peak, rising above Bailey's lower east slopes, is 74 miles away. Working clockwise, you see Union Peak,

almost touching the skyline. On an extremely clear day, you should be able to see Mt. Jefferson just above and a hairline to the left of it, a staggering 156 miles away. The Crater Lake summits, hiding the Three Sisters, stand above and to the right of Union Peak, and Mt. Thielsen (50 miles) shoots skyward behind the cliff of Llao Rock. The easternmost and highest Crater Lake summit is Mt. Scott. Much closer, at the base of your peak, Fourmile Lake spreads below you, while Pelican Butte, a shield volcano behind it, spreads across the skyline. To the southeast, Mountain Lakes Wilderness, the glacier-gutted remains of several overlapping volcanoes, rises high above Lake of the Woods, which lies in a fault-formed trough. How far north can you trace this fault? Brown Mountain, a very youthful volcano with a flow that dams Fish Lake, lies to the south-southeast. Directly above it is usually snowy Lassen Peak (141 miles), visible only on the clearest days. On most days you can make out hulking Mt. Shasta (71 miles) and can identify an often snowy peak to its right, Mt. Eddy (77 miles). To the south-southwest you see, closest to you, Fish Lake, then Howard Prairie and Hyatt lakes. Pilot Rock (31 miles) stands above Hyatt, and to the right of it is the distant, snowy Thompson Peak (77 miles). Continuing clockwise, you'll note that Mt. Ashland (32 miles) almost reaches the horizon while Preston Peak (78 miles), to the west-southwest, certainly makes it, lording it over the northwest corner of California.

After absorbing the panoramas you must face the descent. Before mid-July there's usually a very tempting snowfield that will get you down about 1000 feet. By mid-afternoon, it is usually sufficiently de-iced to provide an exhilarating, somewhat controlled descent *sans* crampons. For most hikers, however, this steep snowfield is too touch-and-go to be safe. By mid-August, a talus slope usually prevails, which is safer. Once you've dropped 1000 feet to the 8450-foot level and regained the bouldery trail, be sure not to lose it, which is easy to do. If you do lose it, contour over to the ridge; don't continue downslope looking for it.

13   Sky Lakes Proposed Wilderness, east of the Pacific Crest Trail

Introduction   This chapter covers the more popular part of the proposed Sky Lakes wilderness—its eastern terrain. There are dozens of lakes you can visit, and two or more routes to most of them. The following list, starting in the north and working south, gives the best lakes (and the best routes to them). Most of the Seven Lakes Basin lakes are worthy goals, but Cliff Lake is the author's favorite (route 3). To the southeast lie the isolated Puck Lakes, the southern one (6) being quite pleasant. Margurette and Trapper lakes lure hikers to the northern part of the Sky Lakes Basin while Isherwood and northern Heavenly Twin lakes lure others to its southern part (all either 11 or 12). Superficially, the Cherry Creek Trail looks like the most direct route to this basin, but it climbs excessively in its last 1¾ miles. Island and Dee Lakes (13), in the upper part of the Blue Canyon basin, are well worth the effort.

Lackluster routes 15 through 17, to shallow lakes in the Fourmile Lake basin, are popular only because they start from a campground that is just minutes away from Highway 140 and the Lake of the Woods Recreation Area. You can ignore these routes plus three more which, though signed in 1982, were essentially abandoned. These are the Cedar Spring (1), Dry Creek (2) and Puck Lakes (5) trails.

Within the wilderness, there are four major connecting routes. From the Seven Lakes Basin you can climb south to Devils Peak via the Pacific Crest Trail (4). That trail (Chapter 16, route 1) also skirts the crest above the Sky Lakes basin. To hike through the basin, you must take the Sky Lakes Trail (7 and 9). Finally, one short, scenic trail (10) makes a loop through the Isherwood/Heavenly Twin lakes area.

Two routes lie just outside the proposed wilderness, and both provide views of a trans-state fault system. The first is the Rye Spur Trail (18), which is of marginal interest to most people; the second is an obvious cross-country route from Pelican Butte to Lakes Francis and Gladys (19). The Pelican Butte lookout road is usually snowbound until mid-August, and before then it makes a fine trail for peak baggers.

1   Cedar Spring Trail (3700)

Trailhead   From Fort Klamath, drive 3.9 miles west on Nicholson Road to Forest Route 32, curving north. You immediately pass the Sevenmile Guard Station and then drive 2.1 miles on 32 to Road 3228, left, which you take west 2.0 miles to Road 3282, which climbs 5.4 miles up to the trailhead. **Maps 12, 13 and 16.**

Distance   6.2 miles, one way.

Low/High Elevations   5650'/6750'

Trail Notes   Although well-signed in 1982, the trail was definitely abandoned. The trail climbs about 2½ miles to its high point at the south base of the Goose Nest. This cinder cone's south slopes are very loose and therefore very tiring. To reach the cone's rim, climb up the forested, stable southeast slopes. For most hikers the view is not worth the effort. A very few strong-legged botanists may be attracted to the cone's vegetation assemblage, which includes some species from eastern Oregon. Don't hike southwest beyond the Goose Nest unless you are an expert pathfinder.

2   Dry Creek Trail (3701)

Trailhead From Fort Klamath drive 3.9 miles west on Nicholson Road to Forest Route 32, curving north. You immediately pass the Sevenmile Guard Station and then drive 1.5 miles on 32 to Road 3208, left, which you take 3.9 miles to where it curves sharply left and up. Straight ahead, follow a deteriorating road 0.6 mile to its end. **Maps 16 and 17.**

Distances 2.8 miles to Cedar Spring Trail, 6.1 miles to McKie Camp, 7.6 miles to Stuart Falls Camp.

Low/High Elevations 5180'/6080' (saddle by Pacific Crest Trail)

Trail Notes At a gully about 260 yards northwest up an abandoned road, this definitely abandoned, yet followable, trail starts a climb to the Pacific Crest Trail. For east-side visitors, this route was the quickest one in to McKie Camp. Today, there is no quick way. However, this abandoned trail still serves as an adequate emergency route out of the wilderness and down to Sevenmile Guard Station.

3   Sevenmile Trail (3703)

Trailhead From Fort Klamath, drive 4.3 miles west on Nicholson Road to Road 3334, which branches north just ⅓ mile past the Sevenmile Guard Station. To reach this junction from Highway 140, first leave that highway ¾ mile west of the Rocky Point Road junction and follow County Route 531 16.8 miles north to its "Mile 0" point (east, it becomes Sevenmile Drive—County Route 1349). From the curve at Mile 0, drive 2.9 miles north on Forest Route 33 to the Road 3334 junction. After either approach, follow Road 3334 5.5 miles to its end, at the Sevenmile Marsh Campground. **Maps 16 and 17.**

Distances 2.8 miles to Ranger Springs, 4.7 miles to Grass Lake, 5.2 miles to Middle Lake, 5.8 miles to Cliff Lake, 7.8 miles to Alta Lake.

Low/High Elevations 5480'/6290', 6830' (Cliff Lake, Alta Lake)

Trail Notes This trail offers the quickest way in to Seven Lakes Basin, and on summer weekends its limited trailhead parking area may be full. The trail begins just uphill from Sevenmile Marsh Campground, which would be a pleasant enough two-site camp were it not for the omnipresent mosquitoes, which don't abate until you reach the Pacific Crest Trail.

From the trailhead you immediately cross Sevenmile Creek, then climb, usually at a gentle grade, 1⅓ miles to a junction with Trail 3706 (route 5), which has fallen into disuse. You then dip slightly to a marshy tributary before climbing ¼ mile west to the Pacific Crest Trail. North, this trail goes about 300 yards before the Middle Fork Basin Trail diverges to the left to wind 0.9 mile over to gushing Ranger Springs, the headwaters of the Middle Fork Rogue River. The trail, unfortunately, doesn't continue west down to the Alta Lake Trail (Chapter 12, route 9), which is a serious shortcoming in this wilderness' trail system.

Those bound for the Seven Lakes Basin climb southwest on the Pacific Crest Trail and in a few minutes hear the unseen Ranger Springs in the canyon below. Just after 2 miles on the "PCT," you reach Honeymoon Creek, with a horse camp that is often used by a ranger on patrol. In another ½ mile you end your climb, fork right from the PCT, and then on the Seven Lakes Trail descend an easy ¼ mile to a junction near Grass Lake. This shallow, grassy lake may be the least desirable of all of the basin's lakes, but because it is the closest to the trailhead, it is very popular. Many folks camp near the trail junction or farther along the spur trail, by the lake's east shore. The lake's best camps are near its south shore, to which you drop from the Seven Lakes Trail.

That trail heads west, staying well above Grass Lake as it makes an easy ½-mile climb to Middle Lake. From here the trail makes a moderate ½-mile climb to Cliff Lake, while the Lake Ivern Trail drops ½ mile to North Lake. Cliff Lake—a must—is described in Chapter 12's route 10, as is Alta Lake (this high lake is most easily reached by that route). The highly desirable Lake Ivern Trail is described in Chapter 12's route 12.

4 Devils Peak via Pacific Crest Trail (2000)

Trailhead Same as for preceding route. **Maps 16 and 17.**

Distance 7.8 miles, one way.

Low/High Elevations 5480'/7582'

Trail Notes As in the previous route, head 1.8 easy miles to the Pacific Crest Trail, then follow it 2.6 miles to the east end of the Seven Lakes Trail. If you plan to camp overnight and tackle Devils Peak the next day, then take this trail to Cliff Lake, camp at its south-shore sites (Chapter 12, route 10), then head ⅓ mile northeast on a lateral trail back to the "PCT." On the PCT we reach that junction in 0.7 mile, which is 1.3 miles shorter than if you detour to camp at Cliff Lake.

You now climb almost 2½ miles, the last half mile of trail switchbacking rather steeply up to the Devils Peak/Lee Peak saddle. Before mid-July, this last stretch is usually under snow. While you catch your breath at the saddle, you can observe the throat of the ancient Devils Peak volcano, which is capped by southward dipping volcanic strata. Chapter 12's route 13 describes the sights you'll see from the summit of this volcano (what little is left of it), which you reach by a very strenuous ¼-mile haul west up a ridge trail.

5 Puck Lakes Trail (3706)

Trailhead None. Links Sevenmile Trail (route 3) with Nannie Creek Trail (route 6). **Maps 16, 17 and 19.**

Distance 6.3 miles, one way.

Low/High Elevations 5700'/6440'

Trail Notes Before the advent of the Pacific Crest Trail, built mostly in the 1970s, the now-abandoned Trail 3706, coupled with the west part of the Nannie Creek Trail, provided a good early-season alternate route to the now defunct Oregon Skyline Trail. Today, Trail 3706 is vague in places, and only the southern ⅓ mile, to the Puck Lakes, receives use (next route). Beyond that, the trail goes 1.2 miles north before dying out, roughly ½ mile short of a shallow lakelet.

6 Nannie Creek Trail (3707)

Trailhead From Fort Klamath, drive 1¾ miles south to County Route 1349 (Sevenmile Drive), then 4¾ miles west on it to County Route 531 (signed "Mile 0"), curving south. Follow it 4½ miles south to Road 3484. To reach this junction from Highway 140, leave that highway ¾ mile west of the Rocky Point Road junction and follow County Route 531 12¼ miles north. Drive 5½ miles up Road 3484 to its end. **Maps 19 and 20.**

Left: Devils Peak reflected in Grass Lake. Right: southern Puck Lake.

Distances 2.4 miles to southern Puck Lake, 6.0 miles to Margurette Lake, 6.3 miles to Trapper Lake, 8.3 miles to Devils Peak.

Low/High Elevations 5970'/6550' (to Sky Lakes Trail)

Trail Notes This route plus routes 8, 11 and 12 provide access to the Sky Lakes Area. To reach it with a minimum of effort, take route 12's shortcut option, which gets you to Trapper Lake, with a minimum of elevation change, in only 4.9 miles. Nannie Creek Trail is ideally suited for visiting the Puck Lakes. Back in the days when these lakes were named, "puck" meant a mischievous or rascally imp. If you're a "nannie" leading an entourage of "pucks," you'll find that southern Puck Lake offers an environment conducive to releasing the shackles of civilization.

The well-engineered Nannie Creek Trail is best for those going to the Puck Lakes. The trail switchbacks up some steep slopes, then climbs moderately northwest up a fault-formed gully. From its head you have a view of Crater Lake's rim peaks, and then you angle west for a pleasant descent to a gully, only to climb briefly up to the abandoned Puck Lakes Trail 3706. This easily followed trail goes to a south-shore camp before reaching, in ⅓ mile, a spur trail that goes ¼ mile to better camps by the northwest and north shores of the southern Puck Lake. Although large, this lake is quite shallow, and it provides some warm swimming. In one section a row of submerged boulders extends across most of the lake—a convenient route for trans-lake swimmers (great for kids). This lake has the distinction of being located at the center of a radiating Ice Age ice cap. Ice flowed in three directions: north past the lower Puck Lake, east over a low divide, and south into Cherry Creek canyon.

Beyond the Puck Lakes Trail, the Nannie Creek Trail drops 1.8 miles to a junction with the Snow Lakes Trail 3739 (last part of next route). Midway along your easy descent, you switchback down "shaly" slopes, which provide good views of upper Cherry Creek canyon and the Sky Lakes Area.

7 Sky Lakes Trail (3762), Trapper Lake north to Pacific Crest Trail

Trailhead None. Links Cherry Creek Trail to the Wickiup, Divide, Nannie Creek and Pacific Crest trails. **Map 19.**

Distance 3.8 miles from the Cherry Creek Trail junction at Trapper Lake north to the Pacific Crest Trail junction near the upper Snow Lakes.

Low/High Elevations 5940'/6680'

Trail Notes The Sky Lakes Trail used to be part of the Oregon Skyline Trail in the days before that oscillating trail, which lept from lake basin to lake basin, was replaced by the better-graded, though largely lakeless, Pacific Crest Trail. For the south half of the Sky Lakes Trail, see route 9.

From the upper end of the Cherry Creek Trail, you walk but a minute north along Trapper Lake to its northeast corner, where you'll meet Donna Lake Trail 3734. This 0.9-mile loop trail makes an initial ascent northeast before curving past Donna and Deep lakes, then climbing back to the Sky Lakes Trail. You can camp near either lake. Donna, being shallow, is a good one for swimming, particularly in early summer, when snow patches still hang around Deep Lake.

The Sky Lakes Trail next climbs 0.3 mile west to a ridge junction just above Margurette Lake. You'll find a couple camps both north and south of this junction. Starting southwest, Divide Trail 3717 makes a well-graded, but unnecessarily long, 2.6-mile climb to the Pacific Crest Trail, at a saddle near Luther Mountain. That peak, the throat of an old volcano, is well worth climbing: scramble east up to the summit. You get a commanding view of the entire Sky Lakes Area plus an aerial view down Cherry Creek canyon.

Past the Divide Trail, the Sky Lakes Trail skirts past deep, attractive Margurette Lake, then climbs ⅓ mile to the northwest end of the Donna Lake Trail. Ahead, you top out near chilly, unseen Tsuga Lake, then descend past a lower pair of Snow Lakes, with a scenic but chilly backdrop. About 200 yards beyond them, you could initiate a westward push through the huckleberries to shallow Wind Lake, though only the most determined fishermen will put up with its usual horde of mosquitoes. Your descent ends at nearby, waist-deep Martin Lake, and then you traverse 0.4 mile to a trail junction. Eastward Nannie Creek Trail 3707 climbs about 200 feet in 2 miles to reach southern Puck Lake (route 6).

Northeastward Snow Lakes Trail 3739 makes an exhausting 0.4-mile start, abating where the abandoned Oregon Skyline Trail continues ahead, making a steep, 1.5-mile climb to the Devils Peak/Lee Peak saddle. Your route turns southwest, then switchbacks up a ridge before switchbacking up to the top of a cliff. On it lie the upper Snow Lakes, which offer scenic, relatively mosquito-free camps. Just 0.2 mile past the second lake, your route ends at the Pacific Crest Trail.

8   Cherry Creek Trail (3708)

Trailhead See route 6's trailhead for location of County Route 531. On it drive either 5¾ miles south or 11 miles north to Road 3450, which you follow 1.9 miles up to its end. **Maps 19 and 20.**

Distances 5.2 miles to Trapper Lake, 5.5 miles to Margurette Lake.

Low/High Elevations 4595'/5940' (to Trapper Lake)

Trail Notes Starting low, this trail provides the most strenuous route into the Sky Lakes Area, so therefore it appeals only to equestrians. With a little imagination, you can set up camp anyplace along or near the first 3½ miles of trail.

The first 2 miles, to the Cherry Creek crossing, are barely uphill. There are two main branches to Cherry Creek, and hopefully the hiker will find a footbridge across the first. You then continue, mostly on a gentle, uphill grade, 1½ miles to the creek's recrossing, which will give you wet feet in early season. You can camp here, or at least rest, for ahead you have a steep, unrelenting 1¾-mile climb to Trapper Lake. In ¼ mile you cross that lake's creek, then more or less climb up its course. It cascades through a miniature gorge, giving music to your ears but hardly consoling your straining joints and muscles. Your totally viewless route ends dramatically as Luther Mountain pops into view and you almost stumble with exhaustion into Trapper Lake. Route 7 describes the trails north of this point, Route 9, south. You'll find some restful camps along the lake's east shore, just a couple of minutes south on the Sky Lakes Trail.

9   Sky Lakes Trail (3762), Pacific Crest Trail north to Trapper Lake

Trailhead None. Links the Pacific Crest Trail to the Cold Springs, South Rock Creek, Wickiup and Cherry Creek trails. **Map 19.**

Distance 4.0 miles from the Pacific Crest Trail junction above Deer Lake to the Cherry Creek Trail junction at Trapper Lake.

Low/High Elevations 5940'/6170'

Trail Notes The crest-hugging Pacific Crest Trail offers a high route past the Sky Lakes Area; the Sky Lakes Trail (routes 9 and 7) offers a much more desirable 7.8-mile route through it.

Leaving the Pacific Crest Trail, you crest a broad divide, then make a moderate ¼-mile diagonal down a fault escarpment, leveling off near mostly shallow Deer Lake. Some folks camp here, but far better camping, fishing and swimming lie ahead. Eastward, you pass, in a few minutes, the north end of Cold Springs Trail 3710 (route 12), then in a few more minutes reach Isherwood Trail 3729 (route 10). Excellent camping, fishing and swimming lie along that route.

Ahead, the Sky Lakes Trail soon passes between the Heavenly Twin Lakes, the smaller, deeper southern one being far less attractive than the northern one. Look for secluded camps along the latter's west shore. At the misnamed South Rock Trail 3709 (route 11), your trail turns north, skirts along the northern lake's east shore and then meets the other end of the Isherwood Trail. From it you continue north past chest-deep "Deep" Lake and its seasonal satellites, reaching, in 0.9 mile, Wickiup Trail 3728. This climbs west 2.0 pond-dotted miles through appropriately named Dwarf Lakes Area, and intersects the Pacific Crest Trail at a crest saddle before dropping 5.2 miles to its western trailhead (Chapter 12, route 16).

Shallow, uninviting Lake Land lies just below the Wickiup Trail's junction. At best, it provides some warm swimming; however, you'd be better off visiting Wizzard Lake, a fairly deep lake just 200 yards northeast below Lake Land's outlet. Beyond Lake Land, you soon pass a knee-deep pond, on your right, then, past a low ridge, two waist-deep lakelets. The south shore of Trapper Lake lies just ahead, and from where you see it you could go 250 yards cross-country southeast to Lake Sonya, easily the basin's deepest lake. More likely, you'll want to camp at the east-shore sites of scenic Trapper Lake.

10   Isherwood Trail (3729)

Trailhead None. **Map 19.**

Distance 1.5 miles, one way.

Low/High Elevations 5980'/6030'

Trail Notes In the Heavenly Twin Lakes area, the Sky Lakes Trail (previous route) visits only the two Heavenly Twin Lakes. A longer, alternate route, the Isherwood Trail, visits five lakes and also passes more campsites.

The southwest end of the Isherwood Trail begins from the Sky Lakes Trail at a junction that is midway between the north ends of Trails 3709 and 3710 (routes 11 and 12). From this junction, Lake Notasha is only a stone's throw away, just beyond a low ridge. This lake, with a camp above its east shore, is the area's deepest, and is the only one stocked with both rainbow and brook trout.

Another low ridge separates Notasha from Elizabeth, which is shallow enough for warm swimming, yet deep enough to sustain trout.

Next, you drop to the brink of a fault escarpment along the west shore of Isherwood Lake, one of the few lakes in the wilderness you can dive directly into; for most lakes, you have to wade out to deep water. From a horse camp midway along the escarpment, you can walk due west to adjacent, chest-deep Lake Liza, with marginal appeal.

Beyond Isherwood the trail winds north to a meadow, then veers east to the north tip of north Heavenly Twin Lake. For isolated camps, look for sites above its west shore. After passing a

Mt. McLoughlin pokes above Island Lake. Beautiful Isherwood Lake, viewed from its up-faulted west shore. A rainbow arcs across the Cascades' eastern escarpment, viewed from Sevenmile Drive.

northeast-shore camp, the Isherwood Trail ends at the Sky Lakes Trail just southwest of shallow Deep Lake.

11   South Rock Creek Trail (3709)

Trailhead Follow Highway 140 to a junction with Road 3651, near the west end of a broad, flat valley. This junction is 3.3 miles northeast of 140's junction with Dead Indian Road and is 2.7 miles southwest of 140's junction with County Road 531 (to Fort Klamath). Drive 7.1 miles up 3651 to its junction with Road 3458, a narrower road that descends 7.0 miles to the county road. Still on 3651, turn left and drive 1.4 miles north to a junction with Road 3659. For the Lost Creek trailhead (routes 13 and 14), follow that road 1.3 miles to a sharp bend. After another 1.2 miles north on 3651, you meet Road 980 (route 19), climbing southeast. Then, in just under ½ mile, your road ends at Cold Springs Campground. **Maps 19 and 20.**

Distances 3.1 miles to Heavenly Twin Lakes, 4.1 miles to Deer Lake, 5.6 miles to Trapper Lake, 5.9 miles to Margurette Lake.

Low/High Elevations 5850'/6020'

Trail Notes Both this route and the next one provide easy, hour-long hikes into the Sky Lakes basin. However, for an even shorter hike, see the next route's shortcut variation.

The misnamed South Rock Creek Trail jogs initially southeast before it crosses, in ½ mile, the very abandoned Pelican Butte Trail, atop a broad ridge. Northward you pass an unseen marshy area before veering west and crossing a low divide. In this vicinity hikers taking route 12's shortcut join your route for a 1.6-mile viewless traverse over to the Heavenly Twin Lakes.

12   Cold Springs Trail (3710)

Trailhead Same as for preceding route. **Map 19.**

Distances 3.0 miles to Deer Lake, 3.2 miles to Heavenly Twin Lakes, 5.7 miles to Trapper Lake, 6.0 miles to Margurette Lake.

Low/High Elevations 5850'/6100'

Trail Notes Because this trail starts in the right direction—north—it is far more popular than the preceding, redundant route, which is just as good. The best route, however, is a combination of the two. You start this shortcut route by hiking about ½ mile up the gradually steepening Cold Springs Trail. The northwest-climbing trail then jogs northeast for about 50 yards before making a steeper, 250-yard climb to a ridge. From the start of this steeper climb, leave the trail and contour 0.2 mile northeast to a broad, level divide. You should end your cross-country walk by the divide's west end, where you'll find the South Rock Creek Trail, which you follow 1.6 miles north to the Heavenly Twin Lakes. By this shortcut route, these lakes are about 2.4 miles from your trailhead. Of course, since both the Cold Springs and South Rock Creek trails are so easy, you may not feel motivated to knock 25% off your hiking effort.

13   Lost Creek and Red Lake Trails (3712 and 987)

Trailhead See route 11's trailhead. **Maps 19 and 22.**

Distances 1.4 miles to Center Lake, 2.4 miles to Island Lake, 2.8 miles to Dee Lake, 3.4 miles to Red Lake.

Low/High Elevations 5720'/6020'

Trail Notes You have an easy 1⅓-mile climb to the outlet of disappointing Center Lake, which is knee-deep in its prime, and only a grassy meadow in late summer. However, from that outlet adventuresome fishermen can contour ¼ mile north to slightly smaller Bert Lake, which nevertheless is deep enough to sustain trout.

Just west of and above Center Lake, you reach the first of three quick junctions, and here the Lost Creek Trail turns south (next route). Starting northwest on the Red Lake Trail, we top a nearby divide and on it find our trail intersected by the Pacific Crest Trail (Chapter 16, route 1). After several minutes of descent, we meet the east end of the Blue Canyon Trail (Chapter 12, route 20), and by going 0.4 mile west on it, we can reach a short spur trail that descends north to some good Island Lake campsites. You can find some hidden ones along this pleasant lake's east and west shores.

The Red Lake Trail heads ½ mile across boggy terrain to Island Lake's northeast corner, where, from a camp, a *de facto* trail goes 0.4 mile west to very pleasing Dee Lake. You'll find an improved horse camp on the low ridge between Dee and Island lakes. Dee is an excellent lake for swimming: shallow enough to have warm water, yet deep enough that it isn't an oversized swamp (like the north half of Island Lake, which is mostly less than waist deep).

Beyond Island Lake your boggy, huckleberry-laden route north passes several ponds that are more suited to mosquitoes than to humans, then arrives at large but grassy and extremely shallow Red Lake, with possible camping and fishing. After another ½ mile northward, the Red Lake Trail becomes abandoned, and the short No Name Trail climbs moderately 0.7 mile east to a crest junction with the Pacific Crest Trail.

14   Lost Creek and Long Lake Trails (3759 and 3713)

Trailhead   See route 11's trailhead. **Map 22.**

Distances   2.6 miles to Long Lake's north shore, 3.7 miles to south shore.

Low/High Elevations   5720'/6100'

Trail Notes   The previous route describes the first 1.5 miles of Lost Creek Trail 3712 up to the south end of the Red Lake Trail. Southward, the Lost Creek Trail becomes 3759, and it makes a gentle climb through a fault-formed trough, passing a grassy, wildflowered meadow just before reaching Long Lake, which stretches along the same fault. This fault runs north past Hemlock and Alta lakes, possibly as far north as Crater Lake's Union Peak. Southward it goes about 70 miles to northern California's Medicine Lake Highland.

Long Lake has two main camp areas. The main one, with more mosquitoes, is at the north shore; the other, at the south shore. To reach the latter, follow the Lost Creek Trail over a low ridge to a junction with Badger Lake Trail 3759 (route 16), then head east up very short Long Lake Trail 3713 to a junction with Horse Creek Trail 3741 (route 15). A short spur trail from here very soon crosses adjacent Long Creek just below the lake's south shore.

15   Fourmile Creek and Horse Creek Trails (3714 and 3741)

Trailhead   From Highway 140 between Lake of the Woods' east- and west-shore roads, start up Road 3661, which climbs 3.0 miles to the Cascade Canal. From here Road 3650 descends ¼ mile southwest to the Mt. McLoughlin trailhead (Chapter 12, route 24), and Road 3633, starting northeast, winds 2.6 miles over to the Rye Spur Trail (route 18). Continue ahead 2.7 miles to Fourmile Lake and go east (right) ¼ mile to road's end (by the dam) for routes 15, 16 and 18; go northwest (left) ¼ mile to road's end for route 17. **Map 22.**

Distances   3.1 miles to Long Lake's south shore, 4.1 miles to north shore.

Low/High Elevations   5730'/6100'

Trail Notes   From the parking area by the dam, start down the Cascade Canal road, passing the Rye Spur trailhead (right) in 30 yards and, in another 30 yards, reaching the Badger Lake trailhead (left). Just 35 yards up this trail you fork right, onto Fourmile Creek Trail 3714, which follows its namesake but 0.3 mile before becoming abandoned. You could follow that trail another ½ mile east, but then it starts a descent through tall, dense tobacco brush.

Leaving the creek, you start up Horse Creek Trail 3741, reaching a knee-deep pond in ¼ mile, a slightly deeper one almost a mile later, and then, in ½ mile more, Horse Creek. You go but ¼ mile up it before crossing it, and from here you could go cross country ⅓ mile upstream to the Badger Lake Trail. Ahead, your trail parallels Long Creek one mile up to Long Lake. This stretch is a joyous one before August, when the creek still flows and wildflowers adorn the landscape. Immediately before Long Lake, a spur trail shoots east to a good south-shore campsite. See the next route for a north-shore campsite. The lake is quite shallow, though deep enough to support trout and to offer some fair swimming.

16   Badger Lake Trail (3759)

Trailhead   Same as for preceding route. **Map 22.**

Distances   1.3 miles to Woodpecker Lake, 1.6 miles to Badger Lake, 3.6 miles to Long Lake's south shore, 4.0 miles to north shore.

Low/High Elevations   5730'/6100'

Trail Notes   From the parking area by the dam, start down the Cascade Canal road, passing the Rye Spur trailhead (right) in 30 yards and, in another 30 yards, reaching the Badger Lake trailhead (left). Just 35 yards up this trail you meet the Fourmile Creek Trail (previous route), forking right. If you ascend the Badger Lake Trail and return via the Fourmile Creek Trail, the total length of your excursion, minus side trips, will be 6.6 miles.

The Pelican Butte Fire Lookout offers this fine view of Upper Klamath Lake.

The Badger Lake Trail visits two of Fourmile Lake's lodgepole-snag bays, presenting you with views of Mt. McLoughlin and its avalanche-prone lower slopes. You then climb ½ mile to Woodpecker Lake, which is mostly less than chest deep. In ¼ mile, you reach more appealing Badger Lake, with better fishing and swimming than its neighbor. Next you pass knee-deep Lilly Pond, then pass a marshy meadow, both of interest to wildflower enthusiasts. Just beyond the meadow, where the trail curves from northeast to north, you could go cross country ⅓ mile downstream to the Horse Creek Trail.

Northward, you have additional boggy terrain to traverse, then you climb ½ mile northeast to a trail junction. To the right, Long Lake Trail 3713 goes 0.3 mile to a south-shore spur trail (previous route). To the left, Lost Creek Trail 3759 goes ¾ mile to a spur trail that is just 75 yards past Long Lake's northwest corner. The trail goes 120 yards east to Long Lake Camp, which has the shallow lake to its south and a seasonal swamp to its north.

17   Twin Ponds Trail (3715)

Trailhead   See route 15's trailhead. **Maps 21 and 22.**

Distances   2.0 miles to Squaw Lake, 2.5 miles to Pacific Crest Trail, 2.9 miles to Summit Lake.

Low/High Elevations   5740'/5840'

Trail Notes   From the west-end loop of the Fourmile Lake Campground, the old, shoreline Twin Ponds Trail heads 1.5 miles northwest to a trail junction at the south tip of Squaw Lake. I would not mention this abandoned route, were it

not so popular (it provides fishing access to parts of Fourmile Lake). The less popular, official route starts at a signed trailhead on the south side of the loop and winds a full 2.0 miles over to the aforementioned junction. Here the defunct but followable Blue Rock Trail 3737 starts a traverse along Squaw Lake's east shore, touches the north end of Fourmile Lake, and then ends, 1.9 miles from our junction, at the Pacific Crest Trail. From that junction, Cat Hill Way Trail 992 (Chapter 12, route 21) heads 3.6 miles north to the Blue Canyon Trail.

The Twin Ponds Trail starts northwest along large Squaw Lake, whose size belies its depth. In some years the lake completely dries up by late summer! Your route then turns west and makes a brief climb to two ponds, perched atop a divide. The Pacific Crest Trail passes between them, and ahead, your trail makes a moderate descent to waist-deep, barren, bouldery Summit Lake, which on occasion also dries up. Not too many hikers will want to camp by it; fewer still will want to go 2 miles past it and drop 480 feet below it to the often stagnant Twin Ponds.

18   Rye Spur Trail (3771)

Trailhead   See route 15's trailhead. **Maps 22 and 25.**

Distances   3.3 miles to viewpoint, 4.5 miles to Cascade Canal, 5.2 miles to Road 3633, 6.0 miles to Highway 140 trailhead.

Low/High Elevations   4980'/6240'

Trail Notes   This 6-mile section of the defunct Oregon Skyline Trail gives long-distance hikers a better route north or south than does the section of Pacific Crest Trail from the Fourmile Lake environs down to Highway 140. However, because the trail is lakeless, it appeals mostly to equestrians. Still, hikers might want to go as far as its scenic viewpoint.

From the parking area by the dam, go just 30 yards down the Cascade Canal road to the Rye Spur trailhead and immediately bridge the seasonal canal. For the first 1½ miles, your route basically contours above the canal, but then over the next 1¾ miles it gently climbs 400 feet to where you reach an open bowl with three outcrops. Climb around the bowl to the highest one, from which you get some fine views of the scenery from Pelican Butte south to the Mountain Lakes Wilderness. You can look right up one of the wilderness' glaciated canyons, which happens to coincide with a major fault. At the base of the canyon, the fault curves north, then heads past the west base of Pelican Butte and continues through the Sky Lakes basin and perhaps on beyond Devils Peak. A similar fault, one of several, passes just below you, near the base of Rye Spur, and it parallels the previously mentioned one perhaps as far north as Crater Lake's Union Peak. The whole set of faults extend about 65 miles south-southeast to northern California's Medicine Lake Highland. At your viewpoint you should see Davidson's penstemons and cliff penstemons growing side by side. The latter, like the also present sulfur flower, is not very common in this part of Oregon.

On your climb to the viewpoint, the vegetation has changed from mostly red firs and lodgepole pines to increasing amounts of western white pines, white firs and Douglas-firs. Just past the viewpoint, you'll see a very close relative of the western white pine, the sugar pine, with pendulous, foot-long cones.

Your views disappear and in 1¼ miles you drop about 500 feet to a bridge across Cascade Canal. You can return to your trailhead via the canal's road, making an 8.9-mile loop. Southward, the Rye Spur Trail drops 400 feet to Road 3633, down which you walk 160 yards southeast to relocate the trail. You then walk past a logged area, plunge steeply down an escarpment, reach a nature trail, and head 0.2 mile east on it to the lower trailhead, near Highway 140. Directions to that trailhead are given in Chapter 14's route 1.

19 Lakes Gladys and Francis

Trailhead   See route 11's trailhead for the start of Pelican Butte's Road 980. By mid-August the road is usually drivable 4.6 miles to the summit. For the "trailhead," first go 1.6 miles to the first switchback, then 2.2 more miles to the 16th switchback. It's easy to recognize, since it's the first one with good views. **Maps 20 and 23.**

Distance   1.3 miles to Lake Gladys, 1.5 miles to Lake Francis by shortest routes.

Low/High Elevations   6510'/7630'

Trail Notes   By starting at switchback 14, 3.3 miles up the road, you could cut about 0.2 mile and 280 feet off your descent but, on your return trip, you probably wouldn't be able to relocate that "trailhead." Therefore, start cross country from switchback 16, which is the one in the northwest corner of Map 23's Section 20. For shallow, fishless Lake Gladys, stay as close as possible to the descending ridge, which finally levels between the two lakes. From there you can descend northwest to that lake or southeast to Lake Francis. Since the latter is seen from the descending ridge, you can choose one of several routes if you want to go cross country directly to it.

Either before or after your hike, be sure to visit the Pelican Butte summit. Its excellent views rival those of significantly higher Mt. McLoughlin, for not only can you study the Cascades, but you can also survey the Klamath Lake basin. Pelican Butte, lying east of the Cascade divide, gets less precipitation, and consequently its vegetation is quite different from lands just a few miles to the west. In that low zone, between the bases of Mt. McLoughlin and Pelican Butte, there lie about a half-dozen north-south faults. The largest one splits into two branches north of Rye Spur, the east branch going through Long Lake and the west one through Island and Red lakes. South of Rye Spur the fault goes through Lake of the Woods, then curves south-southeast, out of sight behind the Mountain Lakes Wilderness, which sits atop a band of parallel faults. All these head south-southeast to the Medicine Lake Highland, an extremely active volcanic area in northern California, which from your summit you can see, 70 miles away.

14   Lake of the Woods Area

Introduction This chapter's first three short trails will attract only nature lovers. Indeed, the first one, to Billie Creek, is specifically designated as a nature trail. It is easily the best of the three routes. The second route, the Lake of the Woods Trail, more or less connects the lake's Aspen Point camping-picnicking area with the Billie Creek nature trail. By itself, the Lake of the Woods Trail provides good botanizing and good bird watching, including occasional sightings of bald eagles. The Brown Mountain Trail's first ⅓ mile is extensively used (and maintained) by scouts at Camp McLoughlin. This Crater Lake Council Boy Scout camp also provides programs for southern Oregon's YMCA youths and handicapped youths. The Brown Mountain Trail, unfortunately, climbs around the mountain, not up to its summit, but that you can reach by a cross-country hike (see route 3).

The last trail, route 4, links the Lake of the Woods area to the Mountain Lakes Trail, which climbs southeast into Mountain Lakes Wilderness. Almost all trail users start at the Mountain Lakes trailhead, not at the Lake of the Woods trailhead, so route 4 sees little use. Finally, there is one more trail, but it won't be described. This is the barely used lower part of the Mt. McLoughlin Trail, the stretch between Highway 140 and Road 3650 (Maps 21, 22, and 25). Even without these 3 miles, the Mt. McLoughlin hike (p. 101-102) is already the book's most strenuous route.

1   Billie Creek Nature Trail

Trailhead From Highway 140 just 0.2 mile west of the Lake of the Woods' east-shore Road 3704, branch north onto a pole-line road. Immediately (in 5 yards) branch right from it, making a hairpin turn onto a minor road. Follow it 100 yards to the trailhead, just before the pole line. **Map 25.**

Distance 0.6 mile, one way.

Low/High Elevations 4980'/5080'

Trail Notes You go 0.2 mile west on Rye Spur Trail 3771, which then switchbacks and makes a short, steep climb. Westward, the nature trail quickly splits, the right branch traversing above Billie Creek's north bank and the left branch soon crossing to the creek's south bank. You can take either branch of this loop trail.

This short trail displays many of Lake of the Woods' conifers, shrubs and wildflowers, and the author has put as many of these species into the botany chapter as space would allow. You should be able to identify several dozen species.

2   Lake of the Woods Trail

Trailhead On Lake of the Woods' east-shore Road 3704, take the signed *Aspen Point* turnoff. This road quickly radiates into five roads, and you take the only one on your right. Follow it ¼ mile to its turnaround loop, at a picnic area. **Map 25.**

Distance 0.5 mile, one way.

Low/High Elevations 4950'/4980'

Trail Notes This short trail passes through several environments, so both the fauna and the flora are quite diverse. The trail starts northwest atop a levee, then follows it north to the lake's often-dry outlet. Lake of the Woods loses far more water through evaporation and underground seepage than stream runoff. Along this short stretch you'll see ponderosa pines—pervasive along the Cascades' eastern slopes—mingling with water-loving willows and lodgepole pines.

Watch for ducks, ospreys and bald eagles in the lake's shallow north end, blackbirds and warblers around a willow-lined lily pond on the

Sunrise over Lake of the Woods and Mt. McLoughlin

right. Past the seasonal outlet, you enter a mixed-conifer forest with Douglas-fir, white fir, Engelmann spruce and western white pine. You'll note that the plants growing on the shady forest floor are quite different from those you saw just a moment ago.

The trail dies out just before Highway 140. If you want to go on to the Billie Creek nature trail (route 1), head northwest across the highway. Be sure to look back at the way you came so that you will be able to find the Lake of the Woods Trail when you return.

3   Brown Mountain Trail (3724)

Trailheads From Highway 140 just west of Lake of the Woods Visitor Center, the lake's west-shore Road 3601 starts south, then Road 3640 quickly branches right. Go either ⅓ mile south on 3601 to Camp McLoughlin's road (no parking) or ⅔ mile southwest on 3640 (minimal parking). **Map 25.**

Distance 4.4 miles to Pacific Crest Trail.

Low/High Elevations 4955'/5660'

Trail Notes This utilitarian trail, which does *not* go to Brown Mountain, was rendered obsolete with the construction of Road 3640 and Road 3774 (just off the map). The only maintained stretch of trail is between the two trailheads. The remaining 4.1 miles generally aren't worth taking.

It's a pity no trail climbs to the summit of 7311-foot Brown Mountain. This recently active volcano has fresh lava flows draped over its north, west and south slopes, so the only respectable cross-country route to its top is from the east. From the trailhead on Road 3640, drive 2⅓ miles south up this road to where it almost levels near a gully. Park here for a roughly 2-mile-long, 1650-foot, forested climb west to the summit (see bottom of Map 24).

4   Mountain Lakes Spur Trail (3721B)

Trailhead At Road 3704, 0.1 mile north of the spur road southwest down to Lake of the Woods Resort and Rainbow Bay Picnic Area. No parking here, though you can park nearby, on a road that starts east almost opposite the paved spur road. **Map 25.**

Distance 1.2 miles, one way,

Low/High Elevations 5000'/5270'

Trail Notes From where this trail begins at Road 3704, a *de facto* trail, following a buried water main west, goes ¼ mile over to the southeast corner of Aspen Point Campground, and this unmarked route is sometimes used by campers. Eastward, Trail 3721B traverses through a logged area to Dead Indian Road (no parking) before it climbs ¾ mile, mostly through a logged area, to the Mountain Lakes trailhead at Road 3660 (Chapter 15, route 2). Most people entering the wilderness on the Mountain Lakes Trail start here, not down by Lake of the Woods.

15   Mountain Lakes Wilderness

Introduction: This compact wilderness, the glacier-gouged ruins of several over-lapping, faulted Ice Age volcanoes, is one of Oregon's most accessible mountain areas. The Varney Creek trailhead—easily the most popular—is barely a half-hour's drive from Klamath Falls. The somewhat less popular Mountain Lakes trailhead is only a few minutes' drive from Lake of the Woods. The shortest way into the wilderness, from the Clover Creek trailhead, should become popular once the last mile of road to it is improved. Using the appropriate trailhead, you should be able to reach any wilderness lake in three hours or less.

The Varney Creek, Mountain Lakes and Clover Creek trails climb to the Mountain Lakes Loop Trail, which weaves a 9.0-mile band through the most scenic part of the wilderness. This loop trail gives rise to two important routes: a trail down to South Pass Lake and a trail up to Aspen Butte (both worthy goals). Aspen Butte, being the wilderness' highest peak, offers the most extensive views: from the Crater Lake rim south to Mt. Shasta and beyond. The wilderness' other peaks, all readily accessible to experienced cross-country travelers, offer instructive views into the heart of the wilderness. One of the easiest peaks is also one of the best: peak 7708, ½ mile north of Whiteface Peak. From the loop trail, its summit is but a quarter mile—and a quarter hour—away.

1   Varney Creek Trail (3718)

Trailhead *From the east:* Drive northwest along Highway 140, pass the well-signed Winema National Forest boundary, and in ⅓ mile turn left onto Road 3637. You immediately pass the county dump as you start a drive 1¾ miles up the road to a junction, left, with Road 3664, which you follow 2.1 miles to a large parking area at its end. *From the west:* Two choices: 1) From the Dead Indian Road junction with Highway 140, drive 5.6 miles northeast down Highway 140 to Varney Creek Road 3610 (this is 0.4 mile before the Fort Klamath road junction). Drive 1.7 miles south up 3610 to Road 3637, and 3.2 miles east on it to Road 3664, mentioned above. 2) From the Highway 140/Dead Indian Road junction, go 100 yards south on the road, turn left onto Road 3610, follow it 5.6 miles to the Roads 3610/3637 junction, mentioned above. **Map 26.**

Distances 4.3 miles to Mountain Lakes Loop Trail, 4.6 miles to Eb and Zeb lakes, 4.7 miles to Lake Como, 5.8 miles to Lake Harriette, 7.5 miles to South Pass Lake Trail.

"Twin lakes:" Eb (top) and Zeb (center). Below, from a 7708' peak, you have a view north-northeast down the Varney Creek canyon. Mt. Harriman is on the far right.

Low/High Elevations 5530'/6700' (up to loop trail)

Trail Notes The trail starts west through a dense Douglas-fir/white-fir forest, arcs around a glacial moraine, and gently climbs almost a mile south to a Varney Creek crossing, which in July is an excellent spot for creekside botanizing. From the crossing, the trail initially jogs northwest, then climbs south, mostly at an easy pace, usually staying just far enough away from the creek to avoid boggy soils. In July you can identify dozens of wildflower species before you cross a dry gully, about 2.2 miles past the Varney Creek crossing. If you were to continue 150 yards ahead and then scramble up the squaw-carpeted slopes of a minor lateral moraine, you'd reach Storm Lake, a seasonal pond.

From the gully that holds a subterranean Varney Creek, you climb moderately for ⅓ mile to a viewpoint, from which you can examine the lodgepole-forested Greylock Mountain basin. Glaciers flowed 5 miles north from this basin, deepening and widening a canyon that was being eroded along a fault. Northward this fault can be traced for about 20 miles, southward for about 55 miles.

In ¼ mile you top off at a pond on a broad divide that was formerly overridden by glaciers. From the pond you can initiate a 2-mile, cross-country jaunt northwest to Mt. Harriman, which in height is second only to the Aspen Butte summit ridge. From the Mt. Harriman summit you can gaze north down the fault-controlled Varney Creek canyon and at a line of small volcanoes, which begins near the north base of your peak. Mt. Harriman is the eroded remnants of one of several medium-sized Ice Age volcanoes. The largest of these was the Mt. Carmine-Aspen Butte volcano, which you can readily identify from your summit. Its maximum elevation was about 9000 feet, possibly less, and it was not much higher than today's Aspen Butte. Contrary to some popular opinions, the Mountain Lakes Wilderness never contained a solitary, 12,000-foot-high stratovolcano.

Beyond the pond you traverse ¼ mile to a trail junction, perhaps unaware that you've crossed an amorphous divide. From that junction you can climb ¼ mile southwest to the very popular Eb and Zeb lakes, or descend almost ½ mile south to equally popular Lake Como. The first two are shallow, with good, fairly warm swimming; the last is quite deep and cool, with better fishing.

2 Mountain Lakes Trail (3721)

Trailhead From Dead Indian Road, just 100 yards south of its junction with Highway 140, go 0.7 mile southeast on Road 3610 to a fork, branch right, and drive 0.8 mile south up Road 3660 to a curve. Limited parking. **Maps 25 and 26.**

Distances 3.3 miles to Lake Waban, 5.4 miles to Mountain Lakes Loop Trail, 6.8 miles to Eb and Zeb lakes, 6.9 miles to Clover Lake.

Low/High Elevations 5270'/7390' (up to loop trail)

Trail Notes See Chapter 14, route 4, for Trail 3721B, which climbs east from Lake of the Woods to your trailhead. Heading east, you traverse across the cryptic crests of two lateral moraines. You then curve southeast and exchange a white-fir forest for a red-fir one as you enter the fault-controlled Mountain Lakes canyon and cross its seasonal creek. Wildflower lovers will appreciate the next ¾ mile, while the trail parallels the creek and then climbs through a sloping meadow. Beyond it, lodgepoles and hemlocks take over, together with their common associate, the lowly grouse whortleberry.

About 2 miles from your trailhead you enter the wilderness and then climb, usually moderately, for 1¼ miles to a spur trail that goes 90 yards west to lodgepole-ringed Lake Waban, more marsh than lake. Its seasonal super-abundance of thumbnail-size tree frogs may be directly related to a superabundance of mosquitoes. Just what animals prey on these frogs is hard to tell. Garter snakes are the usual predators, but at this lake meadow mice may fill the role. These fierce rodents consume their own weight in food about every 24 hours, and basically will eat anything they feel they can tackle—fresh meat included.

Precisely one mile beyond the Lake Waban turnoff, the Mountain Lakes Trail turns east, and wilderness pioneers bound for shallow Avalanche Lake, ½ mile to the southwest, should leave the trail here. That lake site makes an adequate base camp for those intent on climbing Crater Mountain. Next, the trail winds about ⅓ mile east, then makes a rather steep climb one mile up to a crest junction with the Mountain Lakes Loop Trail (route 4). Southeast, this trail descends 1½ miles to Clover Lake; northeast, it first traverses to a nearby saddle and then descends 1 mile to Eb and Zeb lakes.

3   Clover Creek Trail (3722)

Trailhead   From the south end of Lake of the Woods' west-shore Road 3601, drive 3.6 miles southwest up Dead Indian Road to a junction with Clover Creek Road (County Route 603), which lies about one mile east of the Cascade divide. Drive 5.9 miles southeast on Clover Creek Road, branch left onto Road 3852, and follow it 2.0 miles to a fork where the grade steepens. Road 3852 curves north, but you continue ahead, east, up steep Road 190 to a junction with the Buck Peak jeep road, right. Ahead, a logging road quickly forks left while your narrow road goes ¼ mile over to a low ridge. If you have an ordinary passenger car, you won't want to drive any farther. Walk ⅓ mile down the steep, bouldery road to a junction with Road 3840-230, just beyond seasonal Clover Creek, and head ¾ mile up the road to the trailhead. High-clearance vehicles can usually make it all the way to the trailhead. Don't attempt to drive up to the trailhead via Road 3840, for it is definitely worse. Limited parking. **Map 26.**

Distances   2.0 miles to Mountain Lakes Loop Trail, 2.3 miles to Clover Lake, 4.8 miles to Aspen Butte, 5.7 miles to Lake Harriette, 6.0 miles to South Pass Lake.

Low/High Elevations   5620'/6630' (up to loop trail)

Trail Notes   Just beyond the trailhead you cross intermittent, seasonal Clover Creek, then stay close to its west bank as you climb moderately for 1½ miles to the creek's recrossing in a small, grassy meadow. You then climb ⅓ mile up a ridge, leaving it just before a junction with the Mountain Lakes Loop Trail (next route). Straight ahead, this trail climbs ¼ mile to Clover Lake, an oversized pond with an adequate camp above its north shore. Your entire, moderate ascent to this lake has been confined between two fairly large lateral moraines which, due to dense forest cover, stand undetected by most hikers.

From the junction below Clover Lake, you can climb 1¼ miles northeast to a crest above Lake Harriette. Here, you'll see the lake, about ⅓ mile northeast and 600 feet below you. To reach the lake, the loop trail first climbs ½ mile southeast, gaining 300 feet before dropping 2 miles to the lake's outlet. By gingerly working your way cross country down some very steep slopes from the viewpoint, you can reach that outlet in under one mile.

4   Mountain Lakes Loop Trail (3727)

Trailhead   None. Links all the trails together and visits most of the main lakes. **Map 26.**

Distances   Clockwise: 1.7 miles, Mountain Lakes Trail to Varney Creek Trail; 3.2 miles, Varney Creek Trail to South Pass Lake Trail; 0.5 mile, South Pass Lake Trail to Aspen Butte Trail; 1.8 miles, Aspen Butte Trail to Clover Creek Trail; 1.8 miles, Clover Creek Trail to Mountain Lakes Trail; 9.0 miles for complete loop.

Low/High Elevations   6540'/7580'

Trail Notes   This loop trail tends to be more primitive than the three trails (routes 1-3) climbing up to it. The stretch from Eb and Zeb lakes east to Lake Harriette receives the bulk of the use and is quite well defined. However, the remaining 7 miles of trail can have route-finding problems when snow patches are present.

Starting clockwise from a crest saddle at the upper end of the Mountain Lakes Trail, your loop trail traverses almost ½ mile north to another saddle, which lies between 7706-foot Whiteface Peak, to the south, and a 7708-foot peak, to the north. Both summits are about 300 feet above your forested saddle and both are only a 15-minute climb away. I strongly recommend you climb the slaty, northern one, which presents an unobstructed 360° panorama of much of the wilderness area, including all of its major peaks. By looking northwest toward Brown Mountain, Lake of the Woods and Mt. McLoughlin, you look down the exceptionally broad, flat Mountain Lakes canyon. This is not your typical glacier-cut canyon; rather, the upper part was down-faulted, conveniently creating a cirque in which a large glacier developed that flowed northwest 5 miles down-canyon. Similarly, down-faulting occurred in the Clover Creek canyon, and a glacier flowed southeast one mile through it, then continued south 2 miles down unconfined slopes. When that glacier retreated, it left a pair of large, protruding moraines, like those you see along the east side of the Sierra Nevada. Leaving the forested saddle, the loop trail starts a steep, switchbacking, two-stage drop to gentler slopes, across which you ramble ½ mile down to popular Eb and Zeb lakes. In midsummer, the lakes can warm to 70°F, making them highly desirable swimming holes. Most folks camp on level ground between the two lakes.

Just beyond the lakes you make a ¼-mile drop to a junction with the Varney Creek Trail, then drop moderately almost ½ mile to deep Lake Como, with north- and east-shore campsites. The trail then winds east to the rocky moraine that confines slightly higher Zepher Lake, which is too shallow to attract campers. Past it you face a short, steep climb to a notch, which lies below lava cliffs that have produced extensive, slaty talus slopes. In a couple of minutes you drop to Lake Harriette, which is the deepest and most voluminous lake to be found in either Mountain Lakes or Sky Lakes wilderness. Campsites dot its northwest and northeast shores.

From the lake's outlet the abandoned Moss Creek Trail descends 3.6 miles to a closed jeep road. This trail provides access to lots of ponds and lakelets, including grassy, undesirable Hemlock Lake. This area is best left to the ducks, frogs and mosquitoes. Just east of Harriette's outlet, you can descend a ridge to camps above Echo Lake's west shore.

From a seasonal pond east of Lake Harriette, you commence a winding, rather scenic ascent, climbing 600 feet in about a mile to a crest junction with the South Pass Lake Trail (next route). The climbing continues for another ½ mile, and then you traverse briefly west across steep slopes to a junction with the Aspen Butte Trail (route 6). When snow patches are present, usually until mid-July, the traverse is essentially impassable for equestrians. When snow patches are present, also, the 1.8-mile stretch down to the Clover Creek Trail can be very easy to lose. From that junction you climb a better-defined 1.8-mile stretch up to the Mountain Lakes Trail.

5   South Pass Lake Trail (3720)

Trailhead None. Former trailhead, east of and below the wilderness, is on private, inaccessible land. **Map 26.**

Distances 0.2 mile to Mystic Lake, 0.8 mile to Paragon Lake, 1.7 miles to South Pass Lake.

Low/High Elevations 6510'/7360'

Trail Notes The trail descends 135 yards southeast, then goes but 40 yards northeast to a sometimes-missed junction. From it, a 250-yard-long trail heads southeast over a low ridge down to hemmed-in Mystic Lake. At trail's end lies a medium-size campsite with a pleasing view of the Aspen Butte ridge.

The main trail descends through a dense forest, then passes an outcrop of cinders before reaching a meadow. To find shallow, hidden Paragon Lake, head south from the meadow, going cross country about 150 yards. A shallower pond lies in the meadow, and your trail touches its south shore before re-entering forest. You now have a viewless, moderate, 450-foot descent to good-sized South Pass Lake. Although you can camp at the lake's west end, the sites at its east end, about 2 miles from the start of this trail, are more desirable, for they offer a nice view up-canyon and they tend to have fewer mosquitoes. Note the presence of Klamath Lake basin vegetation at these sites.

The northeast ridge of Aspen Butte reflected in South Pass Lake

The heart of the wilderness, from Aspen Butte

6   Aspen Butte Trail (3731)

Trailhead   None. **Map 26.**
Distance   1.0 mile, one way.
Low/High Elevations   7580'/8208'

Trail Notes   This trail is a primitive one, and in places is hard to follow. However, that doesn't matter, since the route is basically along a well-defined ridge. The first ½ mile is an easy climb, but the second half will force most hikers to stop a number of times to catch their breath. Red firs, subalpine firs and mountain hemlocks, which were quite common along the trail's first half, disappear before you reach the summit. Up there the only conifer is the whitebark pine, and the shrubs are mostly pinemat manzanita and Bloomer's goldenbush. Lots of Davidson's penstemons are present, which is typical of so many southern Oregon summits, but you'll also see thigh-high angelicas, which are more common in the Sierra Nevada and Klamath Mountains.

From the summit, you see Mt. McLoughlin and the Crater Lake rim beyond your wilderness' high peaks. Below you, an extensive talus field lies where glaciers formerly flowed northeast about 2 miles, debouching their ice and rubble from the mouth of a hanging canyon, situated about 2000 feet above the Klamath Lake basin. These glaciers also overflowed northwest into the adjacent Moss Creek canyon, which contains most of the wilderness' sizable lakes, and glaciers from that canyon spilled over a low divide into Varney Creek canyon. You'll see, about 3 miles to the west, the Crater Mountain-Whiteface Peak divide, from which glaciers flowed about 5 miles northwest down to the Lake of the Woods environs, while other glaciers flowed about 3 miles south to the Clover Creek trailhead. The view south is unimpressive, but if you look closely, you'll notice that much of the topography consists of lines of northwest-southeast-oriented hills. These are due to faults, about a half dozen of them, which head southeast over to northern California's Medicine Lake Highland, on the horizon about 55 miles away.

16   Pacific Crest Trail

Introduction: The Pacific Crest Trail (PCT) spans California, Oregon and Washington as it runs about 2550 miles from the Mexican border to the Canadian border. In the area covered in this guidebook, the trail runs about 87½ miles, and in this chapter, that stretch is divided into five northbound sections.

The first, from Highway 140 to the Sevenmile Trail junction, is the longest, and it contains *all* the nearby lakes you will *see* along the 87½-mile stretch. Unfortunately, the Pacific Crest Trail is all that its name implies—a *crest* trail—and by hugging the crest, it visits nary a lake. Fortunately, most of the lakes that lie below the trail are accessible from other trails.

The second section, from the Sevenmile Trail junction to Highway 62, hugs the crest as a true crest trail should, and provides a fair number of views—mostly of forests. However, a side trip to Union Peak provides views to make up for all the ones you've missed. After the snow melts, this section is entirely waterless; you will have to go out of your way to get water.

The third section, from Highway 62 to Crater Lake's north-rim access road, has the most water of any section, which isn't all that much after Labor Day. The section, however, is entirely viewless, for it stays far from the crest. A good time to hike it is from mid-July through mid-August, when a fair number of wildflowers garnish the land.

The fourth section, from the north-rim access road to Highway 138, is entirely viewless and, once the snow melts, is totally waterless. There are no creeks to sniff out, for the entire landscape has subterranean drainage. Mercifully, this utilitarian section is the shortest.

The fifth section, from Highway 138 to the Howlock Mountain Trail, generally stays well below the crest, but it does provide mountaineers with takeoff points for routes up Mt. Thielsen, the Sawtooth Ridge and Howlock Mountain. Water is usually reliable only at one place—Thielsen Creek.

The secret to enjoying the lengthy Pacific Crest Trail is to take your time and explore the region. Don't stick to the route; rather, try alternate routes, explore side trails, and even venture cross country to nearby destinations. Soak up all the sights, sounds and fragrances you can, so that you do more than just follow the crest—you commune with this mountain environment.

1   Highway 140 to Sevenmile Trail

Trailhead From the Fish Lake Campground/Resort road junction, drive 2.1 miles east on Highway 140 to Fourmile Lake Road 3650. You go but 15 yards up it before turning left, to follow a short road over to a large trailhead parking lot. From the lot's northwest corner a trail goes 0.2 mile north to the PCT. **Maps 16, 17, 19, 21, 22 and 24.**

Distances 4.3 miles to Mt. McLoughlin Trail, 8.4 miles to Twin Ponds Trail, 13.9 miles to Red Lake Trail, 17.6 miles to Sky Lakes Trail, 23.4 miles to Snow Lakes Trail, 25.7 miles to Devils Peak/Lee Peak saddle, 28.9 miles to Seven

Mt. McLoughlin, from the Pacific Crest Trail across Shale Butte

Lakes Trail, 31.5 miles to Sevenmile Trail, 33.3 miles to Sevenmile Marsh Campground.

Low/High Elevations   4980'/7300'

Trail Notes   The PCT crosses Highway 140 just 0.2 mile west of the Jackson/Klamath county line and 40 yards east of the Cascade Canal. Southward, the trail goes 11½ miles to Dead Indian Road, 54 miles to Interstate 5, and close to 1700 miles to the Mexican border.

Northward, you immediately cross the seasonal Cascade Canal, and then parallel it northeast to a nearby junction with a spur trail to the PCT trailhead parking lot. Just past this junction the trail almost touches the canal before it angles away and leads up open slopes that provide a view south of Brown Mountain and its youthful lava flows. On its ascent to the Mt. McLoughlin Trail, the PCT also crosses lava flows, but most of the climb is through a pristine forest. From where the PCT briefly joins the Mt. McLoughlin Trail, you climb ¼ mile west on an easier grade to the Freye Lake spur trail, just 50 yards past a gully. The ill-defined trail goes ¼ mile over to the shallow, semistagnant lake and its camps.

After you hike another ¼ mile west on the PCT, you leave the Mt. McLoughlin Trail, which climbs—very steeply—3½ miles up to the stratovolcano's summit (Chapter 12, route 24). The PCT crests an immediate ridge, then snakes slowly down through the forest, not once offering a view, and eventually it intersects the Twin Ponds Trail (NW: Chapter 12, route 22: SE: Chapter 13, route 17). This junction lies between two shallow ponds that by late summer are no more than grassy plots. Small campsites may be found at Summit Lake, which can dry up in late summer. To the southeast, the trail goes 2½ miles to Fourmile Lake Campground.

From the junction, the PCT starts northeast, quickly veers north past a stagnant pond, climbs steadily up a ridge, and descends slightly to a junction with the Cat Hill Way Trail (Chapter 12, route 21). Our trail then rounds a gully and veers east up to a gentle slope before curving northeast and climbing to a broad saddle. The route now contours across a forested slope, rounds a linear ridge, and diagonals southeast across its up-faulted slopes to a second saddle. In about a mile, the PCT reaches yet another saddle, on which it crosses the Red Lake Trail. See Chapter 13, route 13, for camping possibilities at Island, Dee and Red lakes.

The PCT now turns north, staying west of a linear divide as it goes 2.6 miles to a trail junction. From the crest junction with the No Name Trail, folks who have used the Red Lake Trail rejoin the PCT, following it gently northeast one mile up to another tempting, alternate route, the Sky Lakes Trail (Chapter 13, routes 9 and 7). The PCT stays high above the Sky Lakes; the Sky Lakes Trail visits them. By taking a variation of the alternate, the Isherwood Trail (route 10), you visit even more lakes.

While the Sky Lakes Trail starts off by crossing an up-faulted escarpment, the PCT starts north, climbs a gentle slope past several ponds, and then reaches a thinning forest as it approaches a cliff above the Dwarf Lakes Area. From here you see Pelican Butte, the prominent summit in the southeast, plus the more subdued Cherry Peak and its western, fault-bound satellite, both directly east. You can't see all the dwarf lakes (ponds) below you because that area is so thickly forested.

Your trail switchbacks slightly up to avoid a cliff, switchbacks slightly down west slopes, and soon encounters a 100-yard spur trail, which goes to an overlook with a view that encompassses most of the rolling western Cascades. We now switchback several times up to a small summit before descending the ridgeline to a saddle and a junction with the Wickiup Trail (W: Chapter 12, route 16; E: Chapter 13, route 9). Here you have your second of four chances to drop into the Sky Lakes basin.

The PCT now heads northeast up to a ridge where the views east into the Sky Lakes basin really begin to open up. The trail then contours to a saddle at the west base of Luther Mountain. Here you have two options: scramble up to the summit of this volcanic plug for unparalleled views of the Sky Lakes Area, or descend 2½ miles along the Divide Trail to that alluring area.

Keeping high, the PCT goes about a mile north to a minor saddle, from which the Hemlock Lake Trail (Chapter 12, route 14) descends almost a mile to that lake. If you need to camp, start up the PCT, then quickly fork left onto the Snow Lakes Trail, taking it ¼ mile to the small but pleasant lakes (Chapter 13, route 7). If you've taken the Sky Lakes Trail alternate route, you'll be climbing up this trail to the PCT.

More climbing lies ahead, as you progress up a slaty ridge before tackling slaty Shale Butte. You then traverse the east slope of Lucifer Peak and on an elongated saddle, meet the Devils Peak Trail (Chapter 12, route 13). Just beyond the saddle, this trail leaves the PCT, climbing up to Devils Peak and then descending too steeply back to the PCT at the Devils Peak/Lee Peak saddle. Most folks climb to the summit for some far-ranging views.

From the saddle the PCT switchbacks down north slopes that can be snowbound through late July. North of the saddle, northbound early-summer hikers have an enjoyable snow slide, while southbound hikers have a strenuous but safe ascent. After the trail's gradient eases, you wind about 2 miles down to a junction with a trail that goes ⅓ mile over to Cliff Lake (Chapter 12, route 10). That lake should not be missed, and from it you can head past Middle and Grass lakes, via the Seven Lakes Trail, back to the PCT. We come to that trail junction in 0.7 mile, then drop about 0.5 mile to Honeymoon Creek, with inferior camping. Past it you rollercoaster across generally viewless slopes for just over 2 miles, and near Ranger Springs, unseen below you, as you approach a junction with the Sevenmile Trail (Chapter 13, route 3). This trail goes an easy 1.8 miles northeast down to Sevenmile Marsh Campground.

2   Sevenmile Trail to Highway 62

Trailhead None. Closest trailhead is at Sevenmile Marsh Campground, 1.8 miles from the Pacific Crest Trail. See Chapter 13, route 3, for trailhead directions and Sevenmile Trail description to the PCT. **Maps 12, 16 and 17.**

Distances 2.1 miles to McKie Camp Trail, 6.5 miles to Stuart Falls Trail, 12.1 miles to Pumice Flat/Stuart Falls trails, 14.5 miles to Union Peak Trail, 17.3 miles to Highway 62 (add 1.8 miles to each destination if you start from Sevenmile Marsh Campground).

Low/High Elevations 5750'/6750'

Trail Notes This section begins at the Sevenmile Trail junction, and ahead your trail will be completely waterless once the snow melts. However, you will be able to get water by going out of the way. Your first opportunity to do this is just 0.2 mile north down the PCT. You meet the Middle Fork Basin Trail, which crests a low, broad divide on its way 0.9 mile southwest down to gushing Ranger Springs. There, at the headwaters of the Middle Fork Rogue River, you can establish camp.

About a mile beyond that trail you meet the Big Bunchgrass Trail, and about a mile beyond it you meet the McKie Camp Trail (both Chapter 12, route 6). Both unite, then go to McKie Camp, which is a pleasant day's hike if you've started from the Seven Lakes Basin. From the camp you can rejoin the PCT or continue off-course to Stuart Falls Camp (see Chapter 12, route 3).

Next, the PCT starts north up toward Maude Mountain, but quickly curves northwest and climbs to its west spur, which is a logical place to start a 740-foot climb up to its eye-opening summit views. It is the highest of a cluster of small, eroded volcanoes, so you have unrestrained views for miles around. Particularly interesting is the view west down the deep, glaciated Middle Fork canyon.

From Maude Mountain the PCT contours north along west slopes past Ethel Mountain, then descends past Ruth Mountain to a saddle just east of Lone Wolf. We now start east, but immediately switchback northwest and descend through a snow-harboring fir-and-hemlock forest before curving north to a flat. Here, where others have camped, a spur trail heads west to a low saddle, then from it drops steeply ½ mile northwest to Jack Spring. Due to the steepness of this descent, plus the difficulty some folks have finding this bucket-size spring, you should take this trail only if you *really* need water.

Your route now winds gently down to the Oregon Desert, which holds a reservoir of water, all of it underground. You traverse the west edge of this open lodgepole-forest flat, and pass a wisp of a trail, heading east, about ⅓ mile before you meet the abandoned Dry Creek Trail (Chapter 13, route 2). On it you scamper northwest over a low divide, leaving it just on the other side. Had you continued northwest a short ½ mile, you'd have reached a junction with the north end of the McKie Camp Trail. North from it, the Stuart Falls Trail goes about 3.4 miles to Stuart Falls Camp (Chapter 12, route 3), and from it you can climb 2.5 miles northeast back to the PCT (Chapter 10, route 10.)

Leaving the Dry Creek Trail the PCT traces out a 5.6-mile course to the last-mentioned junction, staying close enough to the crest, at least north of the Goose Egg, to provide some decent views. The Goose Egg, however, does provide better ones, and its summit is attained in a 20-minute scramble up its north slopes. If you need water when you reach the Stuart Falls Trail junction, head southwest 1½ miles down the "trail" to where this abandoned road levels off in a dry wash. Head 200 yards down the wash and hopefully find water in Red Blanket Creek. If you don't need water, you might as well continue down to Stuart Falls Camp. Because you won't find any surface water anywhere near the PCT north of the Pumice Flat/Stuart Falls trails junction, you should plan accordingly.

North of this junction, the PCT, now an old road all the way to Highway 62, climbs northwest, reaching, in 2⅓ miles, the south end of a long, narrow, open flat. From this end, an old road—the Union Peak Trail—meanders 1⅔ miles west over to the start of a steep summit trail. Weather permitting, you should not pass up the opportunity to scale this prominent landmark. Drop your heavy pack at the end of the old road and scramble, sometimes using your hands, up to the tiny summit of Union Peak (see Chapter 10, route 9).

Onward, the PCT traverses the open flat, then takes you through 2½ miles of dense, viewless forest that contains some of the finest specimens of mountain hemlocks you'll find anywhere. Before mid-July, this shady stretch can be quite snowbound.

Your route ends at a small trailhead parking area along Highway 62. To reach on-trail water, you'll have to continue at least 1¾ miles north to

the Castle Creek headwaters tributaries. But you can also get water by walking ⅓ mile east on Highway 62, leaving it where it bends southeast, and then descending ¼ mile northeast on an abandoned road to the foot of a gully. The Annie Spring Cutoff Trail (Chapter 10, route 6) climbs ½ mile up this fault-line gully back to the PCT, but you head southeast over to the nearby Crater Lake south-rim access road. Get water at Annie Spring, by this paved road's bridge, or get water at Mazama Campground, whose entrance lies about 250 yards south along the road.

3   Highway 62 to North-Rim Access Road

Trailhead   In Crater Lake National Park on the south side of Highway 62, 0.8 mile west of the Annie Spring entrance (south-rim access road). **Maps 4, 8, 9 and 12.**

Distances   2.1 miles to Dutton Creek Trail, 6.5 miles to Lightning Springs Trail, 13.4 miles to Crater Springs Trail, 14.4 miles to Red Cone Spring spur trail, 18.3 miles to north-rim access road.

Low/High Elevations   5450'/6500'

Trail Notes   This entirely viewless section begins by climbing ¾ mile, part of it up a fault-line gully. Then it descends momentarily east to the head of a second fault-line gully. Southward, Annie Spring Cutoff Trail (Chapter 10, route 6) heads down it, ending in a flat just west of Annie Spring. The PCT winds 0.6 mile down to a closed road, on which we'll hike the remaining 16.9 miles of this section. Westward, this road is abandoned but followable; your route starts northeast.

Soon you pass three seasonal tributaries of Castle Creek before you turn west and pass a fourth, which is permanent in some years. About 2 minutes past it you reach very reliable Dutton Creek, with a spur trail southwest down to campsites. Here too, you find the Dutton Creek Trail (Chapter 9, route 2), which climbs 2.4 fairly hard miles to Crater Lake's Rim Village junction. To take in bit of Crater Lake scenery, you can hike up this trail, head northwest on the Discovery Point Trail (route 4), and then descend back to the PCT via the Lightning Springs Trail (route 5).

The PCT descends 1¼ miles to two-forked Trapper Creek, passing two seasonal creeks on the way. Trapper Creek flows most of the summer, but later on you'll have to go downstream to find it flowing. Ahead, you ramble about 1¼ miles over to a divide, then make a noticeable descent north to four forks of South Fork Bybee Creek. The first two flow most of the summer and have potential camps; the third flows just as long but is campless; the fourth is vernal.

Past the fourth, the old road briefly rises, then descends ½ mile to lasting Bybee Creek. Starting up it is an old road, the Lightning Springs Trail, mentioned earlier. You could camp just north of the trail junction, but by continuing 1.1 miles you'll reach an old spur road that descends ⅓ mile to camps along a tributary of Bybee Creek. If the tributary is dry, look for water just downstream.

Beyond the spur road, the PCT soon turns west and then descends ½ mile to a very abandoned road, starting west in a small, grassy area. Our route turns north and soon crosses the fairly reliable South and Middle forks of Copeland Creek. Open, lodgepole-punctuated meadows stretch ¼ mile beyond the Middle Fork, and these, like meadows north of them, are favorite browsing spots for elk. From the second set of meadows, you climb 2⅔ miles to a ridge, follow it briefly east, then continue one mile east up gentle slopes to a junction with another abandoned road. This makes a moderate descent 3 miles west to Crater Springs, at the head of Sphagnum Bog (Chapter 10, route 1). That area is an interesting one for naturalists, but is too far off the beaten track for most PCT hikers. No decent camping exists in that area.

Climbing gently northeast for one mile, we reach the Red Cone Spring spur trail, which traverses a fairly open stretch over to the nearby "Thank God" spring. If you've been heading south on the PCT, this will be your first reliable water since Thielsen Creek, a thirsty 21 miles away. Northbound hikers take note. There are several campsites near the spring, and these may be packed with water-hungry hikers.

Northward, we descend ½ mile to the other end of a loop road, which leads the PCT hiker down to Boundary Springs, a full 6 miles out of the way (as at Crater Springs, no camping is allowed within ½ mile of these springs). If you can't face a 20½-mile waterless slog on pumice to Thielsen Creek, head down to the springs, then follow Chapter 10's route 3 in reverse (down the Rogue River), and follow its trail-head directions in reverse (Maps 4 and 1). The latter will guide you to camping, water and supplies by the southeast shore of Diamond

Lake. There too you'll find the start of the Mt. Thielsen Trail (Chapter 11, route 7), which gets you back up to the Pacific Crest Trail.

Hikers hell-bent for punishment ignore this road and make an easy 3⅓-mile traverse, mostly through an open, lodgepole-pine forest, around avalanche-prone Red Cone and over to the north-rim access road.

The route 3's PCT is through viewless forest, here near Red Cone Spring

4   North-Rim Access Road to Highway 138

Trailhead From the turnout loop near the south edge of the park's Pumice Desert, drive 2.4 miles south up the north-rim access road to a small parking area on the road's west side.

Alternatively, from Crater Lake's Rim Drive, drive 2.6 miles down the north-rim access road. **Maps 5 and 9.**

Distance   8.8 miles, one way.

Low/High Elevations   5915'/6500'

Trail Notes   This short stretch, which can be done in several hours, will be skipped by all but the most loyal PCT adherents. The previous stretch manages to avoid Crater Lake views; this stretch manages to avoid both views and water. From the north-rim access road, you start by walking east over to the nearby base of Grouse Hill, a huge mass of rhyodacite lava that congealed just before Mt. Mazama erupted and collapsed to create the Crater Lake caldera. Its eruptions, occurring about 6900 years ago, "sandblasted" the top of Grouse Hill, and it's unfortunate that the PCT doesn't traverse that interesting surface.

But it doesn't, so you trod north between road and base, both gradually diverging before you reach the Timber Crater Trail (Chapter 10, route 5), almost 3 miles later. On this closed road, you walk 260 yards east to a road fork and thence head northeast, climbing gently up toward Timber Crater. After 1.3 miles the road becomes steeper and you branch left, back onto trail tread again. You climb but ¼ mile northwest before continuing in that direction on a long, viewless, winding, 2½-mile descent to the *old* north boundary of Crater Lake National Park. From here an old trail heads west ⅓ mile along that boundary line to an abandoned road that goes 1½ miles north to Highway 138, then just beyond that to the North Crater Trail, bound for the Diamond Lake area (Chapter 11 route 8).

Heading toward Highway 138, the PCT takes a longer way, first starting east along the old boundary, then traversing north-northeast to reach the new boundary and Highway 138 just 70 yards west of a broad, low, crest pass across the Cascade Range. You won't find any parking here, so cross the highway, go 230 yards on the PCT, then fork left and descend ¼ mile on the North Crater Trail to a well-developed trailhead parking area.

5   Highway 138 to Howlock Mountain Trail

Trailhead   Same as Chapter 11, route 8's *south* trailhead. **Maps 2 and 5.**

Distances   5.9 miles to Mt. Thielsen Trail, 8.4 miles to Thielsen Creek Trail, 11.5 miles to Howlock Mountain Trail (add 0.2 mile to each destination if you start from the North Crater trailhead).

Low/High Elevations   5915'/7370'

Trail Notes   From the end of the North Crater Trail, which is ¼ mile southeast of a trailhead parking lot and just north of Highway 138, the PCT traces a poorly defined Cascade divide almost ½ mile north to an abandoned road that is used mainly by winter snowmobilers. The grade stays gentle for about a mile but then it steepens, eventually climbing into a snow-harboring, glaciated bowl. With your moderate climbing done, you climb easily west out of the bowl, cross Mt. Thielsen's southwest ridge, and traverse across a second glaciated bowl before hitting a junction with the Mt. Thielsen Trail (Chapter 11, route 7). The peak's summit is a worthy though difficult goal, and you certainly won't want to carry a backpack up to it.

Beyond the Mt. Thielsen Trail, the PCT traverses north to the peak's west ridge, then crosses the open, view-packed northwest slopes to the northwest ridge. From it you see the next major Cascade volcano—bulky, often snowy Diamond Peak. Your trail then makes long switchbacks down from the ridge before it descends southeast to Thielsen Creek. Over this last mile of trail, snow sometimes lasts through late July. Thielsen Creek is your first source of reliable water since Red Cone Spring, 21 miles back. Just past the creek ford you reach the Thielsen Creek Trail, on which you can descend about 100 yards to a spur trail that leads 100 yards west down to Thielsen Creek Camp. For the remaining 3.1 miles of PCT, plus route descriptions down the Thielsen Creek and Howlock Mountain trails, consult Chapter 11's route 6.

Books and Articles on the Crater Lake Area

General

Clark, Ella E. 1953. *Indian Legends of the Pacific Northwest.* Berkeley: University of California Press. 225 p.

Darvill, Fred T., Jr., M.D., F.A.C.P. 1983. *Mountaineering Medicine.* Berkeley: Wilderness Press. 60 p.

Schaffer, Jeffrey P., and Bev and Fred Hartline. 1979. *The Pacific Crest Trail, Volume 2: Oregon & Washington.* Berkeley: Wilderness Press. 328 p. plus supplement.

Toops, Constance M. 1983. *Crater Lake National Park Trails.* Crater Lake: Crater Lake Natural History Association. 48 p.

U.S. Department of Agriculture. 1981. "Backpacking." Washington, D.C.: GPO pamphlet 1981 0-351-727: QL 3. 52 p.

U.S. Department of Agriculture. 1974. "Horse Sense on Backcountry Trips." Washington, D.C.: GPO pamphlet 1974 798-604/13 Region 10. 16 p.

Winnett, Thomas. 1979. *Backpacking Basics.* Berkeley: Wilderness Press. 132 p.

Geology

Alt, David D., and Donald W. Hyndman. 1978. *Roadside Geology of Oregon.* Missoula MT: Mountain Press Publishing Co. 268 p.

American Geological Institute. 1976. *Dictionary of Geological Terms.* Garden City NY: Anchor Books. 472 p.

Armstrong, Richard Lee. 1978. "Cenozoic igneous history of the U.S. Cordillera from lat. 42° to 49°N." *Geological Society of America, Memoir 152,* p. 265-81.

Bacon, Charles R. 1983. "Eruptive History of Mount Mazama and Crater Lake Caldera, Cascade Range, U.S.A." *Journal of Volcanology and Geothermal Research* (special issue on arc volcanism).

Baldwin, Ewart M. 1981. *Geology of Oregon.* Dubuque: Kendall/Hunt Publishing Co. 170 p.

Barrash, Warren, and Ramesh Venkatakrishnan. 1982. "Timing of late Cenozoic volcanic and tectonic events along the western margin of the North American plate." *Geological Society of America Bulletin,* v. 93, p. 977-89.

Blinman, Eric, and Peter J. Mehringer, Jr., John C. Sheppard. 1979. "Pollen Influx and the Deposition of Mazama and Glacier Peak Tephra." In *Volcanic Activity and Human Ecology* (P.D. Sheets and D.K. Grayson, eds.). New York: Academic Press, p. 393-425.

Coney, Peter J. 1978. "Mesozoic-Cenozoic Cordilleran plate tectonics." *Geological Society of America, Memoir 152,* p. 33-49.

Crandell, Dwight R., and Donal R. Mullineux, C. Dan Miller. 1979. "Volcanic-Hazards Studies in the Cascade Range of the Western United States." In *Volcanic Activity and Human Ecology* (P.D. Sheets and D.K. Grayson, eds.). New York: Academic Press, p. 195-219.

Cranson, K.R. 1982. *Crater Lake: Gem of the Cascades.* Self-published: Sold through Crater Lake Natural History Association (Crater Lake). 111 p.

Decker, Robert, and Barbara Decker. 1981. *Volcanoes.* San Francisco: W.H. Freeman and Co. 244 p.

Heusser, Linda E., and Nicholas J. Shackleton. 1979. "Direct Marine-Continental Correlation: 150,000-Year Oxygen Isotope-Pollen Record from the North Pacific." *Science,* v. 204, no. 4395, p. 837-39.

Jones, David L., and others. 1982. "The Growth of Western North America." *Scientific American,* v. 247, no. 5, p. 70-84.

MacLeod, N.S. 1982. "Newberry Volcano, Oregon: A Cascade Range geothermal prospect." *Oregon Geology,* v. 44, p. 123-31, and *California Geology,* v. 35, p. 235-44.

McKee, Bates. 1972. *Cascadia.* New York: McGraw-Hill. 394 p.

Nelson, C. Hans. 1967. "Sediments of Crater Lake, Oregon." *Geological Society of America Bulletin,* v. 78, p. 833-48.

Phillips, Kenneth N. 1968. *Hydrology of Crater, East and Davis Lakes, Oregon.* Washington, D.C.: U.S. Geological Survey, Water-Supply Paper 1859-E. 60 p.

Smith, James G., and others. 1982. *Preliminary Geologic Map of the Medford 1° x 2° Quadrangle, Oregon and California.* Washington, D.C.: U.S. Geological Survey, Open File Report 82-955.

Wells, Francis G., and Dallas L. Peck. 1961. *Geologic Map of Oregon West of the 121st Meridian.* Washington, D.C.: U.S. Geological Survey, Map I-325.

127

Williams, Howel. 1942. *The Geology of Crater Lake National Park, Oregon.* Washington, D.C.: Carnegie Institution of Washington, Publication 540. 162 p. plus 31 plates.

Biology

Applegate, Elmer I. 1939. "Plants of Crater Lake National Park." *The American Midland Naturalist,* v. 22, no. 2, p. 225-311.

Arno, Stephen F., and Ramona P. Hammerly. 1977. *Northwest Trees.* Seattle: The Mountaineers. 222 p.

California Department of Fish and Game. 1969. *Trout of California.* 56 p.

Follett, Dick. 1979. *Birds of Crater Lake National Park.* Crater Lake: Crater Lake Natural History Association. 80 p.

Franklin, Jerry F., and C.T. Dyrness. 1973. *Natural Vegetation of Oregon and Washington.* Washington, D.C.: U.S.D.A., Pacific Northwest Forest and Range Experiment Station, Forest Service General Technical Report PNW-8. 417 p.

Hitchcock, C. Leo, and Arthur Cronquist. 1973. *Flora of the Pacific Northwest.* Seattle: University of Washington Press. 730 p.

Horn, Elizabeth L. 1972. *Wildflowers 1: The Cascades.* Beaverton, OR: Touchstone Press. 160 p.

Ingles, Lloyd G. 1965. *Mammals of the Pacific States.* Stanford: Stanford University Press. 506 p.

Keator, Glenn. 1978. *Pacific Coast Berry Finder.* Berkeley: Nature Study Guild. 62 p.

Murie, Olaus J. 1975. *A Field Guide to Animal Tracks.* Boston: Houghton Mifflin. 375 p.

Niehaus, Theodore F., and Charles L. Ripper. 1976. *A Field Guide to Pacific States Wildflowers.* Boston: Houghton Mifflin. 432 p.

Peterson, Roger Tory. 1961. *A Field Guide to Western Birds.* Boston: Houghton Mifflin. 366 p.

Sharpe, Grant and Wenonah. 1959. *101 Wildflowers of Crater Lake National Park.* Seattle: University of Washington Press. 40 p.

Stebbins, Robert C. 1954. *Amphibians and Reptiles of Western North America.* New York: McGraw-Hill. 536 p.

Sudworth, George B. 1908 (1967). *Forest Trees of the Pacific Slope.* New York: Dover Publications, Inc. 455 p.

Thompson, Mary, and Steven Thompson. 1977. *Huckleberry Country: Wild Food Plants of the Pacific Northwest.* Berkeley: Wilderness Press. 183 p.

Watts, Tom. 1973. *Pacific Coast Tree Finder.* Berkeley: Nature Study Guild. 62 p.

Weeden, Norman. 1981. *A Sierra Nevada Flora.* Berkeley: Wilderness Press. 406 p.

Whitney, Stephen. 1983. *A Field Guide to the Cascades and Olympics.* Seattle: The Mountaineers. 256 p.

Yocom, Charles F. 1964. *Shrubs of Crater Lake.* Crater Lake: Crater Lake Natural History Association. 82 p.

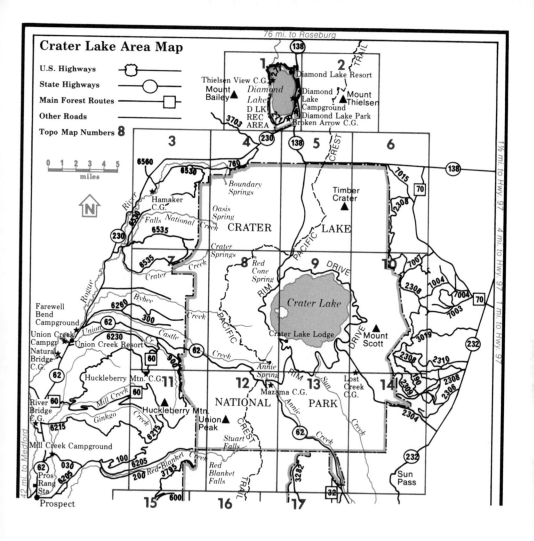

Crater Lake Area Map

SEE CONTINUATION OF MAP ON NEXT PAGE

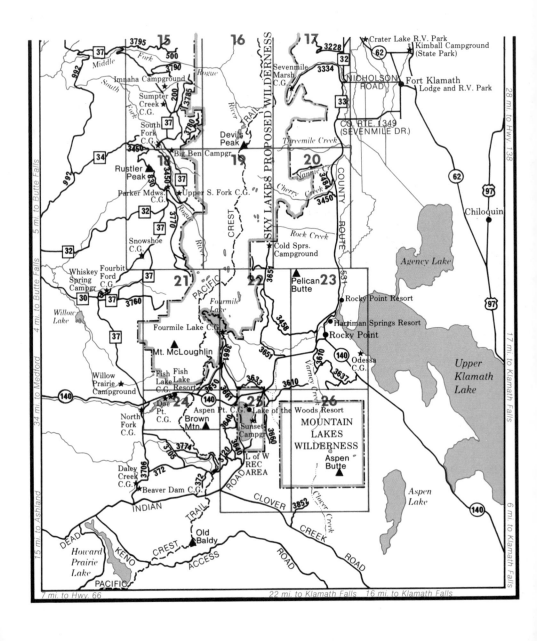

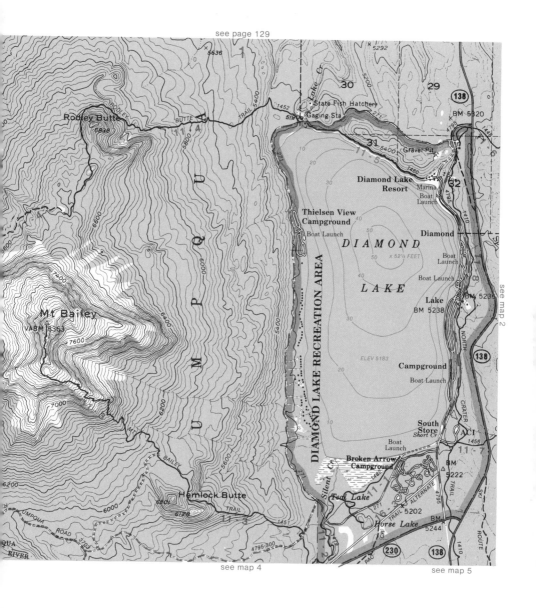

see map 4   see map 5

LEGEND FOR THE TOPOGRAPHIC MAPS

ROADS

Paved, 45+ m.p.h.	================
Paved, under 45 m.p.h.	================
Paved, but not rated	================
Unpaved, 30+ m.p.h.	▬▬▬▬▬▬
Unpaved, 20-30 m.p.h.	▬ ▬ ▬ ▬
Unpaved, 10-20 m.p.h.	▪▪ ▪▪ ▪▪ ▪▪
Unpaved, under 10 m.p.h.	xxxxxxxxxxxxxxx
Unpaved, but not rated	===============

TRAILS

Fair to well maintained	———————
Poorly or unmaintained	– – – – – –
Book chapter—route number	11 · 3

PARK OR WILDERNESS BDY. ▬▬▬▬

SCALE   1:62,500, OR 1 INCH EQUALS ABOUT 1 MILE

NORTH IS AT TOP OF PAGE

131

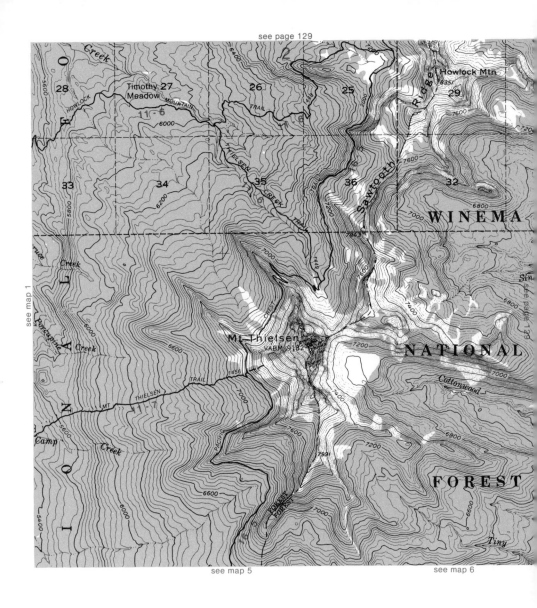

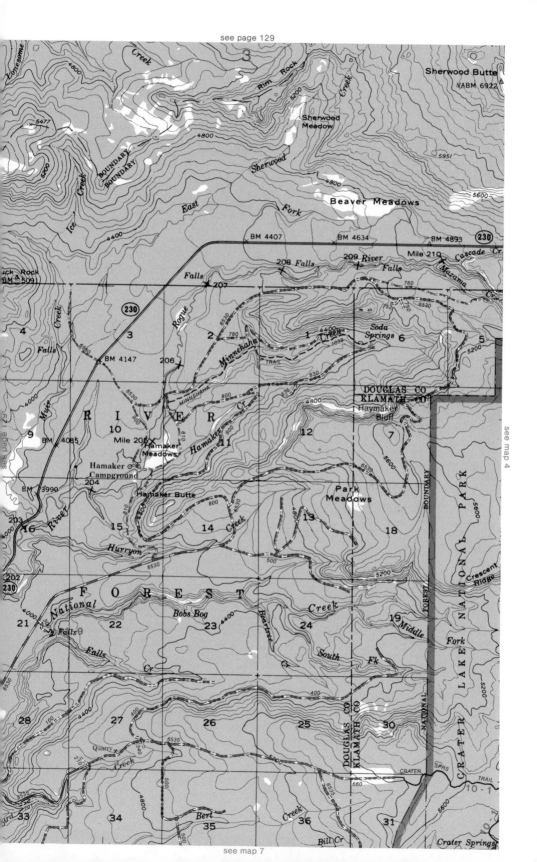

see page 129

Sherwood Butte
VABM 6922

Sherwood Meadow

BOUNDARY
BOUNDARY

5477

4800

5200

Ice Creek

5951

East
Fork

Sherwood

Beaver Meadows

5600

4400

4800

BM 4407   BM 4634   BM 4893   230

Falls   208 Falls   209 River   Mile 210   Cascade Cr

ick Rock
BM 5091

Falls   207   760   Mazama Cr

230   Rogue   752   6530

Creek   6530   6530

4   3   2   1   4400 Creek   Soda Springs   6   5
780   1699   5200

Falls   BM 4147   206   Minnehaha   TRAIL   830

4000   6530   800   4800   DOUGLAS CO
KLAMATH CO

R I V E R   MINNEHAHA   810   Haymaker Bluff

9   10   800   12   7

BM 4085   Mile 205   Hamaker   800   11   6530   5600

Hamaker
Meadows

Hamaker
Campground   Park
Meadows

BM 3990   204   800   6530

Hamaker Butte   810   500   13   18

203   810   4000
16   River   15   14   Creek

Hurryon   6530   500   5200

202   Crescent
Ridge

230   F O R E S T   Creek

National   5600

21   22   Bobs Bog   23   4400   24   19 Middle

Falls   Bearrree Cr   South   Fk   Fork

Falls   Cr   400

28   4400   27   26   25   30

100   Quarry   6535   340   400   CRATER   5200

Creek   500   660   SPRS

TRAIL   10-1

6535   20   4800   5600

33   34   Bert   35   36   31   Crater Springs

Bill Cr

see map 7

see map 4

CRATER   LAKE   NATIONAL   PARK

see page 129
see map 1

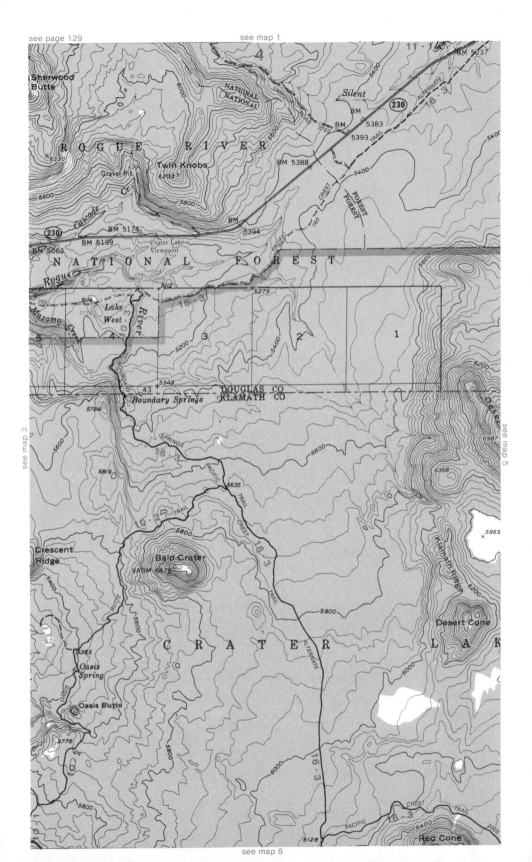

see map 3
see map 5
see map 8

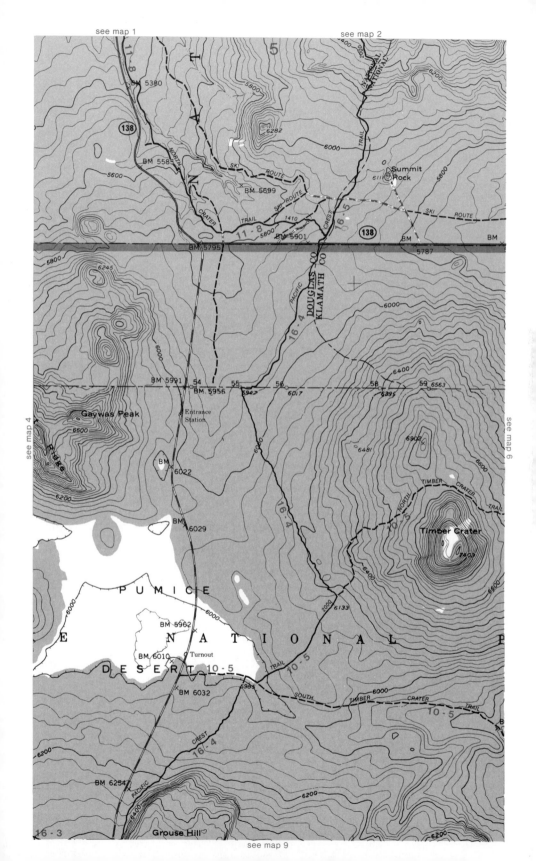

see map 1
see map 2
see map 4
see map 6
see map 9

BM 5380

138

BM 5585

5600

6282

6000

Summit
Rock
5111

5800

NORTH

SKI

ROUTE

TRAIL

BM 5699

SKI ROUTE

138

BM
5787

BM

CRATER

TRAIL

1410

5800

BM 5901

16·5

5800

BM 5795

11·8

CREST

DOUGLAS CO
KLAMATH CO

SKI   ROUTE

5800

6245

PACIFIC

16·4

6000

6400

BM 5991   54   55   56   58   59 6563
       BM 5956   5942   6017   6395
                                                6395

Gaywas Peak

Entrance
Station

6600

6481   6906

6200

BM   6022

16·4

TIMBER   CRATER

NORTH

10·5

Timber Crater
7403

BM   6029

6600

Ridge

PUMICE

6000

6400

6600

E   N   A   T   I   O   N   A   L   P

BM 5962

2000   6133

BM 6010   Turnout

D   E   S   E   R   T   10·5

10·5

TRAIL

10·5

6000

BM 6032   5985

SOUTH   TIMBER   CRATER   TRAIL

10·5

B

6200

CREST

16·4

6200

BM 6254

PACIFIC

6400

16·3   Grouse Hill

6200

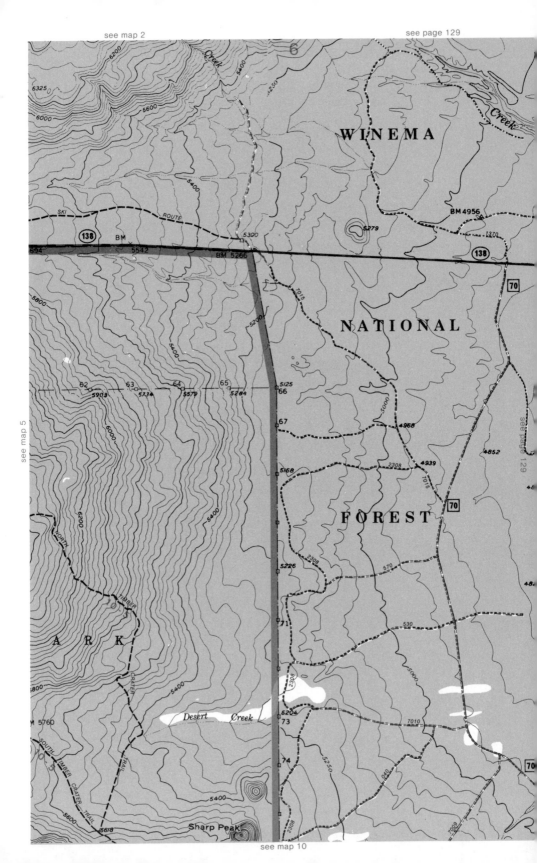

see map 2

see page 129

WINEMA

BM 4956

SKI   ROUTE

138   BM

BM 5266

138

70

NATIONAL

see map 5

62   63   64   65   66
5903 5734 5579 5284

67   4958

5168   2308 4939

70

FOREST

5226   2308

71

5204
73

74

ARK

Desert   Creek

Sharp Peak

70

see map 10

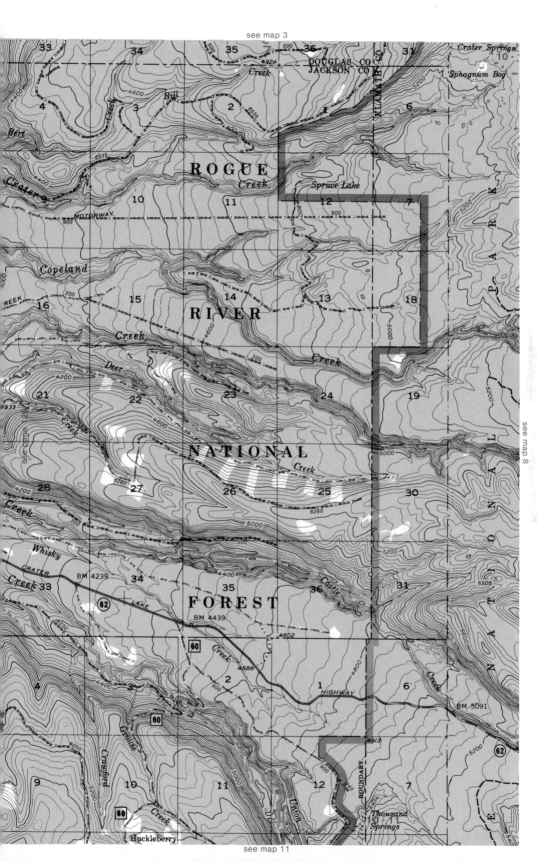

see map 8

see map 4

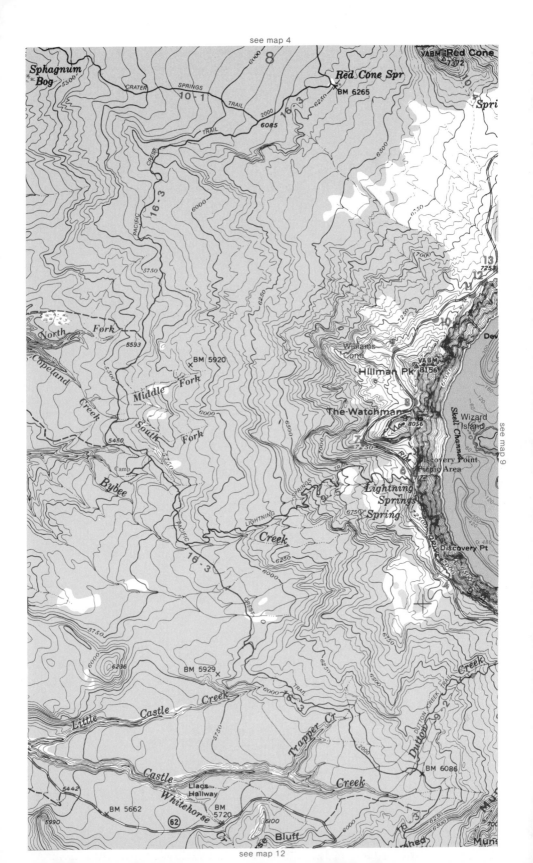

Sphagnum Bog

Red Cone Spr

VABM Red Cone

BM 6265

North Fork

BM 5920

Middle Fork

South Fork

Willams Cone

VABM
Hillman Pk 8156

The Watchman

Bybee

Lightning Springs

Spring

Discovery Point Picnic Area

Creek

Discovery Pt

Wizard Island

Skell Channel

BM 5929

Little Castle Creek

Trapper Cr

Dutton Creek

BM 6086

Castle Creek

Llaos Hallway

BM 5662

Whitehorse

BM 5720

62

Bluff

see map 9

see map 12

MOUNT

R
9

Grouse Hill

M

19 19
Cleetwood
Picnic 17 DRIVE
14 Area Mazama Rock
15 7089 20
16 Rugged Crest
Boat Lw
Cleetwood
Llao Rock Steel Bay Cove
8046 Pumice Pt Palisade Pt 21

Llao Bay 22
Merriam Pt Palisades
Rou
ils Backbone Merriam
x 1788 Cone Wineglass

x 1932
Grotto Cove
ELEVATION 6176 FEET
CONTOUR INTERVAL
60 FEET (10 FATHOMS) Skell Head

L A K E
Wizard
BM
6940
Island C R A T E R Cloudcap
Bay
Governors
Bay possible
site of
Mt. Mazama's
summit Pumice
x 1548 Castle 33

Sentinel Rock Victor view 34
x 1572 35

Danger Bay
Eagle Cove R 6 E R 7 E
Phantom BM 6763 7525
BM 6179 Eagle Pt Ship 6339 RIM
Sinnott Kerr
Memorial Chaski Bay Notch
Rim Lodge
Village 7076 Kerr Valley
Munson Castle Dutton
Sprs Garfield Pk 8000 Sun Notch Cliff Gate
Dyar Rock 7850 VABM VABM 8150 9
Park Headquarters Applegate Pk 8135 A A
Crater Lake PO M Dutton
Castle Crest A Ridge
Wildflower Z
47 Garden A 40
M 42 7500
Creek BM A 41
7025 Vidae BM 6570
Valley Falls BM 7361
44
Picnic
son Pt Area

see map 8

see map 10

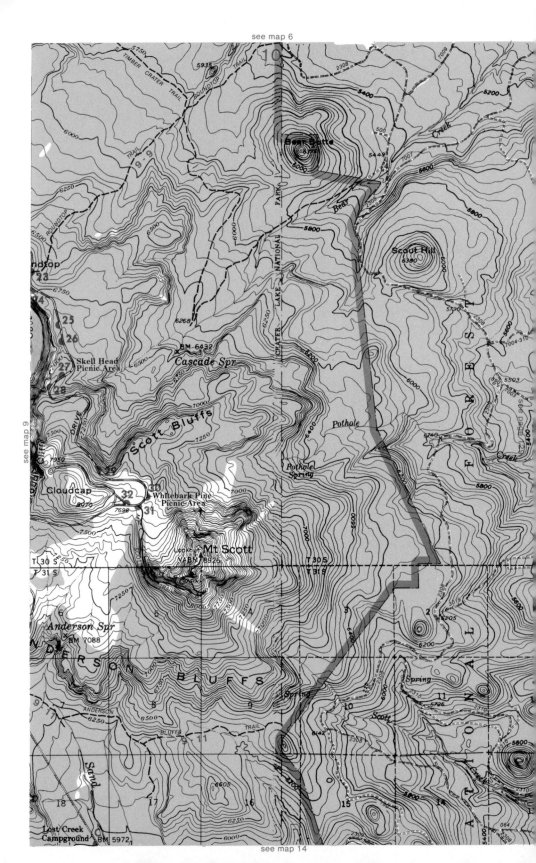

see map 9

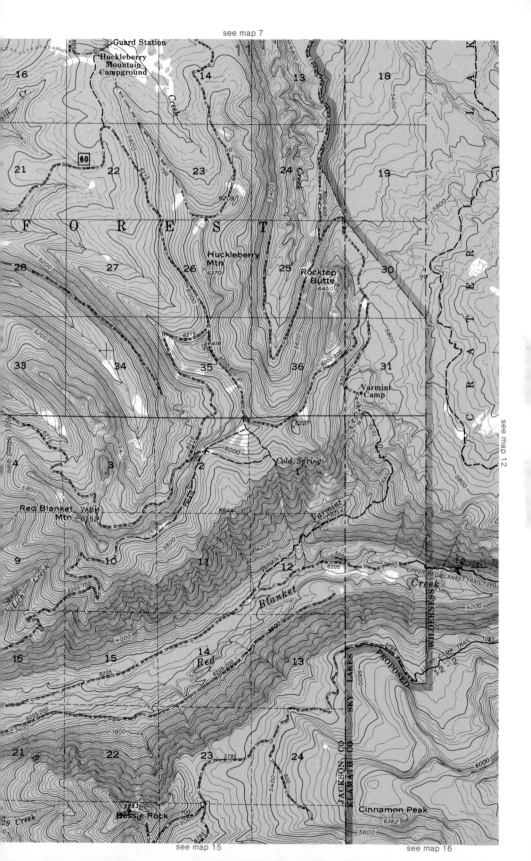

see map 7

see map 12

see map 15

see map 16

see map 8

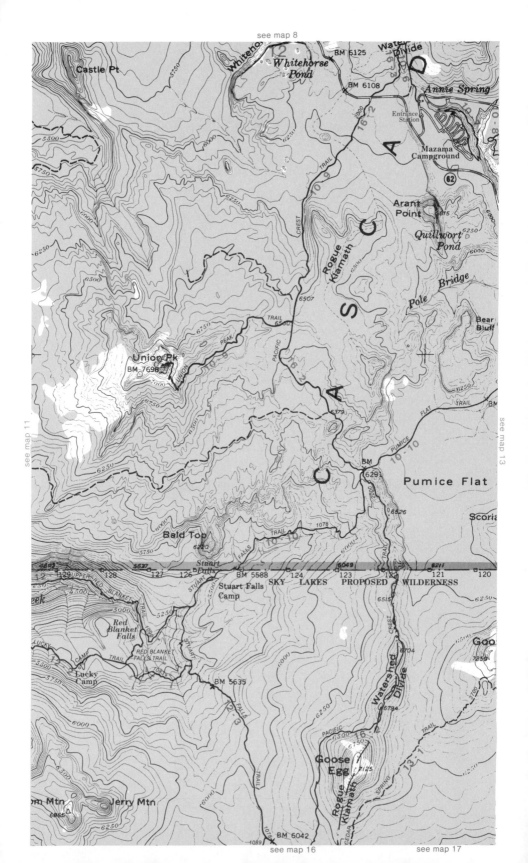

see map 11

see map 13

see map 16

see map 17

see map 12

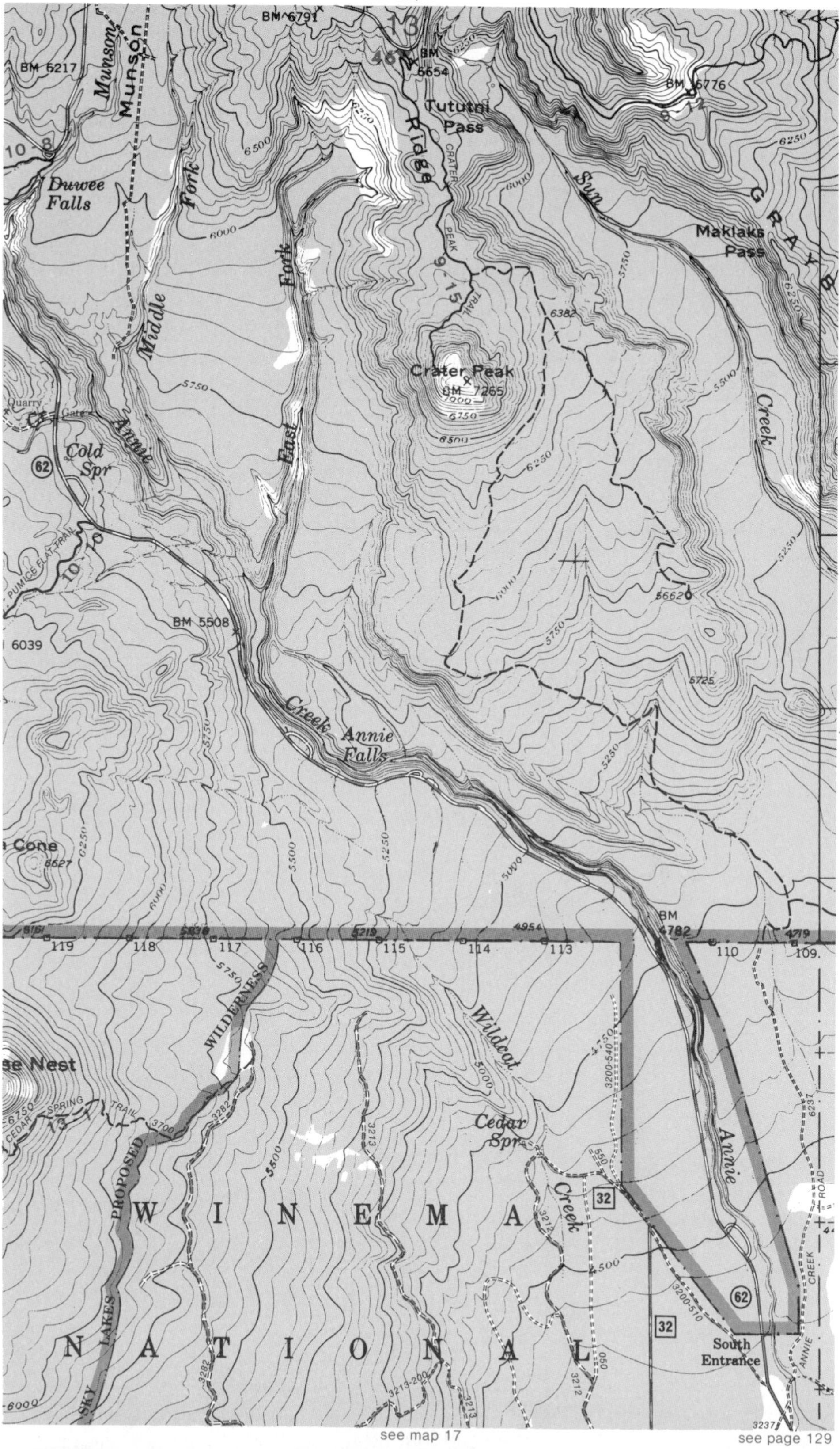

see map 14

Munson

BM 6791

BM 5654

BM 5776

Tututni Pass

Maklaks Pass

Duwee Falls

BM 5217

Middle Fork

East Fork

Annie

Munson Fork

Ridge

CRATER PEAK TRAIL

Crater Peak
BM 7265

Sun Creek

G R A Y B

Quarry

Cold Spr

62

PUMICE FLAT TRAIL

BM 5508

6039

Creek

Annie Falls

Cone
6627

5620

5725

BM 4782

119 118 117 116 115 114 113 110 109.

8151   5830   5219   4954   4719

WILDERNESS

Wildcat Creek

se Nest

CEDAR SPRING TRAIL

PROPOSED

Cedar Spr

32

W I N E M A

Annie Creek

62

SKY LAKES

N A T I O N A L

32

South Entrance

ANNIE CREEK ROAD

3237

see map 17

see page 129

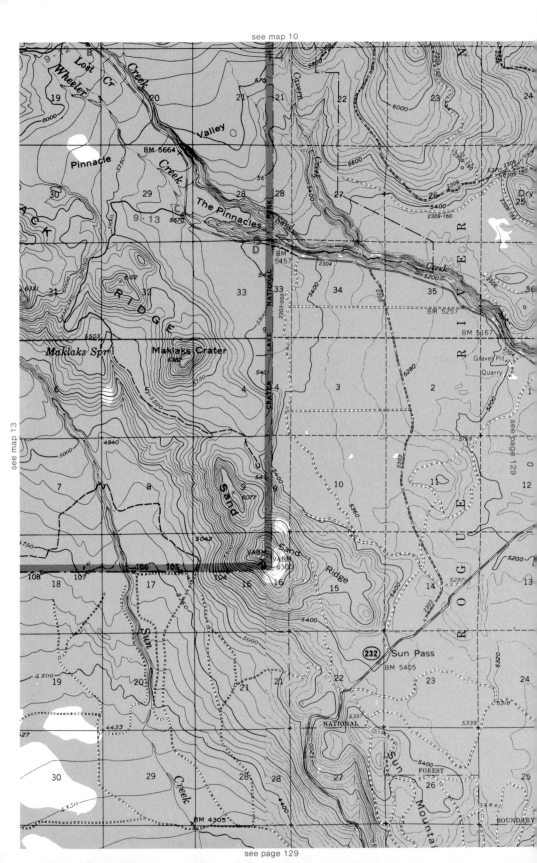

see map 13

see page 129

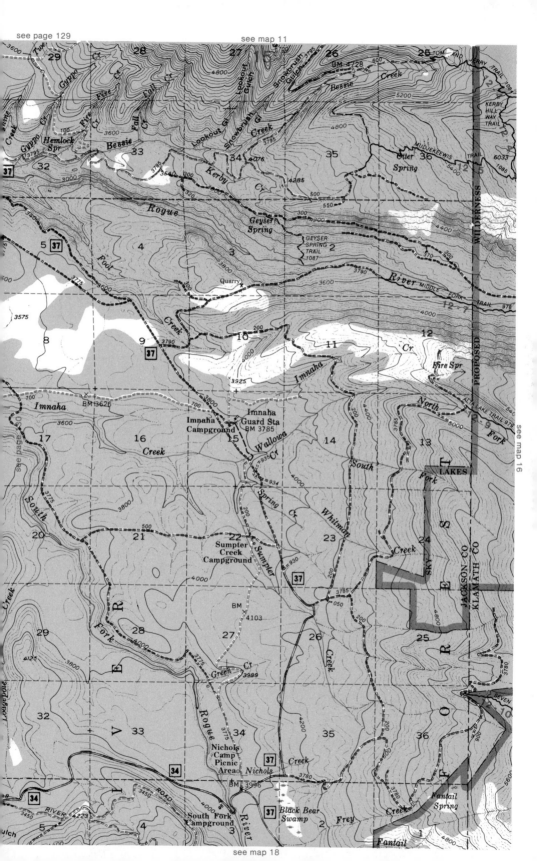

see page 129
see map 11
see map 16
see map 18

see map 11
see map 12

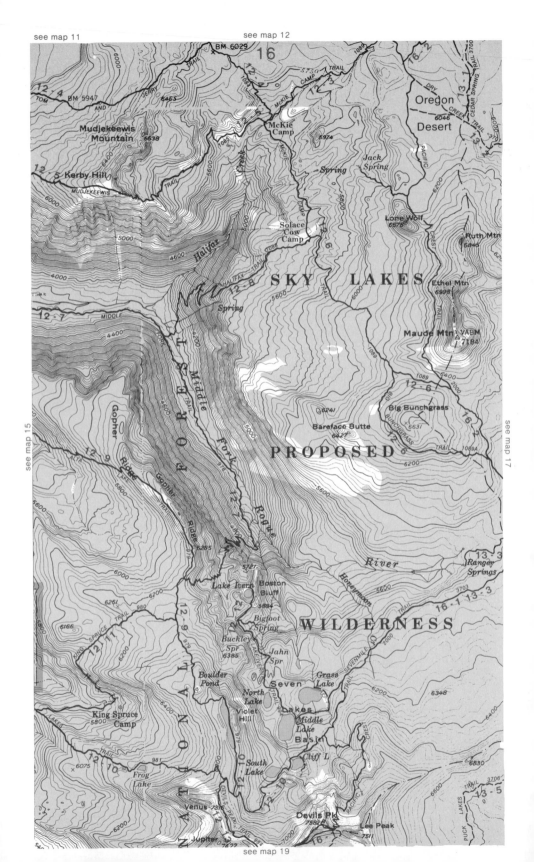

see map 15
see map 17
see map 19

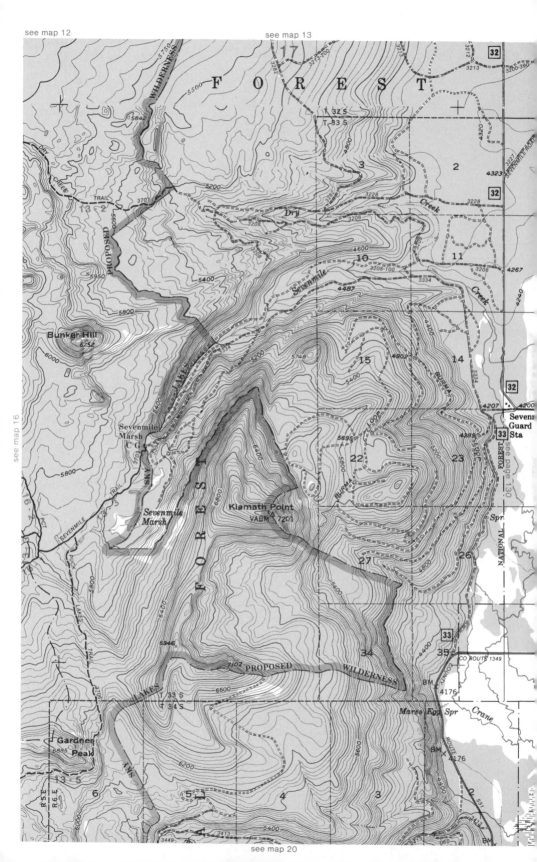

see map 12
see map 13
see map 16
see map 20
see page 130

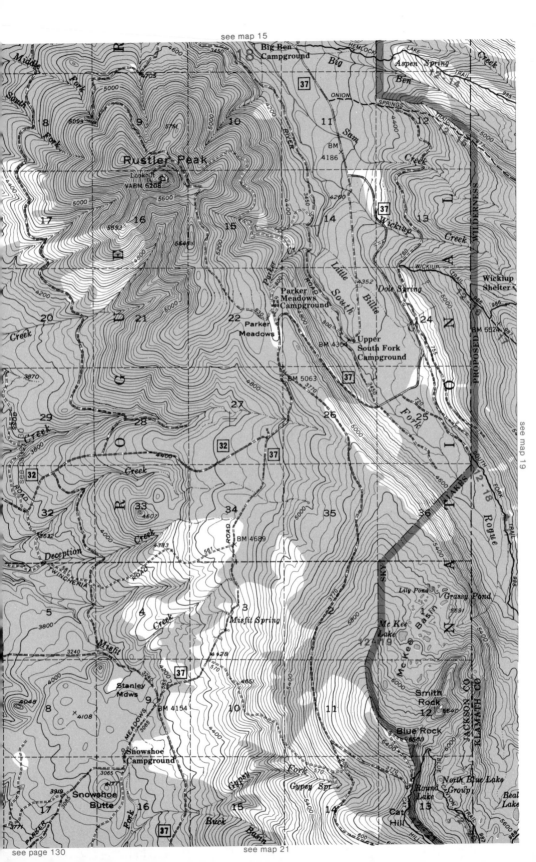

see map 15
see map 19
see map 21

see map 16

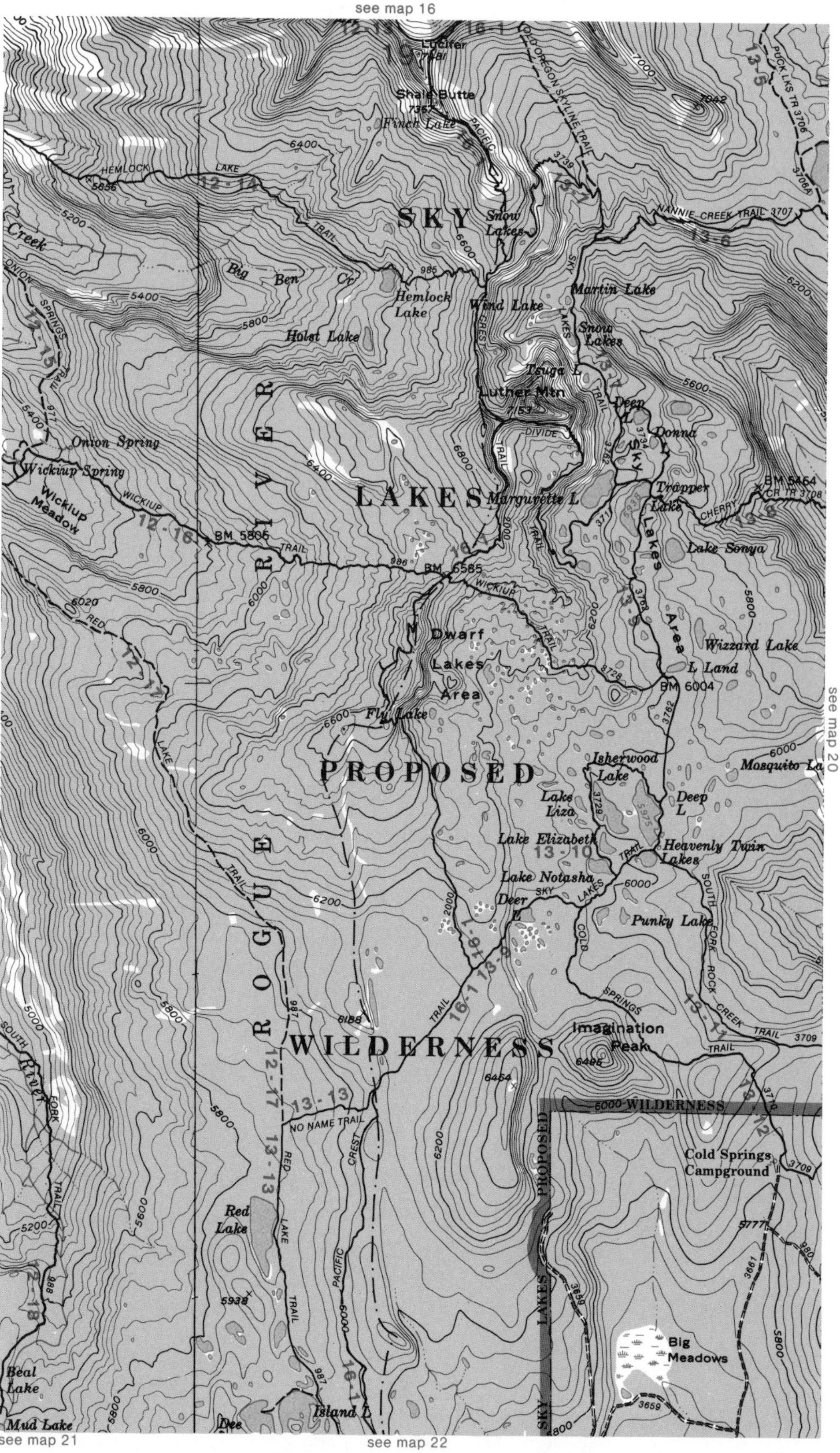

Lucifer

Shale Butte

Finch Lake

SKY

Snow Lakes

HEMLOCK LAKE

Creek

Big Ben Cr

Hemlock Lake

Holst Lake

Wind Lake

Martin Lake

Snow Lakes

NANNIE CREEK TRAIL 3707

Tsuga

Luther Mtn

DIVIDE

Deep L.

Donna

Trapper Lake

Onion Spring

Wickiup Spring

Wickiup Meadow

WICKIUP TRAIL

BM 5805

LAKES

Margurette L

BM 5585

Lake Sonya

BM 5464

CR TR 3708

CHERRY

WICKIUP

Dwarf Lakes Area

Wizzard Lake

L Land

BM 6004

Fly Lake

PROPOSED

Isherwood Lake

Lake Liza

Lake Elizabeth

13-10

Lake Notasha

Deer L.

Deep L.

Mosquito La

Heavenly Twin Lakes

Punky Lake

see map 18

see map 20

ROGUE RIVER

6188

WILDERNESS

Imagination Peak

NO NAME TRAIL

13-13

RED LAKE TRAIL

PACIFIC CREST TRAIL

Red Lake

5938

SOUTH FORK ROCK CREEK TRAIL 3709

WILDERNESS

PROPOSED

Cold Springs Campground

3709

SOUTH RIVER FORK TRAIL

5777

Big Meadows

3659

Beal Lake

Mud Lake

see map 21

Dee

Island L

see map 22

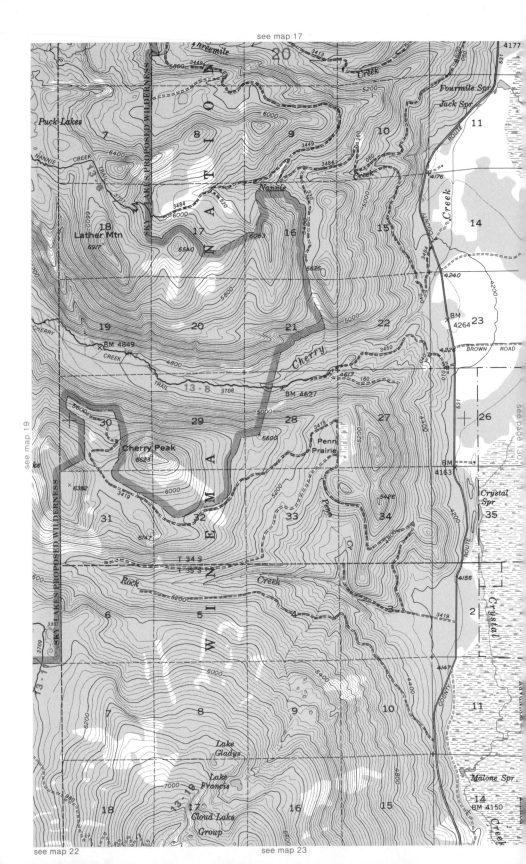

see map 19

see page 130

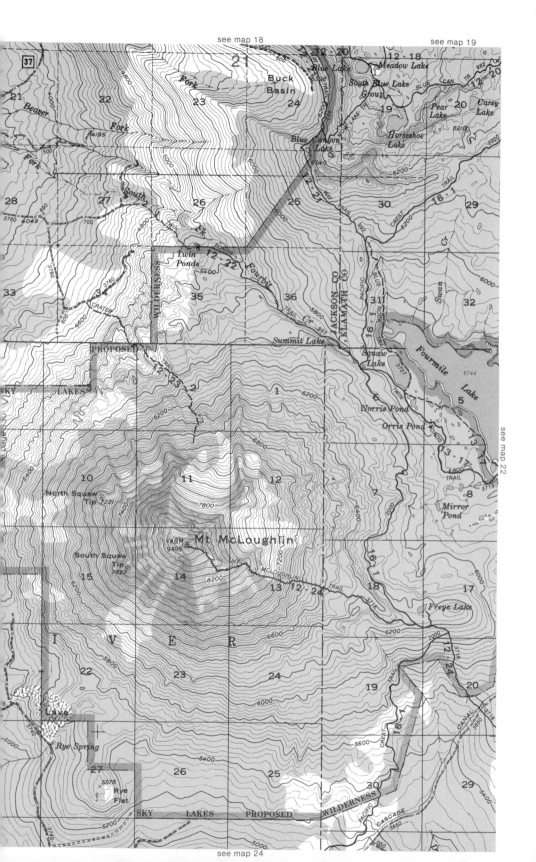

see map 18
see map 19
see map 22
see map 24

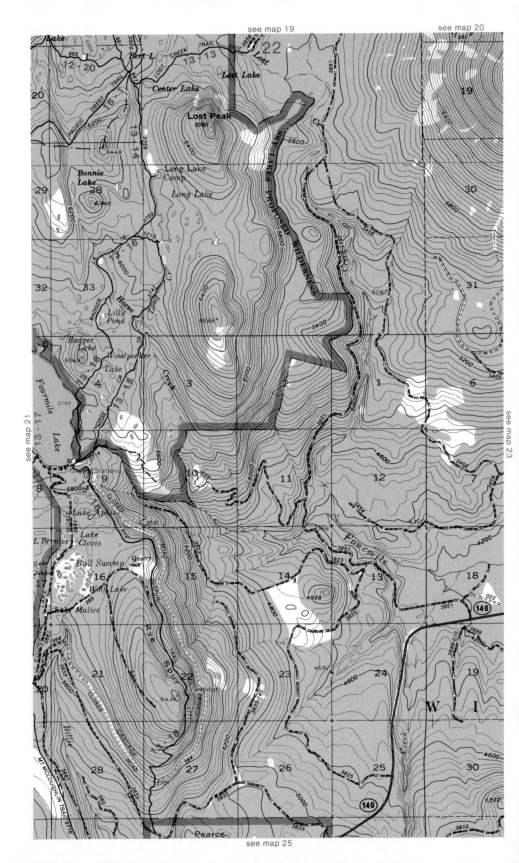

see map 21

see map 23

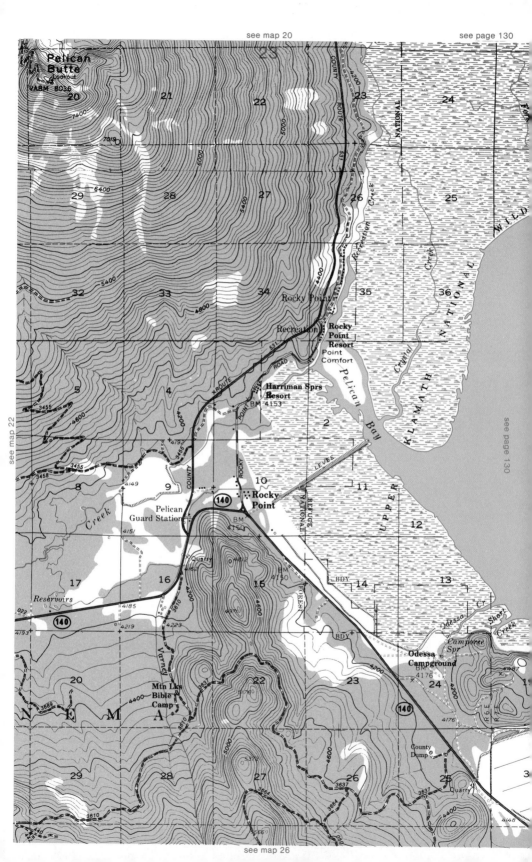

see map 22

see page 130

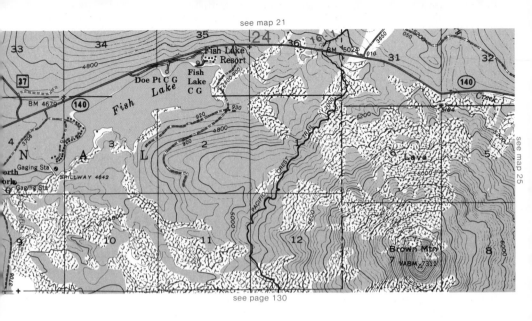

see page 130

154

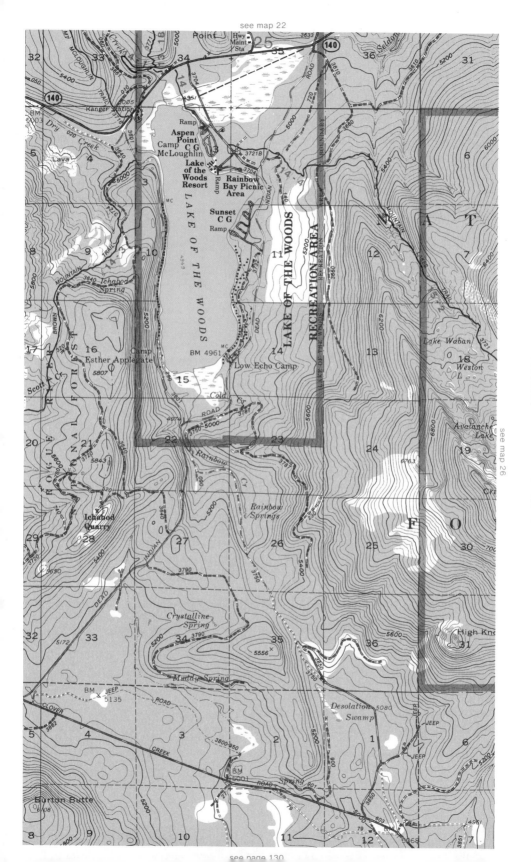

see map 26

see map 25

Index

Numbers in *italics* indicate *illustrations;* numbers in **bold face** indicate **maps.** Maps begin on page 131.

158